India Briefing, 1987

About the Book and Editor

This annual review of major events, issues, and trends in Indian affairs presents an authoritative and insightful assessment of India in 1986. Interpretive essays illuminate the causes and consequences of a tumultuous year, as leading specialists discuss Indian politics, economy, society, culture, and foreign relations. The contributors examine such important developments as the breakdown of the Punjab accord, the resurgence of militant communalism, Prime Minister Rajiv Gandhi's faltering leadership, the dramatic heightening of Indo-Pakistan tensions, the growing resistance to economic reforms, and the impact of the video revolution on Indian culture.

Filling an important gap in the literature on contemporary Indian affairs, this book will be invaluable for students and scholars of South Asia as well as for journalists, policymakers, businesspeople, and serious travelers who wish to understand current and future developments in India.

Marshall M. Bouton is director of the contemporary affairs department of The Asia Society. He is the author of *Agrarian Radicalism in South India* (1985).

India Briefing, 1987

edited by
Marshall M. Bouton

Published in cooperation with
The Asia Society

Westview Press / Boulder and London

Published in 1987 in the United States of America by Westview Press, Inc.; Frederick A. Praeger, Publisher; 5500 Central Avenue, Boulder, Colorado 80301

Library of Congress ISSN: 0894-5136
ISBN: 0-8133-0546-2
0-8133-0547-0 (pbk.)

Composition for this book was provided by the editor.
This book was produced without formal editing by the publisher.

Printed and bound in the United States of America

∞ The paper used in this publication meets the requirements of the American National Standard for Permanence of Paper for Printed Library Materials Z39.48-1984.

10 9 8 7 6 5 4 3 2 1

Contents

Preface

The last few years have been a time of almost dizzying change for India. The escalation of the Punjab crisis and the death of Indira Gandhi in 1984, Rajiv Gandhi's coming to power and his efforts at political and economic reform in 1985, the faltering of these reforms and of his leadership, as well as heightened tensions in India's foreign relations during 1986—all these developments have reminded the world of the magnitude and complexity of India's problems and potential. At the same time such changes occur amidst certain constants: the diversity and yet inherent stability of Indian society, the richness of Indian culture, the size and sheer momentum of India's economy, and India's international roles.

Despite the importance of India's changes and continuities to Americans and others, no single publication has provided a comprehensive annual analysis of recent developments and issues in Indian affairs. The insights of scholars and other specialists into Indian politics, economy, society, culture and foreign relations have not been regularly available in a form appropriate to a general readership.

India Briefing 1987 is intended to fill this gap in publications on India. It is the first volume in what we expect will be an annual series. The purpose is to provide an authoritative, timely and readable assessment of events and trends in India during the previous calendar year, in this case 1986. We hope that *India Briefing 1987* and future volumes will be of interest to policy-makers and analysts, business people, journalists and serious travellers, as well as students and scholars. From year to year certain topics will be singled out for closer examination, such as religion and politics in *India Briefing 1987*. But *India Briefing* will also continue to be quite broad in its coverage, dealing each year with all the major topics in Indian affairs.

The publication of *India Briefing 1987* is a collaborative project of The Asia Society and Westview Press. The Society and Westview have jointly published *China Briefing* for several years, the success of which led us to decide to undertake *India Briefing.* The Asia Society is grateful to Westview and particularly to Fred Praeger and Susan McEachern for their interest in expanding the collaboration of the two organizations.

Several individuals helped make *India Briefing 1987* possible. I am particularly grateful to Owen M. Crowley whose skills, hard work and initiative were critical to every phase of this publication. His command of the research, editing and production requirements was always impressive. I am also deeply indebted to Lorri Kaye who very skillfully and conscientiously transformed the contributions into a manuscript. Valuable assistance was provided as well by Chip Gagnon, Mari Maruyama and Eileen D. Chang. Whatever errors or omissions remain are the responsibility of the editor.

Marshall M. Bouton
The Asia Society
19 June 1987

U.S.S.R.
CHINA
Boundary claimed by India
Aksai
Chin
Cease-fire Line
Kashmir
Srinagar
Boundary claimed by China
Kabul
AFGHANISTAN
Islamabad
Lahore
TIBET
Lhasa
PAKISTAN
Indus River
New Delhi
NEPAL
McMahon Line
Kathmandu
BHUTAN
Brahmaputra River
Karachi
Ganges River
BANGLADESH
INDIA
Dhaka
Calcutta
BURMA
Bombay
Arabian
Sea
Rangoon
Bay of
Bengal
N
Madras
Andaman and Nicobar Islands (India)
Palk Strait
Colombo
SRI LANKA
Indian Ocean
MALDIVES

South Asia

U.S.S.R.
AFGHANISTAN
Kabul
Boundary claimed by India
Cease-fire Line
Aksai Chin
CHINA
Islamabad
Srinagar
JAMMU AND KASHMIR
Chinese Line of Control
Amritsar
Lahore
HIMACHAL PRADESH
PAKISTAN
PUNJAB
Chandigarh
HARYANA
New Delhi
Boundary claimed by China
Lhasa
McMahon Line
TIBET
ARUNCHAL PRADESH
NEPAL
Thimpu
Aligarh
Jaipur
Agra
Lucknow
Kathmandu
SIKKIM
BHUTAN
RAJASTHAN
ASSAM
UTTAR PRADESH
MEGHALAYA
MANIPUR
Patna
BANGLADESH
BIHAR
Ahmedabad
Bhopal
INDIA
MIZORAM
GUJARAT
WEST BENGAL
Dhaka
MADHYA PRADESH
Calcutta
BURMA
TRIPURA
ORISSA
Bhubaneswar
MAHARASHTRA
Bombay
Hyderabad
Bay of Bengal
Rangoon
ANDHRA PRADESH
GOA
N
KARNATAKA
Bangalore
Madras
ANDAMAN AND NICOBAR ISLANDS
Port Blair
TAMIL NADU
Kavaratti
LAKSHADWEEP
KERALA
Palk Strait
SRI LANKA
Trivandrum
Colombo
MALDIVES
Indian Ocean

India

1
Rajiv Gandhi: A Mid-Term Assessment

Myron Weiner

To the acclaim of India's middle class and much of the world's media, Rajiv Gandhi in his first year as prime minister set forth a new agenda for India: to embark on a new economic policy that would accelerate India's industrialization and economic modernization, to reconcile the concerns of India's restive linguistic, religious and tribal communities with the need for national integration, and to improve relations with India's regional neighbors. By his second year in office the economic reforms, though accompanied by signs of economic growth, were faltering, conflicts among ethnic communities showed no signs of abating and India's relations with her neighbors had deteriorated. Worse yet for a political leader, the governing Congress party, which had triumphed in parliamentary elections in December 1984 and state assembly elections a few months later, had lost assembly elections in five states, Assam, Kerala, Mizoram, Punjab and West Bengal, and had maintained a foothold in state elections in Kashmir and Jammu only by allying itself with a popular regional leader. Rajiv Gandhi's hold on his own party, on the bureaucracy, on the middle class that had initially embraced him and on the electorate had plummeted; his own future and that of his party for the parliamentary elections in 1989 were now clouded, and the agenda he had set for the nation seemed to be going nowhere.

To what extent this rapid political descent was the result of Rajiv Gandhi's failure to demonstrate leadership skills, or whether the Indian situation and system makes leadership initiative increasingly difficult and uncertain is a central issue in assessing whether a political recovery is possible and, more broadly, whether major reforms in the near future are likely. To answer this question we need to examine how Rajiv Gandhi became prime minister, how he set about seeking to carry through his agenda, what were the challenges to his leadership and what qualities he brought to bear to deal with these challenges.

The Path to Power

Before June 1980 Rajiv Gandhi was completely outside of politics. The eldest son of Prime Minister Indira Gandhi, and older brother to Sanjay Gandhi, Rajiv Gandhi led a quiet, private life as a pilot for Indian Airlines. His major ambition, it was said, was to pass the examinations that would enable him to fly 747s. Though both brothers, with their families, lived in the private residence of the prime minister, it was Sanjay Gandhi who regarded himself and was regarded by others as the heir apparent to the prime ministership. With Sanjay's death in a daredevil plane crash in June 1980, Congress party leaders pressed Rajiv to step into his brother's political shoes. For nearly a year Rajiv resisted entering politics, supported, it is said, by his Italian wife Sonia. He "helped" his mother but remained out of public life. With some of Sanjay's supporters pressing Sanjay's wife, Menaka, to stand for his seat in Parliament, Rajiv came under growing pressure from opponents of Sanjay's faction to stand on the Congress ticket. In June 1981 Rajiv ran for Sanjay's vacant parliamentary seat; with his victory he was widely regarded as the most likely successor to Mrs. Gandhi as leader of the Congress party and as her successor as prime minister.

The dynastic character of the succession process was a consequence of the transformation of the Congress party after the split of 1969 when the Congress (I) (I for Indira) emerged as the victorious heir of the old Indian National Congress, which had dominated the country's politics for most of the twentieth century. After having successfully defeated the leading Congressmen in the country in a struggle for national power, Mrs. Gandhi created a new Congress organization that was personalized and centralized, where there would be no danger that independent provincial party leaders could threaten her position. No internal elections for party officers were held. State party leaders and Congress chief ministers were not elected by local rank and file, but chosen by the prime minister. Loyalty, not local support, became the basis for party leadership at the state level. This new pattern of party organization—so different from the federal/electoral structure of the old Congress—had two consequences for national governance. One was that since state Congress leaders were appointed by and therefore dependent upon the center they had no independent capacity to deal with local political conflicts, with the result that conflicts within states necessitated intervention by the central leadership. The second consequence was that since the state Congress parties could no longer produce politicians of local popular standing, the prime minister's cabinet soon consisted of politicians without a political base of their own. No one could threaten the prime minister, but there was also no one in a position to be her successor. In the 1970s a few senior Congress politicians remained with Mrs. Gandhi, but even these drifted away when the Emergency was ended and Mrs. Gandhi, her son Sanjay and the Congress party were rebuked by the electorate in the parliamentary elections of 1977.

The Congress (I) that was returned to power in 1980 was the party, as one wag put it, of one and a half leaders. Sanjay was the chosen successor simply because there was no alternative leader, and the rank and file of the party and the members of Parliament consisted of careerists and loyalists—loyalists not to the party but to its leader. With Sanjay's death, Mrs. Gandhi and the party needed Rajiv Gandhi.

For a little over three years Rajiv Gandhi was tutored by his mother. In February 1983 Indira appointed Rajiv as secretary of the Congress (I). As party secretary his style was hardly different from that of his mother. Under his mother's guidance he sought to bring down the handful of opposition party state governments. By providing support to dissident elements he attempted to undermine the Janata government in Karnataka, the Telugu Desam government in Andhra, the Sikkim Sangram Parishad government in Sikkim, and the National Conference government of Farooq Abdullah in Kashmir. It was also reported that Rajiv encouraged Jarnail Singh Bhindranwale, the militant Sikh priest whose call for the creation of an independent Sikh state, a Khalistan, was dividing the Akali Dal, the political party of the Sikhs in Punjab. Rajiv's major political contribution as Congress party secretary was thus to support the prime minister's efforts to weaken those opposition parties that had strong local support in the states. Nonetheless, Rajiv retained a reputation for personal integrity; he was not tainted by any financial scandals nor was he regarded as an aggressive and domineering person as was his younger brother. His close friends were not politicians but classmates from the Doon School, an elite private school located in the hill station of Dehra Dun. They were private businessmen, managers in multinational corporations, advertising executives, people with managerial and (like himself) technical training (Rajiv studied engineering at Cambridge University, though he did not earn a degree).

On 31 October 1984 Mrs. Gandhi was gunned down at her residence by Sikh members of her own personal bodyguard. The assassination was in retribution for her decision to send troops to storm the Golden Temple in

Amritsar, the holy shrine of the Sikhs, then occupied by armed supporters of Bhindranwale. Within hours after her death the Congress leadership chose Rajiv Gandhi as her successor. At the age of forty he had become the prime minister of the world's largest democracy. On 12 November he was unanimously named president of the Congress (I), and the following day he announced that parliamentary elections would be held in late December. Whereas *garibi hatao* ("abolish poverty") was Mrs. Gandhi's theme in the parliamentary elections of 1971, "restore democracy" was the election theme of the victorious Janata party in 1977 and "elect a government that works" was Mrs. Gandhi's theme in 1980, Rajiv's theme was "national unity," a slogan translated by many Hindu nationalists into *desh bachao* ("save the motherland"). In the campaign that ensued Rajiv warned that the country was in danger, that national unity was threatened not only by the Sikh militants and the Akali Dal but by the opposition parties that, he asserted, had endorsed the secessionist Anandpur Sahib resolution of the Akali Dal. (The opposition parties, it should be noted, had not endorsed the resolution, nor was the resolution secessionist.) Rajiv thus tarnished the opposition with the brush of antinationalism. His much quoted comment that "when the tree falls the ground will tremble" seemed to provide a justification for the Hindu attacks against Sikhs in New Delhi in the days following his mother's assassination.

The Congress (I) was reelected with a record 401 seats out of the 515 for which polling took place, the largest parliamentary victory in India's history. In the months following his victory Rajiv Gandhi seemed to do everything right, winning support from the press, the business community, Congress party workers and even grudgingly from opposition leaders who were earlier offended by his campaign tactics. He took on the two major political problems left unsolved by his mother: Sikh militancy in Punjab, and the agitation in Assam against illegal migrants fom Bangladesh. He signed "accords" with the leaders of the two movements. In Punjab the prime minister agreed to transfer Chandigarh, the joint capital of Punjab and Haryana, to the exclusive control of Punjab in return for the transfer of a number of Hindi-speaking villages to Haryana. That, along with a commitment to adjudicate the dispute over the sharing of river waters between Punjab and Haryana and the rehabilitation of Sikhs who had been discharged from the military after the government's attack against the Golden Temple, led the Akali Dal to renounce the demand for a Khalistan and agree to take part in new state elections.

In Assam an agreement was reached to close the international borders, to grant citizenship to those who illegally entered the state before 1967, to delete from the electoral rolls those who had entered between 1967 and 1971 and to expel those who entered after March 1971. The Assam leadership in return agreed to end their agitation and to take part in state elections. For appearing to bring about a settlement on these two issues where his mother had failed, Rajiv Gandhi was hailed by the press, by his own party and even by most opposition leaders for his healing skills. When the two states elected opposition parties which then became responsible for restoring order within the states, Rajiv was praised for putting the needs of the country over those of his own party.

Rajiv was also admired for his new economic policies. Within months after taking office the prime minister announced new policies to accelerate India's slow industrial growth—liberalizing imports, providing new incentives for exports, permitting the import of technologies, encouraging foreign investment through joint ventures, reducing taxes and deregulating the economy so as to make it more competitive. Liberally oriented economists and administrators were placed in charge of the Planning Commission, the Finance Ministry, and in other key economic positions.

Rajiv also promised to restructure the Congress (I), to hold party elections for the first time in fifteen years and to encourage a new, younger leadership to take responsibility in the states and in the central government. He appointed a number of young MPs as junior ministers. An Anti-Defection Bill was introduced to discourage elected members of Parliament and state assemblies from threatening to bring down governments in order to improve their own chances of becoming ministers. At the Congress party's centenary celebration in 1985 he criticized the party for its corruption, for its self-seeking leadership and for its failure to attract new talent. The prime minister's style was decidedly antipolitical and managerial. He spoke of making the Indian government "work faster" and in an uncharacteristic rhetorical flourish, Rajiv promised to lead India into the twenty-first century.

Rajiv Gandhi's new approach, his willingness to take a fresh look at old problems, aroused the hopes of India's large middle class and received enthusiastic support from India's business community and from the press. His youthfulness, his managerial style, his modern attitude toward technology as manifest by his eagerness to expand India's computer industry, his reputation for personal integrity ("Mr. Clean") and his contempt for old-style politicians resonated with India's large modern urban middle class, disheartened by the slow pace of change, the rising tide of violence, the inefficiency of government and the absence of political leadership. Expectations were so high that in early 1986 Rajiv Gandhi warned an interviewer with the influential magazine *India Today* that "the euphoria has to stop."

It did. Rajiv Gandhi's second year as prime minister was marked by disillusionment. His effort to work with the moderate Sikh leadership in the Akali Dal against the militants did not bring an end to terrorism, and the Punjab Accord itself was not implemented as a result of a controversy over the issue of what territory should be transferred from Haryana to Punjab in return for Chandigarh. There was also much criticism in Punjab of the government's failure to take action against individuals accused of killing Sikhs during the Delhi riots that followed Mrs. Gandhi's assassination. Terrorist attacks were resumed in Punjab, followed by retaliation against innocent Sikhs in Delhi by Hindu militants. In Assam, state government leaders expressed their anger at what they regarded as the failure of the central government to remove illegal migrants. By the end of 1986 there were threats of renewed agitations against the central government. In both Assam and Punjab it was clear that Rajiv could not rely upon his subordinates or upon local leaders to take the necessary next steps to implement the agreements.

Elsewhere in the country, violence erupted among a number of linguistic, caste and religious communities. In Gujarat and in Andhra Pradesh "backward" castes (government-designated low castes that are regarded as one rung up from the ex-untouchable castes) demanded reservations comparable to those given to the ex-untouchable castes for admission into colleges and into government employment and were opposed by the upper or "forward" castes; in Gujarat there were communal clashes between Hindus and Muslims; in northern West Bengal a militant party of Nepalis demanded a separate state of Gurkhaland; in Goa a demand was raised for the creation of a Konkoni-speaking state; in Tripura militant tribals clashed with Bengalis; and throughout northern India Muslims agitated against two court decisions, one to subject Muslim divorcées to the civil law of alimony rather than to Muslim law, and another to give Hindus repossession of a shrine regarded by Muslims as a mosque.

Not only had the prime minister not fared well in reducing the level of violence in the country, but, noted his critics, his new economic policy was faltering. Deficit financing increased, the trade deficit worsened, exports failed to grow, many industries were threatened by import liberalization, there was a drop in the output of capital goods industries and industrial growth was slower than anticipated. The business community itself was divided in its assessment of the new policy, and with few exceptions the country's economists were critical.

The prime minister, initially praised for his openness, was now criticized for his lack of accessibility. Although he appeared daily on national television, giving the appearance of accessibility, the reality was that he rarely met with senior Congress politicians, cabinet positions were frequently reshuffled, signifying his lack of confidence in his own party, and for advice he fell back upon a small number of bureaucrats and personal friends. The result was that all too often the prime minister made hasty and politically unwise decisions or issued statements that were politically inept. A decision in early 1986, for example, to increase sharply petroleum and kerosene prices—at a time when international prices were declining—simultaneously antagonized the middle classes and the poor. After a sharp popular reaction and opposition from senior figures in the Congress party, the prime minister hastily reversed the decision.

Some of the criticism of Rajiv Gandhi can be regarded as the inevitable aftermath of a period of excessive euphoria and unrealistic expectations. But some of the criticism represented greater articulateness on the part of Rajiv Gandhi's leftist critics opposed to economic liberalization and by rightist critics opposed to his accommodative attitude toward linguistic and religious demands. Both sets of critics are advocates of a stronger state, the former to manage the economy and to give the government a stronger role over the private sector, and the latter to strengthen state authority against what Indian nationalists call "fissiparous" forces. To the critics of both the left and right, the Indian state is under siege and the prime minister has either failed to meet the challenge or, worse, pursued policies that weaken the Indian state.

Rajiv Gandhi and the Crisis of the Indian State

Rajiv Gandhi assumed the office of prime minister at a time when the capacity of the Indian state to perform three tasks had seriously eroded: to maintain law and order in a sharply divided society; to play a positive role in facilitating economic growth in an economy with a high saving rate, skilled managerial and technical personnel and promising entrepreneurial talent; and to cope with an uncertain international security environment.

Indira Gandhi's assassination was part of a larger pattern of growing violence directed by various groups against one another and against the Indian state. Many of the policies adopted earlier by the Indian government for managing social conflict that had worked reasonably well in the past no longer worked, and the coercive institutions of the state—the police, the paramilitary, the intelligence services and the military—were themselves weakened. The pace of industrial growth, low from the mid-1960s till the late 1970s—especially when compared with the dynamic economies of East Asia—picked up after 1980, but the state sector remained a drag on the economy. Power and transport, both public sector industries, had failed to keep pace with the needs of the economy. Public sector steel was inefficient and overpriced. The state-run capital goods industry was not competitive, and its high cost reduced the efficiency of the consumer goods sector.

India's security environment had also deteriorated. Pakistan's acquisition of new military equipment from the United States, the growing possibility that Pakistan was developing nuclear capabilities, the continued border conflict with China, the strained relationship with Sri Lanka over that country's ethnic conflicts and the presence of Soviet forces in Afghanistan presented new security challenges to the Indian government. Moreover, India's relationship with its neighbors now spilled over into India's domestic politics. The ethnic conflict in Sri Lanka affected India's own Tamil population and the central government's relationship with Tamil Nadu. The decision of the government of India to grant statehood to the union territory of Arunachal Pradesh was denounced by the People's Republic of China since the territory was disputed. The Indian government charged the government of Pakistan with abetting Sikh terrorists and found itself faced with illegal migrants from Bangladesh in Assam, refugees from the Chittagong Hill Tracts and armed tribals in Tripura using Bangladesh as their sanctuary.

Then there was the crisis of the Congress party. Though Congress won an overwhelming majority in the parliamentary elections in late 1984, the party itself remained organizationally weak in the states. In 1985 Congress lost the state assembly elections in Punjab to the Akali Dal, in Assam to the Asom Gana Parishad, in Sikkim to the Sikkim Sangram Parishad, in Karnataka to the Janata party and in Andhra Pradesh to the Telugu Desam. Since Congress had been defeated earlier in West Bengal and Tamil Nadu, by the end of 1985 Congress was largely in control only in the states of central and northern India: Bihar, Gujarat, Haryana, Himachal Pradesh, Madhya Pradesh, Maharashtra, Orissa, Rajasthan and Uttar Pradesh. In assembly elections in early 1987, a Congress-coalition government in Kerala was defeated, and Congress failed to defeat the governing Communist party (Marxist) government in West Bengal. Congress had become the party of the Hindi heartland and its nearby neighbors, while the opposition parties were in control of most of the states in the geographic periphery.

A review of Rajiv Gandhi's attempts to deal with the problems of internal order, to rejuvenate the economy, to shape the country's foreign policy and to restructure the party not only provides an opportunity to assess Rajiv Gandhi's personal leadership but also enables us to consider the kinds of constraints upon the prime minister and the pressures he faces to accommodate to the realities of the Indian state, polity and society.

Confronting Violent Social Conflict

Not since the mid-1950s has any prime minister of India been faced with such geographically diverse and acutely violent social conflicts as those faced by Rajiv Gandhi: the Sikhs in Punjab, conflicts in the tribal areas of Mizoram, Tripura and elsewhere in the northeast, caste conflicts in Andhra Pradesh and Gujarat, language conflicts in Goa and Tamil Nadu, unrest in Assam, demands by Nepalis in north Bengal and Hindu-Muslim clashes in Uttar Pradesh and in other states of northern India. If similar social conflicts were managed more effectively in the 1950s it was because Prime Minister Jawaharlal Nehru could rely upon several well-regarded national and regional Congress party leaders to serve as mediators, the police were more disciplined and less politicized than now, and conflicts within states and between the states and the central government could often be accommodated within the Congress party itself. In addition, conflicts were farther away from the borders and thus were less affected by the policies of neighboring states, and arms for militants were not so readily available.

Central government policies toward ethnic conflicts have largely been reactive: to wait until the movements develop, to allow the conflicts to grow, then to accommodate them. Rajiv was left with a legacy of several ethnic conflicts, especially in Punjab, Assam and Mizoram, and several new conflicts erupted shortly after he became prime minister. He has, in the main, taken an accommodative stance, with mixed results.

The "accord" signed in 1985 by Rajiv Gandhi and the Sikh leader Sant Harchand Singh Longowal (who was subsequently assassinated) failed to end the violence in Punjab. Throughout 1986 Sikh terrorist attacks against government officials, Hindus and moderate Sikhs continued. Assassination attempts against both the head of the police and the chief minister failed, but the former chief of the Indian Army was slain. Random attacks against Hindus led to counterattacks against Sikhs in Delhi, further embittering the Sikh community. The prime minister continued to support the Akali Dal government, though the Akali Dal was divided and opponents of Chief Minister Surjit Singh Barnala won control of the Sikh Gurdwara (temple) Committees, some of which are known to finance the terrorists.

By year's end the problem seemed no closer to solution. No action seemed likely on the disputed issue of transferring Chandigarh to

Punjab at least until state elections are held in Haryana mid-1987. The Barnala government has been ineffectual in coping politically either with the terrorists or with his own party's dissidents, but Rajiv Gandhi was understandably reluctant to replace the Akali government with President's (that is, central government's) rule, nor has he yet found a way to put a more popular and effective government in power.

The violence in India's northeast—in Assam, Tripura, north Bengal, and along the borders of the Chittagong Hill Tract—though unrelated to Punjab, is also in border states where terrorists can readily seek sanctuary across an international border and where it is difficult for the government to control the flow of arms. Rajiv successfully negotiated a settlement with the rebels in the northeastern tribal state of Mizoram, statehood was granted, elections were held and Laldenga, leader of the Mizo insurgency, was made chief minister. In north Bengal the conflict centers around the demand by Nepali migrants for a state of their own, a Gurkhaland, independent of West Bengal. Though the movement is armed the prime minister declared that it was not "antinational." He charged that the neglect of the area by the state government had fueled the Gurkhaland agitation, a statement regarded as an attempt to erode support for the Communist party of India (Marxist) government of West Bengal before the forthcoming state assembly elections. In a speech in Darjeeling, the prime minister subsequently declared his opposition to the creation of a separate state of Gurkhaland. He also asserted—probably incorrectly—that the India-Nepal treaty of 1950 prohibited the Indian government from granting citizenship to Nepalis who entered India after the treaty was signed. The obvious conclusion is that large numbers of noncitizen Nepalis can have no voice in the politics of the state, a conclusion that seems likely to fuel the agitation further. The prime minister also expressed his opposition to the breakup of the Indian states into smaller units and said that it had been a mistake to reorganize the Indian states along linguistic lines in the 1950s. It was not clear whether he was enunciating a new national policy intended to warn linguistic, tribal and subregional groups that claims for statehood within the India union would henceforth be rejected, or whether this was a casual remark intended to reinforce his opposition to the claim for a Gurkhaland.

Another major social conflict erupted in 1986 in the state of Andhra Pradesh. Violence broke out after the state government extended reservations to the backward castes. What was at issue was whether the state should ensure to all economically and socially subordinate groups a position in the modern sector, especially in higher education and in state employment, disproportionate to their numerical place in society. The chief minister of Andhra Pradesh, N. T. Rama Rao, leader of a regional party (the Telugu Desam) and a colorful former film actor whose saffron robes and turban and comic character have earned him the disdain of the educated middle classes but considerable popularity among the peasantry and urban lower classes, sought to win support from the backward castes by announcing that they would be entitled to 44 percent of college admissions and jobs in the state government. These reservations or quotas were to be added to the 15 percent currently reserved for scheduled castes (the ex-untouchables), 6 percent for scheduled tribes and 6 percent for special groups like the handicapped—for a total of 71 percent. The chief minister won approval from the backward castes, but the upper-caste-dominated student organizations agitated against the state government. The students demanded that reservations for the backward castes be limited to the 25 percent previously awarded by the state government. The chief minister finally gave in (he was forced to by the courts), but now the backward-caste associations launched a statewide protest, setting buses on fire, demonstrating and clashing with the forward castes and with the police.

Because the conflict over reservations in Andhra Pradesh was a problem for an opposition state government, the prime minister chose to remain aloof from the controversy, though a year earlier a similar dispute in Gujarat led him to replace the Congress chief minister who had inititated reservations for the backward castes. At that time the prime minister suggested that a national policy was needed on the backward-caste reservation issue, but thus far none has been suggested.

The prime minister was more directly involved in the controversy between Hindus and Muslims over the role of the state in regulating the personal law of religious communities. An elderly Muslim woman by the name of Shah Bano, divorced and left penniless by her husband, filed a case in court demanding alimony. She won the case under a provision of the civil code that provides that a divorced woman must be supported by her husband. Muslim priests informed Shah Bano that she had violated the Shariat (Muslim law) which provides that her family, not her former husband, is financially accountable. She withdrew the case, but the Muslim community was in an uproar, demanding that the civil code be amended so as to enable Muslims to follow their religious law with respect to marriage, divorce and other personal matters. The prime minister, concerned with losing Muslim support, agreed. A bill was introduced and subsequently passed by Parliament, but there was strong opposition from the secular middle class, from Hindus and from the women's movement, which regarded the prime minister's move as a concession to Muslim communalism and a break from secularism. What was at issue was whether a uniform personal law, guided by some conception of justice and equity, should be applicable to all citizens, or whether each community is entitled to follow its own religious code, determined not by a legislative body but by the interpretation of religious scholars and priests.

The Indian government's policies toward demands by caste, linguistic, religious and tribal groups have generally been guided by the notion that within limits the state should be accommodative. India is, of course, more than a country; it is a civilization with a variety of religions, tribes, languages and a complex hierarchical caste system. Identities are fluid, shaped in part by birth, but often by political circumstances, by acts of government and by forces of social change, such as education, migration and economic competition. Indians tend to regard society as autonomous of the state; the state, most Indians believe, should not impose a moral code, nor should it remake group identitites. Individual self-realization through religious rituals, conduct and thought rather than state-imposed norms represents the Hindu view. Rather than the state remaking identities, most Indians believe that state structures and policies should be adopted to suit the variegated identities that make up India. The restructuring of state boundaries to coincide with linguistic boundaries, the creation of reservations to give proportional access to government employment to specified castes and tribes, policies that require of educational institutions that they instruct in the mother tongue, the insistence that official languages of states be those of the local population and recognition of community personal law—all these are examples of state adaptations to social realities rather than efforts by the state to restructure social reality. (The one time, it should be noted, when the state chose to impose its norms upon society—the compulsory family planning program introduced during the Emergency—the government was overturned by the electorate.)

But many of the policies adopted earlier to accommodate ethnic demands no longer mitigate social conflict. Reservations in education and in state employment for scheduled castes, for example, were widely acceptable to the upper castes so long as these reservations were confined to the scheduled castes and tribes, but their extension to other communities now threatens the upper castes. Moreover, there is growing resentment among all groups at the inclusion of individuals who are not "deserving" of benefits by virtue of their income and class, but who have access to reservations because of their caste. Similarly, the principle of giving each major linguistic community a state of its own was adopted in the 1950s and was subsequently grudgingly extended to the tribal areas of northeastern India. But now state governments are unwilling to allow themselves to be fragmented, and, as we have seen, the prime minister himself and others in the central government fear that by acceding to the demands of the Nepalis, the Konkonis and other groups, there will be no end to the process of state formation. There are others, however, who argue that India might be better off with a larger number of smaller states, that states like Uttar Pradesh with 110 million people, Bihar with 70 million and five states (West Bengal, Tamil Nadu, Maharashtra, Madhya Pradesh and Andhra Pradesh) with more than 50 million are too large to be effectively governed from a single capital. Still others have suggested that there be a national policy of devolving greater authority and resources from the state and central governments to popularly elected district councils.

The issue of a uniform secular civil code versus accommodation toward Islamic personal law also remains unresolved. Secularism in India has meant that the state should not patronize any religion and that it should also refrain from interfering in how religious communities conduct themselves. Many Indians, however, regard secularism in the broader sense that there ought to be a uniform civil code, applicable to all, irrespective of religion, based upon a consensus concerning what constitutes justice and equity. These two conceptions of secularism remain in conflict. What now gives this conflict a more visceral dimension is the recent heightening of Hindu nationalism, a reaction to the claims upon the state by Muslims and Sikhs, reports of conversion by ex-untouchables to Islam and the growth of Islamic fundamentalism. There is now a conjunction of interests between militant Hindus and the secular middle class that sharpens the conflict with India's Muslims.

Finally, what has made ethnic conflict more unmanageable in recent years is that the claims of one community are now increasingly resisted by others, making it difficult for government to accommodate to demands by mobilized groups without taking into account the reactions of other mobilized groups. To transfer the capital city of Chandigarh to Punjab, for example, without some territorial concession to Haryana is a political risk for the governing Congress party. Similarly, it is difficult for the central government to accede to the Assamese demand that illegal Bengali-speaking Muslim migrants from Bangladesh be expelled because of opposition from the government of West Bengal and from India's Muslim leaders.

In response to growing and often violent group demands Rajiv Gandhi has taken a piecemeal approach: to deal with each demand on its own, to be accommodative to group claims where possible, to postpone action when contending groups make conflicting claims, to use the police and paramilitary forces when necessary rather than the military and to rely upon advisors within the prime minister's secretariat rather than upon state and local political leaders. There is no conceptual framework to his approach nor does there appear to be any attention to the broader policy issues raised in the individual agitations. The issues, for example, of whether states should be made smaller or existing boundaries kept intact, whether group reservations for specific tribes and castes should be reconsidered, whether there should be a uniform code for personal law and how the laws of citizenship should be applied to migrants from Bangladesh and Nepal have received little attention. The result is that the prime minister's statements often lack consistency, and it is difficult for groups and individuals to anticipate what will be the policy response of the central government to their claims, a situation conducive to extreme demands and popular agitations.

Party Reform and Cabinet Politics

Rajiv's distaste for politics and politicians was articulated in a remarkable speech commemorating the centenary of the Congress party in Bombay in December 1985. Sounding more like a leader of the opposition than of Congress, he denounced the Congress "power brokers," as he called them, "who dispense patronage to convert a mass movement into a feudal oligarchy," and he spoke of Congress party bosses "who thrive on the slogans of caste and religion." Rajiv promised to reform the party and to bring in a new breed of politicians. He appointed his close political associate, Arjun Singh, as the party vice-president, along with new party general secretaries who were charged with the mission of reorganizing the party. New members were to be recruited into the party, scrutiny committees were to be appointed to verify party membership lists and elections for local Congress committees—the first since 1969—were promised. In an effort to maintain contact between the party and the electorate, the party's mass organizations—the Youth Congress, the Mahila (Women's) Congress and the Seva Dal (Service Society)—were to be strengthened.

One and a half years later little had been accomplished. The mass organizations remained ineffective. Party elections were postponed after Rajiv Gandhi's advisors warned that bogus memberships would allow electoral victories for the very power brokers that the prime minister hoped to check. Though the prime minister said he welcomed criticism within the party, Pranab Mukherjee, one-time finance minister and a leader of an Indira Gandhi dissident faction within the Congress, was expelled, while the All India Congress (I) Committee's octogenarian Working President Kamalapati Tripathi was forced to step down after he expressed sympathy for the dissidents.

In the absence of independent leaders within the party, Rajiv continued to maintain centralized control. He seemed to be the only significant voice that mattered in the selection of Congress candidates for the

Rajya Sabha (upper house of Parliament) elections. Rajiv's preferences rather than those of state assemblies and state Congress leaders determined the choice of chief ministers in a number of key states. And presidents of the pradesh (state) Congress committees were changed frequently by the prime minister or his lieutenants. But the newer politicians appointed by the prime minister are unable to use the traditional patronage machine since local party bosses retain their influence within the bureaucracy. Nor do the chief ministers, even those appointed by Rajiv, have easy access to the prime minister.

In short, Rajiv has not succeeded in creating a new party leadership, while at the same time the older party workers are disgruntled. Congress leaders in the states remain weak because of their dependence upon the center; they are, therefore, highly vulnerable to revolts from dissident factions within the party. Moreover, the failure thus far of Rajiv Gandhi to translate his electoral victory in the parliamentary elections of 1984 and the state assembly victories in early 1985 to success in state elections thereafter reduces his capacity to cope with dissident Congress factions in the state organizations.

Cabinet appointees have not fared well at the hands of the prime minister. There were major cabinet reshuffles in 1985, two major cabinet reshuffles in 1986 and another one in early 1987. The influential P. V. Narasimha Rao, the home minister, was demoted to the new Human Resources Development Ministry. In succession three different ministers were appointed to run External Affairs. Arun Nehru, a relative of the prime minister and widely regarded as one of the most powerful figures in the government, was dropped as minister for internal security. Arjun Singh was removed as vice-president of the Congress (I) and given the portfolio of minister of communications. And in early 1987 Rajiv abruptly transferred Raja Vishwanath Pratap Singh, the powerful finance minister and architect of the liberalization program, to the Defense Ministry, reportedly because he had zealously cracked down on income tax evaders—though some critics thought he also wanted to remove a potential political rival.

These repeated changes in key portfolios mean that effective power, especially in Home and External Affairs, has been in the hands of bureaucrats and a handful of personal advisors. The prime minister has been unable to find political leaders upon whom he can rely, at either the state or cabinet level, with the result that day-to-day decisions are largely in the hands of secretaries of ministries and officials within the prime minister's own secretariat.

Rajiv has made a considerable effort to bring back into the Congress "nonloyalists" who had deserted Indira Gandhi after the Emergency. In 1986 he successfully persuaded Sharad Pawar, the leader of a Congress opposition group in Maharashtra, to join the Congress (I), and in Kashmir he forged a legislative coalition and electoral alliance with Farooq Abdullah, leader of the National Conference in Jammu and Kashmir. Although some observers expressed the hope that both men would play a part in rebuilding the Congress, it was more likely that the prime minister was primarily concerned with having their support for the Congress parties in Maharashtra and Kashmir.

Publicists for the prime minister sought to give the impression that he is accessible, and that he confers frequently with party leaders, but most observers believe that the prime minister's confidants are few in number, that they are confined to a few friends and high government officials and that no major Congress party leaders or chief ministers are part of his inner circle. In an effort to give the appearance of accessibility, the prime minister has reestablished the traditional *durbar,* a morning meeting with citizens who make complaints, request favors, or, in the traditional manner, seek the *darshan* or blessings of the prime minister by being in his presence. The prime minister, under close guard because of threats to his life, makes occasional excursions to the countryside or to state capitals where he often announces that he has allocated sums of money for drought and famine relief. The style is majisterial and the impression is given on Doordarshan, the government-controlled television, that the prime minister, in his personal capacity, has generously distributed resources to aid the distressed and needy. In a similar vein the prime minister sometimes travels with a retinue of cabinet members and officials to a state capital so that decisions can be made on the spot.

Critics of the prime minister say that his approach is that of an outsider. His roots are not in the party and he remains contemptuous of most politicians, including members of his own party. He is only at ease with a handful of old friends, those he knew before he became prime minister and who have become ministers, members of Parliament and party officials only since he himself entered politics five years ago.

Rajiv's impatience with politicians has been extended to the bureaucracy as well. Secretaries of ministries are reportedly chastised in the presence of others, though in the past prime ministers treated senior civil servants with considerable respect. A particularly egregious episode occurred in early 1987 when the prime minister in a casual comment at a news conference dismissed the well-regarded foreign secretary, A. P. Venketeswaran, without prior notice. In a rare response, the Indian Foreign Service Association criticized the prime minister, charging that his action had undermined the morale of the entire service. The effect of the incident was further to isolate the prime minister and to undermine his support within the government.

The Foreign Policy of Rajiv Gandhi

In 1985 when Rajiv Gandhi spoke of improving relations with China, the United States and Pakistan, critics warned that he would endanger India's traditional close ties with the Soviet Union, and although he had some support for his new foreign policy thrusts from within the Ministry of External Affairs (especially from those who sought to give priority to an improvement in India's relations with its neighbors) there was clearly little support for any fundamental strategic realignments. By 1986 it was clear that in the area of foreign policy Rajiv had decided to adhere closely to the policies of his predecessors, that he was persuaded by his foreign policy advisors that the military relationship between Pakistan and the United States precluded any significant change in relationship with either country, that lessening tensions with China through concessions on the border dispute was politically too risky and that on balance the close relationship with the Soviet Union was beneficial for India.

Rajiv Gandhi spent a great deal of time in 1986 in trips abroad, meeting with foreign leaders and making pronouncements on foreign affairs. He went to Sweden for Olof Palme's funeral in March, to the frontline states bordering South Africa in May, to Mauritius in July, to the Commonwealth meeting in England in August, to a six-nation meeting on nuclear disarmament in Ixtapa, Mexico, in August, to the Non-Aligned Movement (NAM) summit at Harare, Zimbabwe, in September and to Indonesia, Australia, New Zealand and Thailand in October. As chairman of the NAM the prime minister projected India—and himself—as a leading supporter of the anti-apartheid struggle in South Africa and as an advocate of sanctions. The prime minister also actively supported proposals for superpower nuclear disarmament, a moratorium on nuclear testing, a test ban verification, an end to the US strategic defense initiative, the dismantling of the US bases at Diego Garcia and making the Indian Ocean "a zone of peace."

The prime minister welcomed a number of foreign leaders to India but no visit received greater acclaim and was accompanied by more euphoria than that of Soviet leader Mikhail Gorbachev in November 1986. There were extensive closed discussions between the two leaders, a joint statement which indicated a similar outlook by the two leaders on international issues, a commitment by the Soviet Union to provide more than $1.5 billion in credit, an agreement to expand significantly Indo-Soviet trade and a Soviet offer to build a space center in India. In return Rajiv Gandhi endorsed the Soviet position on arms control and disarmament at the Reykjavik summit and reconfirmed the 1971 Indo-Soviet Treaty of Peace and Friendship. The meeting highlighted the fact that the Soviet Union remains regarded by Indian leaders as India's only significant reliable friend, and that the Soviet leader accords Rajiv the status of a world leader.

Thus in 1986 the prime minister reiterated continuity in two elements of Indian foreign policy, India's close association with the Soviet Union and its role as a leader of the nonaligned movement. What was downplayed was Rajiv's earlier hopes to improve relations with India's regional neighbors, with China and with the United States.

The thaw that had begun in relations with Pakistan in 1985 was reversed in 1986. The major problems, from India's point of view, were alleged Pakistani support of Sikh extremists, indications of progress in Pakistan toward acquisition of nuclear weapons capability, the prospect that Pakistan would purchase airborne warning and control systems (AWACs), in addition to F-16s, from the United States and purported Pakistani support for the Sri Lankan government's efforts to use military force against the Tamils. The handling by Pakistan of a hijacked Pan American plane carrying large numbers of Indians in September led Rajiv Gandhi to criticize sharply the Pakistan government. Two proposals raised in 1985—President Zia's offer of a no-war pact and Rajiv's counterproposal of a friendship pact—floundered in 1986.

Although a memorandum of understanding concerning the transfer of technology was signed by the United States and India, and the US government agreed to sell India engines and possibly other technology for light combat aircraft and a supercomputer and there was a significant increase in the number of joint ventures between Indian and American businessmen, any improvement in US-Indian relations could at best be described as marginal. The Indian government repeated its concern at the flow of arms to Pakistan, continued to be publicly passive on the Soviet presence in Afghanistan and criticized the United States for its attack against Libya.

Attempts to improve relations with the People's Republic of China were also stalemated. Rajiv Gandhi issued a strong statement opposing any border concessions to China and reacted sharply to the Chinese criticism of the Indian government's decision to declare the disputed Union territory of Arunachal Pradesh a state. The appointment of A. P. Venkateswaran, former ambassador to the PRC and a hardliner on the disputed border question, to be foreign secretary was a further demonstration to the Chinese that India had no intention of conceding any of the disputed territory, including territory occupied by the Chinese since 1962. (The subsequent dismissal of the foreign secretary was unrelated to his views on China; indeed there were reports that once he became foreign secretary he was eager to take steps to improve relations with China). Although a few foreign policy analysts in India suggested that India needed to rethink its policies toward China, taking into account the possibility either of an improvement in Soviet-Chinese relations or a settlement between the Soviet Union and Pakistan over Afghanistan, there was no indication that the Indian government was preparing for any major policy change.

In a year in which foreign policy occupied much of the prime minister's time, a great deal of attention was also given to the crisis in Sri Lanka where India played an increasingly important role in attempting to bring about a resolution of the conflict between the Sri Lankan Tamils and the Sinhalese-dominated government. India pressed the Sri Lankan government to seek a political solution in the form of some kind of devolution of authority to the Tamils, while at the same time urging the Tamil militants to give up their claim for Eelam, or an independent state. Early in the year the Indian government alleged that the Sri Lankan government was seeking a military solution and that unless it came up with credible proposals for a settlement, India's "good offices" would be withdrawn—with the implication that Indian-armed Tamils working out of Tamil Nadu would escalate their attacks against the Sri Lankan government. By mid-year the Sri Lankan government came up with new proposals, including a willingness to create a Tamil province in the north and several provinces (one with a Tamil majority) in the east. Rajiv Gandhi was himself deeply involved in these matters and has indicated that if an agreement can be reached between the government of Sri Lanka and the moderate Tamil elements, the government of India would undertake to ensure its implementation—implying that India would withdraw its support from the militants if they opposed a reasonable settlement. Although the Sri Lankan crisis still seems far from a solution, Rajiv appears to have demonstrated considerable skill in simultaneously pressing the Sri Lankan government to seek a political solution, while pressing the government of Tamil Nadu to restrain the Tamil militants.

Rajiv Gandhi, the Indian State and the New Economic Policy

It was in economic policy, especially industrial policy, that Rajiv Gandhi in 1985 promised a totally new perspective. Although to some Indians the new policy represented a continuation of Indira Gandhi's policies, commencing in 1980, to liberalize imports, to others Rajiv seemed to offer a new view of the role of the state in the economy. To his sympathizers—journalists like Arun Shourie and economists like Delhi University's Mrinal Datta Chaudhuri—the prime minister was trying to come to grips with an industrial structure that had become rigid and inflexible as a consequence of its protection from the competition of the international market and, more broadly, from the failure to use market signals to make decisions for the more efficient use of capital resources. The system of industrial licensing gave an assured domestic market to producers while import controls eliminated the threat of competition from foreign sellers. The public sector was absolved from performing efficiently by a doctrine that emphasized that they had "social goals" rather than profit making as their objective. Rajiv's new strategy—liberalized imports, greater reliance on market signals and liberalized rules of entry and expansion—all implied a new recognition that the state should no longer shield industry, public or private, from competition. The prime minister did not explicitly articulate the new policy in any systematic fashion, though the specific actions he, his finance minister and the planning commission took were consistent with this view.

During Rajiv Gandhi's first year in office the critics of the new policy were relatively quiet, for there was considerable enthusiasm from the business community, the press, much of the middle class and the international aid community. By 1986 there were many critics. His opponents included a large portion of the economics community committed to socialism and self-reliance, Indian businessmen in protected sectors of the economy, managers of public sector firms, especially those engaged in the production of high-cost capital goods, union leaders in firms in danger of bankruptcy as a result of competition from importers and most of the bureaucracy engaged in the enforcement of a variety of regulations that gave the bureaucracy the opportunity to extract rents from businessmen seeking licenses. There was also opposition from sections of the prime minister's party, loyalists to socialist doctrines who are also financial cobeneficiaries of the system of bureaucratic controls. The academic community was generally critical, reflecting its socialist orientation, but also reflecting the traditional hostility of India's educated classes to the *banias*, the traditional dhoti-wearing merchants, or to the new safari-suited managers. And there was opposition from the entire left, charging the prime minister with being too concerned with technological modernization aimed at catching up with the developed world, rather than pursuing programs that would cope with the needs of India's poor.

Supporters of the prime minister's strategy were also critical, but from an entirely different perspective. They were concerned that in practice much of the liberalization had been eroded by the bureaucracy.

Though many import items had been placed on Open General License (OGL) and therefore did not require government approval, new tariffs had been imposed on many of these items. Heavy budget deficits were a threat to the new policies, made worse by a $2 billion increase in wages for government employees, major increases in nonplan expenditures, large increases in defense expenditures and the prime minister's practice of doling out money to some of the states for political reasons. Raids on prominent businessmen, launched by the finance minister, presumably with the approval of the prime minister, alarmed the business community. But most disturbing to the business community was that the bureaucracy had delayed implementing many of the prime minister's proposals for deregulation and had found new ways to prevent the decontrol of the private sector. The number of clearances has only been marginally reduced, and the bureaucracy continues to have extraordinary discretionary powers that are used to protect some sections of the business community while limiting others. Clearances still take months, even years, and new investments by Indian businessmen and by foreign investors move slowly. Particularly notorious has been the Chief Controller of Imports and Exports in New Delhi, an office that can and has effectively undercut many of the prime minister's liberalization policies. Moreover, many foreign collaborations approved by the government never move into production, and a host of obstacles impede carrying out approved projects. Supporters of the prime minister's overall strategy also fear that the decline in foreign exchange reserves, the slow pace with which exports are growing and protests from India's capital goods sector may lead the government to further slow the process of liberalization.

By year's end it was not clear which group would have the greater influence on the prime minister. Though he seemed personally committed to continued liberalization, his capacity to make the bureaucracy implement his policies seemed limited. A century earlier British officials complained that their policies were undermined by lower-level Indian officials who had learned to use bureaucratic rules to sabotage policies that did not suit their interests or those outside the bureaucracy with whom they were aligned. Without good staff work, effective support from cabinet members and strong intervention by the prime minister himself, many of the proposed reforms have languished, effectively sabotaged by bureaucrats, public sector managers and private businessmen who fear the competition that comes with liberalization and the loss of state protection. In India, even more so than elsewhere, the politics of policy making is often less critical than the politics of policy implementation; those who are too weak to affect the former can often decisively influence the latter. As the prime minister's policies of liberalization falter through the lack of implementation, and there are no indications that the policies are leading to more rapid industrial growth, his supporters fear that the pressures to return to the policies of protection will grow and that Rajiv's efforts to liberalize, to expand trade and to make the Indian economy more competitive at home and abroad will fail.

Conclusion

Midway through Rajiv Gandhi's term as prime minister any assessment should begin with a recognition that Rajiv has substantially improved the tone of Indian political life. Rajiv may not have the enthusiastic loyal supporters of his predecessor, but neither does he have the bitter enemies. He is not a divisive person—what he has done and said since he became prime minister has thus far not sharply divided the country. He is admired for his reasonableness, his personal honesty, the absence of deviousness and his willingness to meet with critics. In spite of the violence throughout the country, he has been cautious in the use of the coercive powers of the state. He has not been a passive leader: he has put forth a set of goals that have won considerable popular approval, and he has been reasonably innovative in suggesting new policies.

And yet, halfway through his five-year term as prime minister Rajiv Gandhi has clearly faltered in each of his major initiatives. His accommodative approach to the demands of religious minorities and to the anxieties of linguistic and tribal communities has not resulted in an abatement of violence and conflict. His commitment to economic liberalization—a code word for policies intended to reduce controls and to facilitate foreign trade has been stymied by a coalition of public sector managers, government bureaucrats and business executives in protected sectors of the economy. His goal of restructuring the Congress party to make it more democratic and to attract younger people has been held back by his own fear that the "power brokers" would wrest the party from his control. And his desire to improve relations with India's regional neighbors, with China and with the United States has made little progress, constrained partly by the actions of others, partly by the Indian foreign policy establishment and partly by domestic political considerations.

Powerful interests within the state bureaucracy and public sector enterprises, a foreign policy establishment that remains cautious and reactive, the inheritance of a weak party organization and the international environment have thus combined to frustrate a young and politically inexperienced prime minister at every turn. His first months as prime minister were a period of enunciating new directions, a heady time both for himself and for the country as a whole. The country, certainly the middle class, the business community and the media, were pleased to have a new prime minister who was self-confident, open and innovative. His overall perspective that the state, once regarded as a locomotive of change, had itself become an impediment to change won a sympathetic hearing from much of the new middle class. But in his second year in office Rajiv Gandhi was confronted with the hard reality of implementing the new policies. At critical stages he faltered: he hesitated to implement the Punjab accord; he failed to follow up on his economic reforms by actually removing powers from the hands of bureaucrats; he cancelled Congress party elections; he did not pursue the option of policy changes toward Pakistan and China. Deeply frustrated, he snaps at civil servants, publicly quarrels with the president of India, is flip and unnecessarily combative in answering questions in Parliament and is dismissive of both bureaucrats and politicians.

Major policy changes invariably create opposition. A political leader initiating new policies needs to build a team with which he can work, and he needs to forge a new coalition from among those who will gain from the new policies. Rajiv mistakenly assumed that his electoral mandate was sufficient for carrying out reforms, forgetting that Mrs. Gandhi's mandate in 1971 and 1972 was followed by political disarray and the declaration of an Emergency of 1975, and that the Janata landslide of 1977 was followed two years later by the fall of the government. The Congress party as presently constituted is too weak and his support too fragile for Rajiv Gandhi to be confident that his electoral victories two years ago mean assured support. Rajiv has not won over the old Congress politicians or attracted new politicians to his party; he has not built support within the bureaucracy nor has he been able to elicit popular support for himself. Rajiv is in danger of becoming politically isolated, a leader who may become less concerned with implementing policies than with maintaining his own political position. During the first half of his term in office observers were asking whether he would be able to carry out the reforms he had promised. The question for the second half of his term is how will the prime minister deal with a situation in which his personal political stock is declining, where there is dissension within his own party and where his party's electoral prospects for the 1989 parliamentary and state assembly elections have fallen. For a brief historical moment there was an opportunity for significant change. That moment appears to have passed.

2
Politics: The Failure to Rebuild Consensus

Francine R. Frankel

Introduction

The debate in 1986 within and outside the Congress (I) (long the dominant party in India's politics) on whether the Congress had become a regional party or remained a national party threw into sharp relief the changes in the political landscape since the early 1970s. The classic description of the Congress as the "party of (national) consensus" had its origins in the Nehru years. During 1950-1964, opposition parties, including those of the Marxist left, as well as the Hindu communal and secular right, exercised their greatest political influence through pressures on sympathetic factions within the umbrella Congress organization. The "single-party dominant system" worked well so long as the level of politicization was low, the distribution of patronage was narrowly directed and arbiters "above politics" were available to settle factional disputes.[1]

After Nehru's death, opposition groups, often with the help of defectors from the Congress party, occupied more political space on both the right and left and reduced the broad center of Congress control. Within Congress, moreover, the demands of the newly politicized backward classes (i.e., socially and educationally disadvantaged castes) for an independent share of power frequently overwhelmed the machinery for allocating ministerial posts and other patronage resources. Beyond that, in November 1969, the polarization between younger socialist radicals and the older conservative party bosses over the content and pace of economic reforms helped push the party organization into a debilitating split.

Prime Minister Indira Gandhi's tactical success in simultaneously discrediting the parties of the right and neutralizing the Communist

Party of India (Marxist) by identifying herself—rather than her party—with the aspirations of the poor aborted polarization along class lines. Not surprisingly, these tactics also accelerated the institutional decay of the Congress party. Indira Gandhi put an end to intraparty elections, which could no longer function as a mechanism for conflict resolution. She centralized party and governmental power in her own hands to insure that opposition groups identified with "antinational" forces would not get out of control.

The late prime minister's antipoverty programs, which reached out to the underprivileged by defining target groups in terms of their caste or ethnic identities (i.e., scheduled castes of former untouchables, scheduled tribes and backward classes), avoided class issues and maintained the Congress "culture" of an umbrella party that absorbed all interests. These programs, however, also set the stage at the state level for the emergence of regional populist parties that competed fiercely for the support of local linguistic, ethnic and religious voting blocs, a process that accentuated social differences at the expense of secular unity. Mrs. Gandhi's death in 1984 at the hands of Sikh extremists made her the tragic victim of the divisive forces she helped to sharpen. Her assassination set the stage for Rajiv Gandhi to inherit his mother's mantle.

Rajiv Gandhi's commitment to purge the party of corrupt powerbrokers and his promise to restore intraparty democracy encouraged hopes of reviving Congress as a party of consensus. Yet, the young prime minister's enthusiasm for modern technology, and the economic liberalism that seemed necessary to make India's industry internationally competitive, most immediately favored the burgeoning urban middle classes. Fundamental differences on economic and social policies which had earlier pulled apart the Congress party were, unwittingly perhaps, raised again.

As this chapter shows, by the end of 1986 it was clear that in the absence of shared principles for national economic and social policies, Rajiv Gandhi's politics of reconciliation could not recreate cohesion within the Congress party. Making matters worse, his overtures to alienated regional minorities in the interests of national unity led to Congress defeats at the polls, which further deepened intraparty divisions. The future of the Congress (I) and that of the prime minister came to rest more and more on his ability to win votes at the state level for partymen who were fighting among themselves rather than closing ranks to link party programs with effective grassroots organization.

Electoral Trends

The collapse of consensus in the Congress (I), with partymen unable to cooperate in mobilizing voter support around a coherent program, had a swift effect on the electoral performance of the ruling party. Indeed, the main political trend during 1986 was the weakening of political authority at the center. Only two years earlier, in December 1984, the Congress (I), led by Prime Minister Rajiv Gandhi, won an unprecedented 63 percent of votes and 80 percent of seats in general elections to the Lok Sabha (the lower house of the national parliament). This achievement underscored the position of the Congress (I) as the only party with a truly national following. It suggested that a return to the "Congress system" of one-party dominance at the center and in the states was a reasonable possibility. Only in 1967, when Congress suffered its first major electoral setback and won a modest majority in the Lok Sabha, had the national ruling party failed to win a majority in eight states. Otherwise, parties elected overwhelmingly at the center had also been able to capture power in most states.

In retrospect, the massive mandate for Congress (I) turned out to be a personal victory for Rajiv Gandhi under tragic circumstances.[2] The assassination of his mother, Prime Minister Indira Gandhi, on 31 October 1984 evoked widespread sympathy for the novice pilot-turned-politician chosen by the Congress (I) leadership to succeed her. Rajiv's appeal for popular support during the general elections in December 1984 in the name of India's inviolable national unity aroused an emotional response among voters of diverse social and economic backgrounds in all corners of the country. The young prime minister also symbolized the aspirations for a better future of the younger generation—the 75 percent of all Indians under the age of thirty-five. Even the disaffected middle classes saw hope in his candidacy.

Nevertheless, results of elections in eleven states (and the union territory of Pondicherry) in March 1985, held within ten weeks of the unprecedented Congress (I) victory at the center, revealed that Rajiv's vote-getting ability was not strong enough to compensate for the underlying weakness of the party organization. The outcome created concern that the Congress (I) could become a regional party of the North, and in particular of the Hindi heartland.[3] The party emerged victorious in the Hindi-speaking states of Uttar Pradesh, Bihar, Rajasthan and Madhya Pradesh, while continuing its northern sweep through Gujarat, Himachal Pradesh and Orissa. Even in this area of its greatest strength, a decline in popular support was evident compared to its performance in the national poll. The opposition Lok Dal managed to improve its strength in Uttar Pradesh, Bihar and Rajasthan, and the Bharatiya Janata party improved its position in Madhya Pradesh and Rajasthan.

Outside the North, serious weaknesses emerged. The Congress wrested a victory from Sharad Pawar's splinter Congress (S), only with difficulty, in its long-standing western bastion of Maharashtra. More sobering were the losses sustained by the party in the South. From 1967, a permanent retreat had begun under pressure from the Dravidian movement in Tamil Nadu led by the rival factions of the Dravida Munnetra Kazhagam (DMK).[4] In fact, the Congress (I)'s only success in the region was won in Pondicherry, where it entered an alliance with the All-India Anna Dravida Munnetra Kazhagam (AIADMK). By contrast, in Karnataka, where the Congress (I) confronted a minority Janata government (which had come to power only in mid-term elections of 1983 after an unbroken string of Congress victories since Independence), and where party leaders were confident of winning an overwhelming majority, the Janata triumphed by a better than two to one margin in the Assembly. Similarly, in Andhra Pradesh, where the regional Telugu Desam ended uninterrupted Congress rule in the midterm election of 1983, and where Rajiv Gandhi concentrated his campaigning with appeals to national unity, the charismatic Andhra Pradesh chief minister N. T. Rama Rao turned back the prime minister's challenge.

Weakened in the West, routed in the South (except for the state of Kerala where Congress (I) held on to power as the leader of the coalition United Democratic Front), the party was also decimated in the tiny, but strategic, northern border state of Sikkim by the local Sikkim Sangram Parishad. The general picture of declining national support was sharpened by the results of by-elections to seven Lok Sabha and nine Assembly seats in December 1985. The Congress (I) lost three seats in Parliament and five in the states, and its votes dropped significantly in almost all of the contested constituencies.[5]

The by-election defeats, no less than the unexpected reversals in state assembly elections, established that Rajiv Gandhi's attractive personal qualities notwithstanding, his plea that only Congress governments at the center and the states could protect India's national unity was unpersuasive where alternative popular leaders were able to articulate strong regional sentiments. Equally disturbing was evidence that traditional vote banks of the Congress (I), especially among scheduled castes and Muslims, were being eroded, and that this process had started even in the North.

The scheduled castes (formerly untouchable castes)[6]—about 15 percent of the population—had remained loyal to the memory of Mahatma Gandhi in supporting the Congress party after Independence.

Indeed, the leadership, as a measure of respect for Gandhi, wrote into the 1950 Constitution provisions that legally abolished untouchability, and provided reserved seats in the Lok Sabha and state assemblies, as well as reserved places in educational institutions and government administrative services for the scheduled castes in proportion to their population. Over the years, however, only a small elite in these communities proved successful in reaping the advantages of "protective discrimination." The majority remained in much the same condition of economic and social deprivation. Among younger scheduled caste voters, heightened political awareness led to greater autonomy in political behavior. In 1983, for example, the Janata party in Karnataka had received more support than the Congress (I) from the scheduled castes. Moreover, in the Hindi states of Uttar Pradesh and Bihar, the Bahujan Samaj party (BSP), formed in April 1984 by scheduled caste leader Kanshi Ram, made a militant attack on oppressive "Brahmanical Hindu society" in the name of the majority ("Bahu") of poor people. In some constituencies, the BSP challenge made the difference between a Congress (I) victory and a defeat.

The 1985 elections also revealed losses to Congress (I) of support among India's Muslims—more than 11 percent of the population. After Independence, fears among the Muslims about the rise of Hindu communal parties (such as the Jan Sangh, the composite Janata which included the Jan Sangh and Lok Dal, and the Bharatiya Janata party, which incorporated elements of the Jan Sangh after the Janata split) made the community as a whole lean toward the secular Congress party. However, Muslims gradually became alienated by their community's relative economic backwardness and experience of discrimination in finding employment. Some Muslims began to listen to the promises of opposition leaders or to turn toward their own local Muslim parties. This process was perceptible by the late 1970s, in part fed by the funds remitted from Muslim workers in the Gulf countries. But it reached unprecedented proportions during 1985 and 1986. Court judgments on seemingly minor disputes inflamed Muslims across the country who perceived that their religious identities or communal rights were in danger.

Militant Ethnic and Religious Movements

The electoral reverses of 1985 appeared especially alarming to the Congress (I) against the background of warnings sounded by Mrs. Gandhi before her death that "antinational" forces were gaining strength by appealing to regional sentiments in a bid to weaken national unity. On a number of occasions the late prime minister had implied that opposition parties that displaced the Congress (I) in the states were advancing interests of external powers, who wanted to prevent India from playing its natural role as the predominant power in South Asia and the wider Indian Ocean area. Extremist movements in strategic border areas were portrayed as having the support of India's hostile neighbor Pakistan, or its Asian rival China. Partly for these reasons, Mrs. Gandhi believed that efforts to displace state governments headed by regional parties, even through manipulation by New Delhi, served the national interest. Similarly, she repeatedly rejected any political agreements with militant ethnic and religious groups suspected of harboring secessionist sentiments when such accords would risk Congress (I) control of a state.

Rajiv Gandhi, who adopted his mother's confrontational approach against regional opposition parties during the 1985 electoral campaign, reconsidered his position afterward. He appeared willing to concede that the electorate might prefer a regional party at the state level without weakening the nation. Moreover, he was prepared to follow a conciliatory policy toward militant ethnic and religious groups, even at some risk to Congress (I) rule. He saw this as an effective way to strengthen national unity by providing a place for dissidents within the democratic polity. This approach led him to sign a series of "accords" with dissident groups which, in fact, did end in Congress defeats at the polls. The reverses, which were viewed as the result of the prime minister's departure from Mrs. Gandhi's uncompromising pursuit of national unity under the Congress (I), aggravated the crisis of confidence about the party's future.

The Assam Accord

The Assam Accord, signed by Rajiv Gandhi with leaders of the All Assam Students Union (AASU) and the All Assam Gana Sangram Parishad (AAGSP) in August 1985, ended the bloody six-year agitation by ethnic Assamese demanding the expulsion of illegal Bengali immigrants from East Pakistan/Bangladesh who were swamping the indigenous population. The provisions of the accord, which called for the expulsion of all migrants entering the state illegaliy after 24 March 1971, and the disenfranchisement for a ten-year period of illegal immigrants who entered Assam between 1966 and 1971, created a backlash against the Congress (I) from the Bengali Muslim population, who previously had looked toward Mrs. Gandhi for protection. The Congress (I), which led the caretaker government until elections scheduled on 16 December

1985, was nevertheless confident of being returned to power. Their opposition, the Asom Gana Parishad, Assam Peoples Council (AGP), formed sixty-seven days before the election mainly of student militants drawn from the AASU and AAGSP, was completely inexperienced in electoral politics. The formation of the United Minorities Front, however, which drained away the Congress (I) vote among the Muslims and Bengalis, contributed to a stunning victory for the Asom Gana Parishad, which captured a clear majority of seats. Congress (I) not only lost its last stronghold on the northeast border but failed to eliminate the threat of secession in the volatile region. The AGP government, by December 1986, confronted fresh agitations by AASU for the more rapid implementation of the accord. More ominous, a new terrorist organization called the United Liberation Front of Assam (ULFA) emerged and started to loot banks and to kill political rivals, coordinating its activities with tribal rebels belonging to the Tripura National Volunteers (TNV) in neighboring Tripura state.

The Punjab Accord

The "historic" accord, signed on 24 July 1985 by Rajiv Gandhi and Sant Harchand Singh Longowal, the Akali Dal president, was hailed for ending the three-year agitation for autonomy in Punjab, which had claimed 4,500 lives and was responsible for Indira Gandhi's assassination by followers of the slain extremist leader Sant Jarnail Singh Bhindranwale and the worst communal riots since Partition. The accord addressed the major demands of moderate Sikh leaders: Chandigarh, the union territory and joint capital of Punjab and Haryana since the old state of Punjab was divided in 1966 into Punjab, Haryana and Himachal Pradesh, was to be transferred to Punjab on Republic Day, 26 January 1986; the issue of greater autonomy for the state was referred to the Sarkaria Commission on center-state relations; Sikh army deserters reacting to the June 1984 Operation Bluestar against the fortified Sikh shrine of the holy Golden Temple in Amritsar were to be rehabilitated; and compensation was to be paid to innocent persons killed in communal riots. At the same time, the central leadership gave assurances to the Congress (I) chief minister of Haryana, Bhajan Lal (and his successor Bansi Lal), that Hindi-speaking areas of Punjab would be transferred to Haryana simultaneously with the transfer of Chandigarh to Punjab. In addition, the dispute between the two states over allocation of the Ravi-Beas river waters was referred to a tribunal with the expectation that water would start flowing into Haryana after completion of the Sutlej-Yamuna link canal (SYL).

From the outset, the Rajiv-Longowal Accord encountered powerful opposition in both Punjab and Haryana. Sant Longowal managed to persuade the reluctant senior leaders of the Akali Dal, Parkash Singh Badal, a former chief minister, and Gurcharan Singh Tohra, president of the Shiromani Gurdwara Pradbandhak Committee (SGPC), the elected management committee of all Sikh gurdwaras (temples) combining spiritual and temporal powers, to endorse the agreement. But the breakaway United Akali Dal, led by Baba Joginder Singh, the father of Bhindranwale, as well as a section of the militant All India Sikh Students Federation (AISSF) condemned the agreement as falling far short of their demands for autonomy. Meanwhile, in Haryana, the opposition Lok Dal, led by Devi Lal, himself a former chief minister, launched a mass movement against the accord on the grounds that it sacrificed Haryana's interests. In particular, the Lok Dal charged that the center had gone back on Mrs. Gandhi's 1969 "award" of the cotton-rich Abohar and Fazilka tehsils of Punjab to Haryana.[7]

The potential for successful implementation of the accord against such potent enemies was considerably diluted when on 20 August 1985 Sant Harchand Singh Longowal fell before an assassin's bullets. His successor as president of the Akali Dal, Surjit Singh Barnala, a former central minister and a staunch supporter of the Rajiv-Longowal Accord, did not enjoy the same stature as a mass leader of the Sikhs. Nevertheless, Barnala prevailed against dissidents inside the Akali Dal, including Joginder Singh, who called for a boycott of the state elections. The poll was held as scheduled on 25 September 1985, and for the first time since Independence, the Akalis won a majority in their own right with two-thirds of the seats in the Assembly. The surprising strength of the Sikh party, while hailed as a national victory for democracy, represented an unmistakable defeat for the Congress (I). Many partymen were upset that they had lost all representation in still another government in a strategic border state outside the Hindi heartland.

After the election, Chief Minister Barnala faced renewed violence from terrorists determined to sabotage the Rajiv-Longowal Accord. He was, for the time being, strengthened by the preparations underway for the transfer of Chandigarh and successfully contained the extremists in the United Akali Dal and the AISSF with the use of the state police.

However, close advisers to the prime minister (especially Arun Nehru, then minister of state for internal security), conveyed their worries and those of Haryana Chief Minister Bhajan Lal that the Congress (I) could expect another defeat, this time in its Hindi heartland, when elections scheduled for May 1987 were held in Haryana. An implication was that the entire base of the Congress (I) in North India could be threatened. The prime minister seemed literally to shift ground. He acquiesced in Bhajan Lal's demand—intended to neutralize his Lok Dal opposition—that only Abohar and Fazilka could be considered in exchange for Chandigarh. When technical and political obstacles made it impossible to conclude such an exchange by Republic Day on 26 January 1986, the center made the fateful decision that saw the unraveling of the accord. The transfer of Chandigarh, for which all administrative arrangements had been completed by bureaucrats of Haryana and Punjab, was postponed.

The Barnala government's ability to control the extremists was dramatically eroded. On 26 January, in a bizarre development, about 20,000 fundamentalist Sikh youth from the AISSF and the Damdami Taksal, the seminary for Sikh priests formerly headed by Bhindranwale, captured control of the Golden Temple complex. They convened a *sarbat khalsa* (a general assembly of Sikhs), declared the SGPC temple management committee disbanded and forced its members to withdraw from their offices; dismissed the head priests appointed by the SGPC for collaborating with the Indian government; named the nephew of Bhindranwale, then under detention for sedition, as their own nominee for head priest; and announced they alone would organize *kar seva* (voluntary labor) to demolish and rebuild the Akal Takt. The seventeenth-century "throne of the immortals," which had been damaged during Operation Bluestar, had subsequently been reconstructed by a heretical sect of Nihang Sikhs with government help and was thereby considered defiled.

Barnala's attempt to retrieve his position without further bloodshed only left him isolated. The moderates held their own *sarbat khalsa* at Anandpur Sahib outside Amritsar on 16 February and passed a resolution recognizing the SGPC as the only legal religious body of the Sikhs. However, Gurcharan Singh Tohra, who had served as SGPC president for fourteen years, resigned in February. Barnala named one of his own associates as acting president, but the new chief could not command Tohra's authority.

As the toll taken by terrorist killings mounted, Barnala's government became increasingly dependent on help from New Delhi. The state police force was so demoralized, by poor training and outmoded weapons as well as terrorist sympathizers in their own ranks, that they could no longer function as a reliable security force. Two central appointees, Julio Ribeiro as state police chief and Siddharta Shankar Ray as governor, increasingly assumed the role of the prime minister's chief advisers on Punjab. Over time, the Punjab Armed Police (PAP) relied more and more heavily on reinforcements from the Central Reserve Police Force (CRPF) in operations against extremists.

Nevertheless, on 29 April 1986 terrorists using the Golden Temple as a sanctuary felt sufficiently secure to proclaim the formation of the independent state of Khalistan from its grounds. The chief minister could no longer avoid a direct confrontation with them. On 30 April he ordered 1,300 Punjab police, paramilitary forces and commandos to enter the sacred complex. Operation Search succeeded in clearing out the extremists and reestablishing the SGPC in its old headquarters. Subsequently, the SGPC leadership set up a task force of discharged soldiers to prevent future infiltration. The price of this success, however, was very high. On 30 April, one-third of the Akali Dal legislative party, led by Parkash Singh Badal and Gurcharan Singh Tohra, left the party in protest and formed a new group headed by Badal, the Akali Dal (B). Subsequently, Barnala's government depended for its existence on the support of the Congress (I). His detractors ridiculed him as a puppet of New Delhi who had acquiesced in "proxy rule" of the state.

By the summer, terrorism had entered a new phase. In July, fourteen Hindus traveling by bus in Muktsar were segregated from other passengers and shot dead. A few weeks later, retired General A. S. Vaidya, the commander of Operation Bluestar, was assassinated in Pune, Maharashtra, by members of the "Khalistan Commando Force," demonstrating the long reach of the extremists in a far-off region. The first clear successes of the PAP under Ribeiro's leadership in making daring arrests of several most wanted terrorists were overshadowed by the attempt in early October on Ribeiro's life inside his own PAP complex, with the complicity of his own PAP men. Moreover, in November 1986, the election for president of the SGPC revealed that Barnala's followers had become a minority: the chief minister's nominee was easily defeated by Gurcharan Singh Tohra. One of Tohra's first acts was to disband the SGPC task force guarding the Golden Temple against extremist infiltration.

Terrorist violence escalated further in December. In one incident alone, in Hoshiarpur district, twenty-six persons were gunned down on a state bus. During the fifteen months of Barnala's ministry, some 500-700 persons were killed in Punjab.[8] Barnala himself conceded that the terrorists were able to strike at will and that their ranks were swelling in the absence of any political initiative from New Delhi.

Both the state government and the center prepared to return to the reliance on force that had marked the Congress (I)'s approach before hopes of a political solution were raised by the Rajiv-Longowal Accord. In December the Barnala government arrested Badal, Tohra and scores of AISSF activists under the National Security Act. Meanwhile, the Lok Sabha empowered the Punjab government to employ sweeping powers of electronic surveillance, search, arrest, detention and punishment of persons suspected of a terrorist act under the Terrorist and Disruptive Activity Prevention Act of 1985. Almost at the same time, the Punjab government conferred enabling powers on the army to conduct raids, searches, interrogations and detention of suspected terrorists, and to issue shoot-at-sight orders in an all-out war on terrorism in eight districts, parts of which were declared "disturbed areas."

At year's end, few victories could be counted by the Punjab government in its war against the terrorists. The extraordinary powers conferred on the army failed to prevent the extremists from getting their candidates installed among the five Sikh head priests of the Akal Takt in the Golden Temple. The head priests, moreover, were not intimidated from issuing a directive to Barnala to resign from office, or from announcing his excommunication from the Sikh community after he refused to do so.

Mizoram Accord

Against the background of events in Punjab, the Mizoram Accord of 26 July 1986, which ended a twenty-year insurgency of the Mizo National Front on the northeastern border with Bangladesh, provoked criticism. The agreement, ratified by Parliament in August, recognized Mizoram as a "special category state," autonomous with respect to making laws concerning religious and social practices, customary law and the sale and transfer of land. Skeptics inside the Congress (I) were concerned that the caretaker government, a coalition of the Mizo National Front (MNF) and the Congress (I), headed by the charismatic Mizo leader Laldenga, would be transformed into an MNF government after scheduled elections in February 1987. And events were to prove them right.

The opposition parties, such as the Lok Dal and Bharatiya Janata party, charged the government with post facto appeasement of secessionist elements that would fuel similar demands elsewhere. They stepped up their attacks after the shock of a violent new agitation, this one by the Gurkha National Liberation Front (GNLF), which demanded a separate state of Gurkhaland for the Nepali population of Darjeeling district in Northwest Bengal. Additional tremors shook the political landscape when the small union territory of Goa was convulsed by riots in December, after activists demanded that Konkani be made the sole official language, and that Goa be given full statehood.

Power Struggle Inside the Congress (I)

Among the many factors accounting for the absence of consensus inside the Congress (I) was the uncertainty about Rajiv Gandhi's leadership abilities. His late entry into politics in 1981, combined with his technocratic approach to rebuilding the party organization—symbolized by the effort to compile computerized files on fresh candidates with good reputations—pointed to a dangerous naïveté about the depth of the party's problems. In addition, Rajiv Gandhi's commitment to liberalize the economy and to remove controls that sheltered high-cost inefficient industries from foreign competition met with mixed reactions inside the party. The reforms struck at the prestige and power of several senior bureaucrats. They also created apprehension among sections of the business community whose products were not competitive with similar foreign imports. Moreover, the government's policy of carrying out highly publicized "raids" against some of India's most prominent industrialists to unearth black money earned opprobrium even among businessmen who supported the liberalization policy. Many Congressmen also viewed the emphasis on economic liberalization as a departure from Mrs. Gandhi's antipoverty programs that would widen the gulf between the impoverished majority and affluent upper middle classes, promote runaway consumerism and heighten social tensions.

Amid all these concerns, the growing challenge to the Congress (I) in the states, in a manner that raised fears for India's national integrity, intensified doubts about the prime minister's leadership abilities. The 100,000 Congressmen who attended the party's centenary celebrations (1885-1985) at Bombay in December 1985 met under the shadow of the poor performance in the state assembly elections and the dramatic defeats in Punjab and Assam. They viewed the accords, in particular, as the policy of a well-intentioned but inexperienced leader, who unlike his mother did not understand or appreciate the Congress culture of integrating diverse, and even unsavory, elements to maintain the party's umbrella character. On the contrary, the prime minister remained intent on purging the "power brokers" from the party and putting his own inexperienced aides in key positions. The challenge of the states to central authority thereby became entangled with the challenge by dissidents inside the Congress (I) to Rajiv's authority as party leader and prime minister.

It is difficult to say whether the disillusionment of the "Indira loyalists" with the leadership of their new party chief or the contempt of Rajiv Gandhi for those among them he derided as "power brokers" was the greater. Certainly, no Congress president had ever indicted his own party leaders in the language that Rajiv used to admonish the delegates at the Bombay centennary "celebration": "We (Congressmen) obey no discipline, no rule, follow no principle of public morality, display no sense of social awareness, show no concern for the public weal. Corruption is not only tolerated but even regarded as the hallmark of leadership."[9]

The issue on which both sides entered into a test of strength was Rajiv Gandhi's promise to restore intraparty democracy by holding the first elections to party committees since 1972. The prime minister, who was also the Congress (I) president, set 31 March 1986 as the last day for the membership drive and directed that party elections be completed by the end of June. He was adamant that party workers be selected who were loyal to the party and to the political leadership.

The pace at which "Indira loyalists" were displaced quickened. On 19 January 1986 Pranab Mukherjee, a former minister of finance considered to have been the most powerful member of Mrs. Gandhi's last cabinet, was dropped from both the Congress (I) Working Committee and the Parliamentary Board. Gundu Rao, a former chief minister of Karnataka, who also claimed a close association with Mrs. Gandhi, was removed from the Congress (I) Working Committee. In addition, Rajiv Gandhi isolated the octogenarian Congress (I) "working president," Kamalpathi Tripathi, who was an appointee of Mrs. Gandhi and the epitome of the "Old Guard"—a fifty-year veteran of the party and former chief minister of Uttar Pradesh. The prime minister created a new position of All-India Congress Committee (I) (AICC (I)) vice-president and named his close associate Arjun Singh (until then commerce minister) to fill it. The new vice-president's mandate was to complete the membership drive and conduct the party elections.

Arjun Singh's greatest political strength was in Uttar Pradesh and Madhya Pradesh, the two North Indian states that between them would send over one-third of the members to an elected AICC (I). He was, moreover, adept in winning factional fights for control of district Congress committees and pradesh Congress committees, whose members constituted the electorate for delegates that selected the AICC (I). Even he, however, could not stop the fraudulent practices by rival groups of enrolling bogus members for the purpose of controlling the voting at local levels. Moreover, just as the membership drive was reaching its climax, Rajiv Gandhi, as prime minister, took a particularly unpopular decision. He supported the Muslim Women (Protection of Rights on Divorce) Bill, which broadly upheld Muslim personal law on divorce. His position was interpreted as a calculated concession to fundamentalist elements to win back the Muslim vote. It not only tarnished the prime minister's image as a principled leader of liberal convictions but enraged the Hindu middle classes (and educated Muslim women), for giving priority to Muslim rights over the constitutional directive to move toward a uniform civil code for all communities.

The prime minister's obvious vulnerability emboldened party dissidents. Pranab Mukherjee publicly expressed criticism of the Muslim Women Bill and characterized the government as weak and blundering. More damaging, Kamalapathi Tripathi sent a four-page letter to the prime minister, which was leaked to the press, expressing his anger at the large-scale enrollment of bogus members into the party, accompanied by huge deposits for "membership fees" left at Congress offices by unidentified persons. Other parts of Tripathi's letter represented a catalogue of the dissidents' complaints against Rajiv's leadership:

> Congressmen are puzzled and bewildered at the rapid disintegration of the party at all levels and shocked at the casual, ad hoc and inept handling of party matters by you and your so-called operatives. My contention is that Congress is rapidly losing its contact with the masses and that you are surrounded by a number of sycophants who were not only 'Indira-baiters' but 'Indira-haters.' In handling some of the issues like problems in Punjab and Assam, you have shown impatience and your measures have not only been casual and ad hoc, but have aggravated the problems. This Government is primarily concerned with the welfare of the well-to-do sections of society. The pro-poor stance of your mother's policy is a story of the past.[10]

Tripathi's letter and the large number of dissidents reported to be meeting regularly at his residence were interpreted as a plot to force a split in the Congress (I). This danger was averted by a "preemptive strike" in which Pranab Mukherjee and three other prominent party leaders were expelled from membership.

As scrutiny of the party membership rolls got underway, it became clear that perhaps 60 percent of those listed were not eligible for membership, or simply were nonexistent.[11] The entire enterprise of restoring intra-party democracy had to be abandoned. After June 1986, all talk about holding party elections ceased. Moreover, in August, the expelled leaders held a dissidents' convention and announced the formation of the Indian National Congress (Indira Gandhi), charging Rajiv with failure to follow his mother's policies for strengthening national unity. A follow-up convention in January 1987 changed the name of the new party to the Rashtriya Samajwadi Congress (National Socialist Congress).

The final outcome of the effort to rebuild the party organization ironically decimated what was left of the national apparatus. On 22 October Rajiv Gandhi inducted Arjun Singh back into his cabinet as communications minister, tacitly abolishing the post of AICC (I) vice-president. In mid-November he asked for the resignation of Kamalapathi Tripathi as working president, and those of the seven general secretaries, citing plans for reconstituting the AICC (I) secretariat. On their own initiative, all members of the Congress Working Committee (I) also resigned. At year's end, all the top positions in the national party were still vacant. The pradesh Congress committees in most states hardly met. Rajiv continued to appoint state party chiefs and chief ministers without regard for local political sentiments. Opposition leaders openly speculated on whether the ruling Congress (I) was headed for a split, and they urged their members to be prepared for midterm elections.[12]

Opposition Political Parties

It is a telling commentary on the state of the Indian party system in 1986 that no opposition party was in place to provide alternative national leadership had the Congress (I) acted on its suicidal urge toward a party split. Until 1967, Congress had successfully preempted the opposition by functioning as both a ruling party and a loose coalition in which newly politicized groups were accommodated with a share of power in the organization.

Even after the integrative capacity of Congress declined, the opposition remained fragmented in the absence of a common ideology or an all-India base of social support. The most potent challenges to Congress predominance were raised at the regional level by state parties that could appeal to shared identities rooted in language or ethnicity. For this very reason, the leaders of the opposition parties found it virtually impossible to agree on a single opposition leader (as potential prime minister) that could head a united opposition party and provide a national alternative to Congress. Moreover, Rajiv Gandhi's conciliatory approach toward regional opposition parties proved to be more effective than Mrs. Gandhi's strident attack against them as "antinational" in blunting initiatives by regional leaders to develop an all-India united opposition.

The difficulties of opposition leaders representing narrow and/or opposing interests in establishing stable united front governments were apparent from the end of the 1960s, after Congress lost power in more than half of the states in India. Constant conflict among the coalition partners over allocation of ministerial portfolios and other offices as well as policy disagreements on economic planning, land reforms, language, communalism and reservations for "other backward classes"[13] produced chronic instability. Defections and counter-defections of state legislators to rival party groupings, which led to President's Rule in several states, discredited the practice of forming united front governments based on loose alliances among disparate parties.

The resurgence of Mrs. Gandhi's Congress after the 1969 party split and its sweeping victory at the center in 1971, and in most states in 1972, demoralized the opposition. The one exception was the Communist Party of India (CPI), which welcomed the government's movement toward the left. Indeed, Mrs. Gandhi's decision to push through major constitutional amendments that weakened fundamental rights and removed all limitations on Parliament's powers for legislating radical economic reforms raised the alarm that the government was on the way to imposing a communist-style dictatorship. The resort by the opposition parties to extra-parliamentary agitations for the removal of Mrs. Gandhi from office triggered the prime minister's decision to suspend all political freedoms during the Emergency, between June 1975 and January 1977.[14]

Leaders of the opposition made their first serious attempt to organize a united party only when faced with the extreme danger that democracy itself could be liquidated if Mrs. Gandhi were returned to power during the national election in March 1977. Four parties agreed to fight the elections under one flag and one program, and to merge into a single party after the poll. These four parties were different in their social base, ideological orientation and geographical spread. The Congress (O), formed after the 1969 Congress party split, was a secular and conservative party with a national following but having its greatest strength in Gujarat, the home state of its leader, Morarji Desai. By contrast, the Socialist party, founded in 1971 after numerous splits of the democratic left, found its strongest support in Bihar, among scheduled caste landless laborers, and in Bombay, among unionized factory workers. The Bharatiya Lok Dal (BLD), formed in 1974 under the leadership of Charan Singh, had a broader base than either the Congress (O) or the Socialists. Its supporters were drawn from among the small peasantry belonging to the diverse backward classes of Uttar Pradesh, Bihar and Haryana. Finally, the Jan Sangh, the oldest of the parties, dating to 1951, promoted an ideology based on Bharatiya (Indian) Culture and maintained a close association with the Rashtriya Swayamsevak Sangh (RSS), a militant Hindu youth organization, which supplied many of its political cadre. The Jan Sangh also had its greatest strength in North India, but primarily among the urban middle classes.[15]

The meteoric rise of the Janata party to national power in March 1977, and in seven states three months later, was based on its ability to unite public opinion against Mrs. Gandhi's Emergency rule. Once in office, however, the various constituents were unable to agree on their proper share of power, both in the central government and at the states. The energies of the leadership were consumed in factional struggles, especially schemes for enrolling the largest number of members in order to capture key posts in organizational elections. These elections could never be held. The top party leadership engaged in such bitter conflict that the BLD left the Janata, charging that the Jan Sangh group was seeking to control the party through its cadre raised from the communal RSS.[16]

The experiment of a united opposition party lasted only twenty-seven months. The disillusionment left in its wake paved the way for the return of Mrs. Gandhi as prime minister. By 1980, after precipitating another split in the Congress, she won a two-thirds majority in the Lok Sabha, as head of her own Congress (I), and also swept elections to the state assemblies.

The breakup of the Janata party left the noncommunist opposition more divided than ever. The Janata, which retained most of its socialist members, became a regional party, controlling only the state government of Karnataka. The Lok Dal lost its influence over the governments in Haryana, Bihar and Uttar Pradesh, which it had prized after the Janata's 1977 victory. The Congress (O) was virtually destroyed as a national party, resurfacing as the Congress (S) in Maharashtra under the leadership of Sharad Pawar. The Jan Sangh sought, unsuccessfully, to broaden its social base by reconstituting its organization as the Bharatiya Janata party (BJP).

The CPI, if anything, fared worse. Discredited by its support for Mrs. Gandhi during the Emergency, it won less than 3 percent of the vote nationwide in 1984. Its rival on the left, the Communist Party of India (Marxist), performed twice as well but remained confined to its regional bases in West Bengal and Tripura.

Nevertheless, the animus of virtually all opposition leaders against Mrs. Gandhi provided the continuing impetus for still more opposition unity moves. These gained momentum in 1984 when the Congress (I) successfully toppled the National Conference government of Farooq Abdullah in Jammu and Kashmir and attempted, but failed, to unseat the popular N. T. Rama Rao's Telugu Desam government in Andhra Pradesh.

During 1983 and 1984 as many as fourteen to sixteen opposition parties attended four "conclaves" aimed at reviving a united opposition party. Although this goal eluded them, they did achieve a broad consensus on the issue of center-state relations, which was by no means reassuring to the leadership in New Delhi. The major "consensus document," adopted at the third conclave in Srinagar in October 1983, outlined the need for a new balance in the powers between the center and the states. Among the recommendations were several proposals for constitutional amendments to weaken or abolish the center's power of dissolving state governments and assemblies, appointing governors, legislating on any subject on the state list, deploying central police forces without the consent of state governments, and exercising discretionary control over financial grants to the states.[17]

Rajiv Gandhi's conciliatory approach, as signaled by his unexpected decision in October 1986 to drop Arun Nehru from the cabinet, succeeded in reducing the antagonism between the center and the states. Toward the end of the year this strategy won over two of the most effective leaders in the opposition. In Maharashtra, Sharad Pawar, the leader of the formidable Congress (S), agreed to merge his party with the Congress (I). Moreover, Rajiv Gandhi relinquished President's Rule over Jammu and Kashmir and entered into an agreement with Farooq Abdullah to head a caretaker coalition government of the National Conference and Congress (I) pending new elections.

The Collapse of Consensus Politics

The most significant feature of India's politics in 1986 concerned a hoped-for development that did not take place. Rajiv Gandhi's policies of reconciliation failed to restore the Congress (I) as a party of consensus. The failure of the Congress (I) in 1986, and of the Janata almost a decade earlier, to manage internal competition between rival factions within a framework of party discipline suggests that conflicts eroding the cohesion of national parties have deeper causes than the personal ambitions of power-hungry politicians. Seen from this perspective, Indira Gandhi's political style of centralizing power in her own hands, her substitution of personal rule for the party system, appears as much a symptom as the cause of the progressive breakdown in the consensual Congress culture. Indeed, starting from the 1969 Congress split, Mrs. Gandhi was responding to changes in the political environment that made impossible a return to the "Congress system" of bargaining politics among a plurality of competing social groups.

The rapid rise in political awareness among socially and educationally disadvantaged castes as well as linguistic, religious and tribal minorities transformed the competition for political power between factions that cut across divisive caste and communal lines to fights between more or less homogeneous social classes and ethnic groups. In several states, group-based political mobilization around intensified caste, ethnic or religious identities led to a competition for primacy with dominant castes, classes or communities that could not be resolved by compromise.

The most important type of social polarization arose from the political mobilization of the more advanced caste groups among the backward classes. Their entry into the Congress party organization directly challenged the power of entrenched upper caste faction leaders, whose own leadership position had depended on their ability to co-opt the support of aspiring backward class politicians who commanded the votes of their numerous caste fellows. The struggle for precedence between established elites and their erstwhile subordinates could not be settled through accommodation. Either the dominant agricultural castes that controlled the party organization in the countryside and the merchants, contractors and factory owners influential in the cities became reconciled to giving up real power or the backward classes could defect from the Congress party. This option, in fact, was chosen by Charan Singh, who left the Congress party in Uttar Pradesh soon after the 1967 election to form his own Samyukta Vidhayak Dal or united front government. Thereafter, as head of the Lok Dal, he emerged as a serious contender to the Congress/Congress (I) in Haryana, Uttar Pradesh and Bihar.

Clearly, Mrs. Gandhi understood the nature of the explosive changes in political mobilization that were overtaking the mechanisms of controlled patronage managed by narrow elites which served in the 1950s and the 1960s to secure Congress in its dominant position. In the 1971 and 1972 elections to the Lok Sabha, and in the states (after the 1969 split sloughed off the old party bosses), she made a phenomenally successful class appeal. Mrs. Gandhi received popular support cutting across regional, communal, ethnic and caste divisions, by asking the electorate to "strengthen my hands" to remove poverty. Initially, she also endorsed proposals to rebuild the Congress party as an ideologically committed, cadre-based organization. But she drew back amid fears that plans were underway by radical Congressmen aligned to the CPI for capturing key posts.

The suspension of party elections after 1972 created a "pyramidal decision-making structure in party and government."[18] Central intervention in Congress-ruled states to impose chief ministers and party heads loyal to the prime minister, and the appointment of partisan governors in non-Congress-ruled states who would be helpful in "toppling" opposition governments, became the norm. Yet it is missing the point to argue that Mrs. Gandhi's departure from intraparty democracy weakened the capacity of the Congress for managing factional conflict through the use of bargaining. At the time she took these decisions ideological polarization among the central party leadership was so sharp that the bargaining culture had already been destroyed.

The achievement often attributed to Mrs. Gandhi by her defenders is that by using these tactics she neutralized the left inside the Congress party. Indeed, sidestepping the party, she won over the poor by making herself the personal embodiment of their aspirations. Mrs. Gandhi's detractors have paid more attention to the very high price exacted in weakening institutionalization across the whole spectrum of the party, administration, police and judiciary. Ultimately, her leadership style led to the "cult of personality" and "dynastic democracy."

There were other risks in following this strategy that were less apparent at the time, risks to India's secular values as the basis of national integration. It must be remembered that Mrs. Gandhi governed India during most of her fifteen years as prime minister without an effective party organization to mobilize grassroots support for implementing land reforms and other institutional changes at the core of her antipoverty programs. On the contrary, the dominant castes and classes remained in place to thwart any such changes. As a result (except during the Emergency), Mrs. Gandhi could not launch a direct attack against the privileges of these groups. Instead, she fell back on various social welfare policies that avoided raising the class issue. A series of schemes, targeted at the scheduled castes, the scheduled tribes and small and marginal farmers, heightened the social awareness of these poor and dispersed groups without providing the political organization to weld them into a cohesive force.

In addition, starting with the 1972 elections, the Congress party increased the number of tickets it gave to persons belonging to the backward classes, scheduled castes, tribals and Muslims, albeit without dramatically displacing the dominant castes. This effort to shift the social base of the Congress party was most apparent in Karnataka and Andhra Pradesh, although it was also important in Maharashtra, Gujarat and Rajasthan.[19] In Karnataka and Andhra Pradesh, this shift was also accompanied by increasing the percentage of reserved places for the backward classes in educational institutions and government services.

Such tactics could not be successfully applied in most of North India where the dominant upper castes were more numerous and enjoyed cumulative advantages of ritual rank, economic power and political influence. In this region, the Congress (I) used the reverse approach of holding the backward classes at bay by forging alliances between the elite castes and the more pliant scheduled castes and Muslims. By 1977, the breakdown of the Congress as an integrative party in the North was symbolized in the rise of backward caste chief ministers who swung their support behind Janata (and its Lok Dal constituent) in Haryana, Bihar and Uttar Pradesh.

Other problems surfaced in the Congress (I) bastion of the South by the early 1980s. Since the pro-poor programs of the Congress (I) were populist in character and did nothing to change the structure of economic power, the upper castes were able to shift their financial and other resources to regional opposition parties. Attractive leaders like the Janata's Ramakrishna Hegde in Karnataka and the Telugu Desam's N. T. Rama Rao in Andhra Pradesh, appealing to regional self-respect against growing central intervention in state politics, found it simple to outbid the Congress (I) by promising even more social welfare, with less corruption, and in the name of Telugu or Kannadiga honor.

Moreover, there was a limit to the tolerance of the "forward castes" for higher and higher reservations in favor of the backward classes in both Congress (I)- and opposition-governed states. In Gujarat, Rajiv Gandhi faced a protracted and violent antireservation campaign after the Congress (I) government, in January 1985, announced an increase in reservations for the backward classes shortly before legislative assembly elections. By July 1985, Gujarat's chief minister was forced to resign, and his successor to revoke the higher quotas. In Andhra Pradesh, N. T. Rama Rao's government polarized "forwards" and "backwards" across the state by announcing a steep increase in reservations for the backward classes in colleges and government employment in July 1986. The agitations that followed seemed headed for a similar violent struggle when the state high court intervened to rule that the higher limits (exceeding 50 percent) were unconstitutional.

If the Congress (I) and the regional opposition parties suffered from similar problems in integrating their polarized constituencies into parties of national consensus, their only response was to compete more strenuously with each other for the allegiance of the same groups. The opposition parties, in addition, blamed the center for the capricious allocation of funds and sought to attribute their difficulties in removing poverty to the imbalance of powers between the center and the states.

In such a political climate, it is not surprising that the Congress (I), on the eve of the 1984 Lok Sabha elections, should have sought to fortify its position by seeking to win over larger communal groups. Sanjay Gandhi and, after his death, the then central Home Minister Zail Singh, sought to undermine the Akali Dal by bringing Bhindranwale into the political limelight. They chose him precisely because as the most uncompromising champion of Sikh fundamentalism, with a following among unemployed and underemployed youth, he was best fitted to embarrass the moderate and relatively affluent Akali leadership.[20] From there it was a short step to rally support among the

"Hindus" by demonstrating the government's firmness against the extremists' demands in a manner that led many of the RSS cadres to desert the Bharatiya Janata party in the 1984 elections for the Congress (I).

The question raised by events in 1986 is a fundamental one for India's political system. How long can economic, social and political inequalities underlying regional, caste and communal polarization be ignored without weakening the center's political authority and undermining the secular basis of the Indian state? Already, militant Hindu revivalist organizations are proliferating in small towns across the country, condemning conciliatory policies toward the Sikhs and Muslims as evidence that "Hinduism is in danger." The efforts of leading groups like the Vishwa Hindu Parishad and the RSS to bring all Hindu sects into a single movement, and to foster Hindu unity by schemes to uplift scheduled castes and tribals, may have a greater appeal to the old elites and the affluent new middle classes than the out-of-control populism of the secular party system. The synthetic unity it proffers holds out the promise of religious equality for all castes, but it does nothing to disturb the cumulative inequalities that are inseparable from the structure of the Hindu social order.[21]

Notes

1. For the most influential formulation describing the Congress "system," see Rajni Kothari, "The Congress 'System' in India," *Asian Survey* (December, 1964); also his "The Congress System Revisited: A Decennial Review," *Asian Survey* (December, 1974).

2. See G. G. Mirchandani and K. S. R. Murthi, *Massive Mandate for Rajiv Gandhi, 1984 Lok Sabha Elections* (New Delhi: Sterling, 1985).

3. A. S. Abraham, "A Patchy Congress Mandate," *Times of India*, 9 March 1985.

4. The Dravida Munnetra Kazhagam (DMK), or Dravidian Progressive Foundation, identified with Tamil language and culture since its formation in 1949, succeeded in ousting the Congress party from state government in 1967. The party's support for Tamil and opposition to the imposition of Hindi as the official language, was only one element that distinguished it from the Congress party. Since the period of the nationalist movement Congress had been identified in the cities with the urban professional and business classes, and in the countryside with the dominant landowning castes. By contrast, the DMK mobilized the new lower middle classes in the urban areas and small agriculturalists, artisans, shopkeepers and laborers in the countryside. Moreover, the DMK

pioneered populist policies, including reservations for "backward" Hindus to places in educational institutions and posts in government services. The DMK split in 1972 primarily reflected a clash in personalities. The popular film star M. G. Ramachandran charged the chief minister with corruption, and formed the All-India Anna DMK, AIADMK, invoking the name of the DMK's founder, Annadurai, to suggest a return to principled politics. The AIADMK, sparked by M. G. R. 's personal charisma emerged victorious in the 1977 elections, and retained its hold on the state government during the following decade. See Marguerite Ross Barnett, *The Politics of Cultural Nationalism in South India* (Princeton, N.J.: Princeton University Press, 1976), pp. 188-95.

5. *India Today,* 15 January 1986, pp. 36-38.

6. The British first compiled a list of "depressed classes," a euphemism for untouchables, and appended it to the 1935 Government of India Act, which reserved seats in the central legislature and the provincial legislatures for members of these "scheduled" castes. Although untouchability was legally abolished by the 1950 Constitution, these castes were also identified as scheduled castes for purposes of establishing which groups were eligible to benefit from "protective discrimination. "

7. Mrs. Gandhi yielded, in 1969, to Akali Dal leader Sant Fateh Singh, who threatened to fast to death unless Chandigarh was transferred to Punjab. At the time she conceded Punjab's claim to Chandigarh, she asserted that the Hindi majority areas of Abohar and Fazilka would be given to Haryana. The provisions of this "award" were never implemented. Mark Tully and Satish Jacob, *Amritsar, Mrs. Gandhi's Last Battle* (London: Cape, 1985), p. 45.

8. *India Today,* 31 December 1986, p. 28.

9. *India Today,* 15 January 1986.

10. *India Today,* 30 June 1986, p. 73.

11. *India Today,* 15 June 1986, p. 34-37.

12. *Times of India,* 5 January 1987.

13. The term "other backward classes" refers to low castes exclusive of untouchables, who are economically, educationally and socially backward. The Constitution empowers the states to make reservations for members of the "other backward classes" in educational institutions and government services. Most states have identified such communities on the basis of low ranking in the local ritual hierarchy which subjected them to a variety of disabilities in educational and social areas, and in turn left them economically depressed. See Marc Galanter, *Competing Equalities, Law and the Backward Classes in India* (New York: Oxford University Press, 1984), ch. 6.

14. Francine R. Frankel, *India's Political Economy, 1947-1977, The Gradual Revolution* (Princeton, N.J.: Princeton University Press, 1978), chs. 11,12.

15. Robert L. Hardgrave, Jr. and Stanley A. Kochanek, *India, Government and Politics in a Developing Nation* (New York: Harcourt Brace Jovanovich, 1986), pp. 237-241.

16. C. P. Bhambhri, *The Janata Party* (New Delhi: National Publishing House, 1980), chs. 1-6.

17. Mirchandani and Murthi, op. cit. , pp. 31-40.

18. Stanley A. Kochanek, "Mrs. Gandhi's Pyramid: The New Congress," in Henry C. Hart, ed. , *Indira Gandhi's India: A Political System Reappraised* (Boulder: Westview Press, 1976), pp. 104-5.

19. George Mathew, ed. , *Shift in Indian Politics, 1983 Elections in Andhra Pradesh and Karnataka* (New Delhi: Concept Publishing Company, 1984), chs. 3-5.

20. Mark Tully and Satish Jacob, op. cit., chs. 4, 5.

21. Romila Thapar, "Syndicated Moksha?" *Seminar,* September 1985.

3
Religion and Politics

Ainslie T. Embree

Religion was much in the news in India in 1986, more so perhaps than at any time since 1947, when the coming of Independence was marked by what seemed to many observers to be a religious war in North India between Hindus and Muslims. In India, as elsewhere, when religion is in the news it is almost always bad news, and this prominence of religion in public affairs as a factor in conflict is one of the most unexpected phenomena in national and international life at the end of the twentieth century. It was long accepted by historians and other analysts of the past and present that religion would have a decreasing role in the modern world. It was assumed that the great issues of political discourse would be constitutional arrangements, the solving of economic problems, and the resolution of conflicts of interests between nations. In 1878 one of the earliest spokesmen for Indian nationalism could tell a gathering of young people that while there had been bloody strife over religion in the past, India had had enough of "past jealousies, past dissensions, past animosities."[1] Henceforth, he said, they would raise aloft the banner of progress, on which there was no place for religious differences. This point of view found frequent expression in the writing of Jawaharlal Nehru, India's nationalist leader and first prime minister, with his reiteration that religious strife was the creation of the British to divide the Indian people to prevent them uniting against the imperial power.

The insistence that religious identity was irrelevant to the struggle for freedom, that the alleged animosity between Hindus and Muslims was an artifact of exploitative imperialism for dividing and ruling India, had fateful consequences. It meant, in effect, that by refusing to take religion seriously the nationalist leaders misunderstood a potent factor that was shaping the development in Indian social and political life. The demands expressed in Muslim majority provinces that Muslims should be guaranteed political representation and that there should be constitutional safeguards for their development as a community were dismissed by Nehru and the other leaders of the Indian National Congress as the self-serving tactics of Muslim leaders like Jinnah. According to Indian nationalist rhetoric, "Muslim fanaticism" was being used to undermine secular ideals of Indian nationalism.

Secularism and Communalism

"Secularism" is a much-used and amorphous word in India, a legacy of the pre-1947 nationalist movement, and its interpretation is a continuous factor in the function of religion in relation to politics. It indicates a number of concerns: that despite the numerical superiority of Hindus—85 percent of the population—India is not a Hindu state; that all citizens by constitutional right are free to profess, practice and propagate their religion; that no one will be discriminated against on the basis of religion; that no religion will be favored over another. All of these provisions project values of the liberal democratic tradition, which, probably any knowledgeable observer would agree, have been respected by the state and upheld by the courts. But at the same time, the Indian constitution, the legislative bodies and the courts have involved themselves in the beliefs and practices of religious groups in ways that have led to friction and conflict. The constitution, in Article 25, for example, rather off-handedly suggests that Sikhism is a part of Hinduism, which is a statement of little importance to Hindus and was not much noticed by Sikhs. When Sikh political autonomy became an issue in the 1980s, however, the innocuous reference became, in the eyes of many Sikhs, a reflection on the integrity of Sikhism and denial of their rights. The legal system also makes explicit provision for the guarantee by the state of the laws relating to marriage, divorce and inheritance for Muslims and Christians, but not, it is very important to note in the context of the troubles of 1986, of Hindus. For Hindus, all such matters of personal and family law are governed by the general laws of India, passed after India became independent. In 1986, there was a rising demand that all Indians, as Indians, should come under a common law, that special provision for the enforcement of laws for specific religious communities was both a violation of the spirit of the constitution and a threat to national integrity and unity.

In the simplest formulation, issues involving religion and politics can be stated in terms of national unity versus what Indian newspapers are fond of referring to by the strange euphemism, "fissiparous tendencies," or religious communalism. Communalism is another Indian term that defies precise definition, but it is always used in a pejorative sense, implying that religious groups stress the importance of membership in their group over national identity, and that these groups seek their own advantage over those of other groups and of the nation as a whole. What this definition conceals is that the majority community can equate its own interests with the national interest, and see even rational claims for justice by a minority religious community as an attack on national unity. "National unity" thus can become a code phrase to denigrate legitimate assertions of cultural pluralism. It is in this fashion that such innocuous abstractions as communalism and secularism become part of the terminology of conflict situations in India.

At the end of the century, then, in India as elsewhere, the banners under which warring factions array themselves are inscribed with the ancient devices of religion. In Northern Ireland, the symbols are those of Roman Catholicism and Protestantism; in the Middle East, they are those of Islam, Judaism and Christianity; and in India, in 1986, Muslim, Hindu, Sikh and, to a modest extent, Christian symbols find a place in political discourse and conflict. In December 1984, a *Chicago Tribune* headline neatly summarized an editor's perception of the violence that wracked Delhi following Indira Gandhi's assassination: "Holy War Erupts in India." At the beginning of 1987 a headline in the *New York Times* continued the story: "Violence in India Revives Old Fears," fears, in the words of the article, of "spectacular or gruesome massacres" carried out by extremist Sikhs against Hindus. The article also mentioned seventeen people being killed in the southern state of Karnataka after a local paper had published a short story called "Mohammed the Idiot," which deeply offended the local Muslim population.

All of this confirms the relevance of religion to politics in India, but it is also misleading if it suggests that religious differences are the fundamental or sufficient cause of the conflicts that are given religious labels. Very often commentators use the labels of religious terminology as a convenience for avoiding careful analysis of complex situations. It is assumed that if the protagonists can be given religious identifications that are rooted in historic antagonism, this will be an adequate explanation for an outbreak of violence. This is not to say that such identifications are not important, for although it would be absurd to argue that views on the nature of the deity or memories of the smashing of Hindu idols by tenth-century Turkic invaders led to the riots in Karnataka, it would be equally absurd to refuse to recognize that religious identifications and preferences were important factors. What is essential in looking at religion and politics in 1986—and in looking forward—is to see how complex, indeed, how convoluted, the relationship is. And the place to start is not, I am convinced, with reference to the historic antagonisms rooted in the conquest of India by Islamic invaders a thousand years ago but with the nature of contemporary political and social life.

Political and Socioeconomic Factors

Antagonisms that seem so obvious and self-evident if one stresses historic memories are, instead, very often products of the political and social processes that created modern India. It is in the working out of what is one of the most admirable features of India, the process of political democracy, that religion and politics formed their explosive mixture. Five elements, all part of the historical experience of modern India, seem to be of particular relevance in explicating the relation of religion to politics in India, and after their brief identification, three situations will be noted where they interacted in 1986. The three are what were known in the headlines of Indian papers as the Shah Bano case, the Babri Mosque affair and Sikh terrorism in Punjab. All the elements that were active in these situations will certainly be active again in the coming years.

The first two situations involved the position of Muslims in India, and that more attention is given to them than to the Sikhs reflects a personal conviction that while Sikh activities are far more dramatic and more agonizing, in the long run movements within the Muslim community are more significant for India and, therefore, for the rest of the world. Islam in India does not mean what it does in Iran or Pakistan or Saudi Arabia, where the population is overwhelmingly Muslim and Muslims possess all the mechanisms of power. Muslims in India are a minority—but, it should always be remembered, a minority of about 80 million people, making India the fourth largest Muslim population in the world, after Indonesia, Pakistan and Bangladesh. According to 1986 estimates, 83.6 percent of the population of India was Hindu, 11.0 percent was Muslim, 2.6 percent was Christian, 2.5 percent was Sikh and 0.2 percent were listed as other.

Perhaps the fundamental causal factor in the relationship between religious communities and politics in India has to do with the nature of political representation. Somewhat paradoxically, some of the decisions that led to India's present political structure, while ensuring democracy, also made inevitable the intertwining of religion and politics and the conflicts that follow from this relationship. At the beginning of the century, before a measure of representative government was instituted in India in 1909 (through the Indian Councils Act, usually known as the Morley-Minto reforms), the great issue had been what form such representation should take. The leaders of the dominant nationalist group, the Indian National Congress, were insistent that representation, however the franchise might be defined, should not recognize any difference between Indians on the basis of religion. What they wanted, they insisted, was the establishment in India of responsible, representative government on the pattern of Great Britain and Canada, with the will of the numerical majority being the will of the people. The British answer was that Western political institutions had grown up in a particular society and could not be transferred to another one so different in its composition as India, which was not a nation but a subcontinent composed of many nations. For the vocal Muslim leadership, representative government on the Western model, as demanded by the Congress, meant the permanent subjection of the Muslim minority to the Hindu majority. They demanded separate electorates so as to ensure the Muslims a share of power in the new framework of government. The 1909 act was a curious compromise in that it conceded separate electorates to the Muslims, to the intense anger of the Congress leadership, but at the same time it established the principle of majority rule.

But the question was insistently asked: how are the rights of minorities to be safeguarded? This is a point that had received little consideration in the nineteenth-century British liberal political thought upon which the Indians had drawn. Liberal political thinkers had been concerned with the rights of minority opinions, but the issue in India was very different: not the right of dissenting opinion and individual freedom, but the rights of groups in terms of customs and social practices, which were seen as having a religious basis. This included all the vast corpus of law dealing with inheritance, marriage and family relationships. Could the majority legislate for minority groups in these matters, or were the internal laws of religious groups parallel to those of the state and enforceable by it? In 1986, it was the question of the applicability of the nation's laws to all its citizens, in regard to such matters as marriage, divorce and inheritance, irrespective of membership in religious groups, that was challenged most notably by Muslim leaders, although some Christian groups were also involved. There appeared to be some confusion in India, as in other liberal democracies, between the concept of religious freedom, one of the most cherished rights that has emerged in the long struggle of the individual against the state, and group rights. Religious freedom, in the language of the Indian constitution, means the right to practice and propagate one's faith, without hindrance from the state, but increasingly this has been interpreted to mean that the government should, in effect, support through law the customs that a community claims are basic to its internal life.

The assertion that groups have rights that cannot be challenged by majority decision, as expressed through the legislature, on the grounds that the nation is an aggregate of groups, not of individuals, is, on one level, merely an interesting theoretical proposition. That it is also an intensely practical issue, of immediate political consequence, was shown in 1986 in the Shah Bano case and the Muslim Women (Protection of Rights on Divorce) Bill, to which further reference will be made, when they elicited such enormous passion both among Muslims and Hindus. In a less publicized case, but one involving the same issue, a Christian woman won a case for her right, as a daughter, to share in the family inheritance along with her brothers. The argument against the legal decision was that the courts should uphold what was regarded as an essential custom of the community. The rights of a group, or in the common Indian terminology, of a community, against the will of the numerical majority was also a dominant factor in the behavior of the so-called Sikh extremists during the past year, as it has been since 1980.

A second situation that provides occasion for religious identity becoming central to political concern is the very frequent perception by minority groups that in a rapidly changing society members of other groups are benefitting economically while they are being deliberately excluded. The economic basis for antagonism between religious and ethnic groups in India is a complex and controversial issue. During the nationalist struggle, Nehru's view was widely shared, that it was not religion that divided Muslims and Hindus, but disparities in economic opportunities. Imperialism and capitalism, he argued, had worked together to create Hindu-Muslim hostility, and the disappearance of imperial rule and the creation of a socialist pattern of society would lessen the economic competition on which hostility was based. Nehru and his followers misunderstood both the power of religious identity and the difficulties of creating a society that would be free of economic rivalries. Before independence, the majority of Muslims belonged to the poorest sections of the population, but after 1947 the situation worsened as many of the better educated and more affluent Muslims, who might have provided community leadership, opted for Pakistan. Competition for jobs was felt most keenly by the poorest people, both Hindus and Muslims, and it is easy to see how in the struggle for survival it was easy to identify religious and ethnic differences as causal factors in disputes that were almost wholly economic in origin. In Moradabad in Uttar Pradesh, for example, the cause of the serious riots in the 1980s was almost certainly the growing prosperity of Muslim groups, which was seen as a threat by groups of Hindu workers and traders. Somewhat the same situation seems to have been an important factor in riots that broke out in Bombay in 1984 in a working-class area; Muslims who had traditionally been at the bottom of the economic ladder were seen as making gains at the expense of Hindu working-class groups.

What is reasonably clear in these situations is that religious leaders and politicians have made skillful use of the frustrations of poverty and unemployment to mobilize constituencies under the banner of religion. Perhaps the most dramatic example of this was the riots in slum areas of Delhi following the assassination of Indira Gandhi in which over two thousand Sikhs were killed. Both the victims and the killers generally came from the poorest classes, with politicians for their own ends legitimizing the killings in the name of religion.

Thus the factors at work may be almost wholly economic and social, but it is easy to make the transition to seeing one's group as victimized for religious reasons by the majority community. The Sikh agitation is almost a textbook illustration of this, since, on the surface, it can be argued that no community has benefitted from social change more than the Sikhs, but the reality is that within the Sikh community there are elements that feel their exclusion had been deliberately engineered by the ruling Hindu majority. In such a situation, grievances that may be purely economic in origin are perceived as coming from a bias against one's religious identity, the very core of one's being. A reasonable form of action is to respond to the enemies of one's faith with violence, especially when, as is the case with the so-called Sikh extremists, the government is identified with the Hindu majority. When the government uses its power with overwhelming ruthlessness, as it did in the attack by the army on the Golden Temple, the Sikhs' holiest shrine, in 1984, this is seen as an attack by the Hindus. Furthermore, within the Sikh ethos there is what may be called a theology of martyrdom, not martyrdom in the Christian sense of being willing to die rather than abjure one's faith, but, on the contrary, an injunction to fight fiercely to death against the enemies of the faith. All religions have legitimized violence against the wicked and unbelieving, and in the current situation in Punjab this legitimization appears to the extremists to be obvious. The newspapers speak of senseless, random violence, as in the unprovoked shooting of Hindu passengers on buses by the Sikh extremists, and undoubtedly from one angle of vision it is precisely that. But from another angle it is part of a war, not of individuals against individuals, but of a righteous community against an unrighteous one. In this context, the innocence of an individual caught in the cross-fire of war is a regrettable irrelevancy.

A third factor that has to be taken into account in understanding the interplay of religion and politics in India is in some ways the obverse of the second. It comprises the activities and attitudes of groups from the majority Hindu community who feel that their religious and cultural traditions, which they identify with the nation, are being threatened by concessions being made to minority communities. This has always been a factor in modern Indian politics, with the assassination of Mahatma Gandhi in 1948 being the most dramatic example of its consequences. His death was the outcome of the sense of outrage by a group of nationalistic, committed Hindus to whom Gandhi seemed to be responsible for concessions being made to the Muslims that threatened the integrity of the nation. Indian commentators often referred to this "backlash" phenomenon in politics in 1986, with alleged concessions being made to Sikhs and Muslims as evidence that the time had come when India must assert its national cultural identity, which means, in effect, its Hindu culture. A comment not infrequently heard in 1986 was that the partition of India in 1947 meant that the Muslims who remained in India had chosen to become second-class citizens.

A fourth factor in trying to explicate the connections between religion and politics, particularly where violent confrontation is involved, is in some ways of a quite different character from the other three, but is related to them all, having to do with the actors in situations of violence. They are not members of an older generation, schooled in traditional learning and critical of a new order that is destroying the ancient landmarks of their youth. On the contrary, one can safely make the generalization that the most vociferous and violent guardians of religion in India are young men. They usually live in urban areas, are often employed in relatively low-status occupations, have some education but feel marginal to the social and economic changes taking place around them. The cry that their religion is in danger, that their group is being overwhelmed, reinforces their frustrations and anger and turns them against those who seem responsible for their situation. It is not necessary that the young men who respond to these appeals should be piously attached to the beliefs and practices of their religious group, although very often this is so. It is certainly the case with members of the nationalistic Hindu organization, the Rashtriya Swayamsevak Sangh, familiarly known as the RSS, as well as with its Muslim counterparts, such as the Jamaat-i-Islami. But in the current situation the best-documented example is that of the young Sikhs who are followers of Bhindranwale, who fit very well this profile of the violent guardians of religion: This peculiar role of young men in the conjunction of religion and politics, along with the other three factors noted above—the claim that groups, not individuals, should be represented in the political system, the perceived grievances of minorities, the identification of nationalism with Hindu culture—were all interwoven in the complex mosaic of Indian life in 1986. A fifth component must be added that seems present in almost all incidents of religious or communal violence—the role played by the class referred to in India by the untranslatable word *goondas.* The media sometimes refer to them as "known miscreants" or "antisocial elements," and these phrases are apt enough. They are not exactly gangsters in the American sense, but they belong to the subculture that appears to be present in all Indian cities and probably in much of the countryside. They are important because they are for hire by politicians, religious leaders and businessmen who want to cause trouble for their opponents. Their wages are not so much money as the loot that comes from riots as well as the undoubted psychological satisfaction that comes from participating in mob violence. There is much less individual violent crime in India than in countries like the United States, and one plausible explanation is that social behavior is under the very strong constraints imposed by family and society. There are few opportunities for individual expression against frustration, so that group violence, if it can be given religious sanction, however spurious, provides enormous psychic satisfaction and release to young men. It may not be easy to distinguish between the *goondas* and the young men referred to above as motivated by religious identification, especially among the young Sikhs in rural Punjab, but there is a real difference that is of great importance in understanding such incidents as the seizure of the Golden Temple and what appears to be random violence against individuals who are on a hit list. It is perhaps not overly glib to say that, because of this, the religiously motivated are more dangerous to Indian polity than the *goondas.*

The Muslims

As far as Hindu-Muslim relations are concerned, all of these factors converged in 1986 in what was known as the Shah Bano case. This was one of those issues where the surface events conceal the reality, which, reduced to its essentials, was the great unfinished question of Indian political life: In a democratic system, what special concessions are to be legally guaranteed to minorities, whether ethnic, linguistic or religious? All through the twentieth century this problem, in one form or another, had haunted India as it constructed its framework of political representation. It did not suddenly become an issue in 1986, but, according to many observers, the political strategies of politicians, especially during Indira Gandhi's long period of dominance from 1966 to 1984, had been to politicize religion through calculated appeals to religious fears and prejudices. This took many forms, some of them contradictory, such as at times the appeal to Muslim voting blocs and, as will be noted later, at times an appeal to Hindu resentment against the activities of religious minorities such as the Sikhs.

Shah Bano

The Shah Bano case was almost trivial in itself, but if one were to do a word count of the Indian press for the year, it almost received more attention than any other single issue, and it had repercussions that raised fundamental questions about the nature of Indian politics. The factual background can be fairly easily summarized. Although attention in the press reached a high point in 1986, the case had its obscure beginnings in 1978 when Ahmed Khan of Indore in Madhya Pradesh divorced Shah Bano, to whom he had been married for forty-four years. He gave her back the Rs. 3,000 (about $300) which had been her *mehr,* or marriage settlement from her family, as required by Islamic law. All of this was commonplace enough, but what was not common was that Shah Bano, probably on the instigation of her sons, who were said to be on bad terms with their father, sued for maintenance under the Criminal Procedure Code of India. When the lower court magistrate awarded her Rs. 25, she appealed to a higher court, which raised the award to Rs. 180. The husband then appealed this judgment to the Supreme Court of India on the grounds that as a Muslim he had to obey the Shariat, the law of Islam, which required only that he pay her maintenance, or *iddat,* for three months. A bench of five Supreme Court judges ruled that under Section 125 of the Criminal Code a husband was required to pay maintenance to a wife without means of support. Chief Justice Chandrachud did not, however, conclude his judgment with this interpretation of the Code; he went on to say that this ruling of the Supreme Court was more in keeping with the Quran than the traditional interpretation by Muslims of the Shariat. He then said that the time had come for a common legal code for all Indians, irrespective of their religion.

These rather gratuitous comments by the chief justice, combined with the Supreme Court's ruling, which would become a precedent in similar cases, led to both violent protests in the streets and lengthy debates in Parliament and in the press. In Bombay, for example, a procession of 100,000 people denounced the Court's verdict, while in Ahmednagar, another city in Maharashtra, a group supporting it was stoned by opponents. An ironic, even if somewhat irrelevant, twist was given to the situation when Shah Bano refused to accept the alimony payments awarded her by the court on the grounds, as she put it, that it had been brought to her notice that acceptance of maintenance was against the teachings of the Shariat, since the obligations of the marriage contract for both parties ended with divorce. The Imam, or head of the mosque, of Indore had explained this to her, she said, and she added a sentence that summarizes the argument that the will of the religious community has primacy over that of the individual: "If the majority of the community thinks it is wrong, how can one individual be correct?" But the feisty old lady added another twist to this pious ejaculation when she gave notice that she was going back to the Court to get the current value of her *mehr;* since it was Rs. 3,000 in 1932 when it was given, it was worth at least Rs. 120,000 now.[2]

In the debates that began in earnest in 1986 over the ruling, the lines were by no means so neatly drawn as they appeared to be in the streets. At first, when the Court's ruling was criticized by Muslim religious leaders for interfering in the rights of the Muslim community, Prime Minister Rajiv Gandhi seemed to support the Court's decision. This was expected, as he had been presented to the Indian public as a modern man, and, moreover, as one with a special concern for the rights of women. Here surely was a case where modernity and compassion would march hand in hand, for, as a writer in a magazine put it, "an old and indigent woman, after forty-three years of marriage was being callously discarded and made to fend for herself."[3] The minister of state in the Ministry of Home Affairs, a position of high responsibility although not a cabinet post, was Arif Khan, who was a Muslim, and therefore a suitable spokesman for the government on such an issue. He made a spirited defense of the court's decision in Parliament, and the prime minister was said to have congratulated him for his speech, which, he said, had evoked widespread enthusiasm throughout the country.[4]

Political realities, however, soon asserted themselves. Rajiv Gandhi's Congress party depended in many constituencies on the Muslim vote—the figure often given is that Muslims make a decisive difference in nearly 150 seats out of a total of 542 in Parliament. Although this seems a high estimate, it is an indication of the importance of the Muslim vote. Muslim religious and political leaders began to make clear their opposition to the Court's judgment in favor of alimony for a divorced Muslim wife and to the chief justice's claim to interpret the Quran. This, they argued, was intolerable interference in the internal life of the Muslim community. The point that the religious leaders made was not the negative one that the Shariat freed the husband from the obligation to pay maintenance but that it forbade a woman to take such a payment, on the grounds that divorce had abrogated the marriage contract. This was the argument that the Imam of Indore had made to Shah Bano, and undoubtedly it was one that was widely accepted by Muslims. Najma Heptullah, a Muslim woman who is deputy chairman of the Rajya Sabha, the upper house of Parliament, and the granddaughter of Maulana Azad, one of the most famous Muslim leaders of the nationalist movement, noted that among Muslims there is "no business of till death do us part"; the husband's responsibility ends with the legal termination of the marriage contract.[5]

In his original speech in defense of the Supreme Court's decision, Arif Khan had pursued a line of argument that many people pointed out played into the hands of his critics, in the same way that the chief justice had. Not content with insisting on upholding the law of the land for all Indian citizens, irrespective of their religion, he had argued that the conservative Muslim legal scholars and the religious leaders, the imams and maulvis, were wrong in their interpretation of the Quran and the Shariat. As sympathetic observers pointed out, this line of reasoning exposes the fundamental weakness of the ideology of secularism, because it accepts the validity of the argument of the religionists that the precepts of religion are truth that must be accepted. All that the religious specialists have to do to defeat the theological arguments of politicians like Arif Khan is, first of all, to show the frequent factual errors in their expositions and, secondly, to assert the authority of the tradition over individual interpretation.

Not only did the imams and the maulvis have the authority of their learning on their side; they also probably had the support of the majority of the Muslim community. No opinion surveys were made, no referendums held, but a Muslim college teacher from Calcutta summed up what many people felt was true, that "among a largely illiterate and socially backward Muslim community," the Supreme Court judgment was projected "as a threat to Islam and to the identity of the Muslims in India."[6] Nor was it only the illiterate masses, but also the Muslim middle classes, including liberal intellectuals, who saw the judgment, and the enthusiastic support it received from Hindus, as a threat to the integrity of the Muslim community. This seemed to be the clear message of a by-election in December 1985, in Kishanganj, Bihar, when Syed Shahabuddin, the general secretary of the Janata party, defeated the Congress candidate, who was also a Muslim, by a large majority. Shahabuddin was by no means a demagogic Muslim fanatic, as his opponents in Gandhi's party were fond of picturing him, but like many educated Muslims he saw the Shah Bano case not as an issue over the right of an aged divorcee for a minimal maintenance, but as an indication that a Supreme Court made up of Hindus and a government dominated by Hindus would use their power to weaken further the Muslim community.

Babri Mosque Affair

The Shah Bano case was not the only issue that aroused Hindu-Muslim antagonisms early in 1986. More dramatic, and the cause of more violence and bloodshed, but of less reasoned discussion, is what became known as the Babri Mosque affair, which became inextricably interwoven with the fears and emotions aroused by the Shah Bano decision. If the bare facts of the Shah Bano case are known and easily summarized, those relating to the Babri Mosque are not, because they involve ancient Hindu myths, actions of a Muslim invader in the early sixteenth century and decisions in a local district court. Here it may be mentioned in passing how central the legal system is to Indian life in general and to religious controversies in particular. Not only is the commitment to secularism constantly undermined, as noted above, by the willingness of judges to include theological pronouncements in their judgments, but the courts are frequently asked to intervene to settle disputes between religious factions. To cite a digressive example, some years ago, in Indore, Shah Bano's city, the Christian congregation became involved in a bitter dispute over the authority of the bishop. The issue was a technical one, having to do with ecclesiastical governance, but the local magistrate was asked to intervene, and he responded by padlocking the church door. His justification was simple: the function of a magistrate was to prevent the violence that might have ensued. The Hindu judge is alleged to have quoted Saint Paul to the quarrelling Christians: magistrates are not a terror to the good, but to the wicked.

In the Babri Mosque case, the magistrate's issues had larger ramifications, for the quarrel was between Muslims and Hindus. The violence that erupted in 1986 had its immediate origins in 1970 when idols of Rama and Sita were placed or appeared in the Babri Mosque in Ayodhya, Uttar Pradesh. These action verbs, placed and appeared, are the key to the dispute. The local Muslims said that Hindu revivalists had entered the mosque and set up the idols of the Hindu deity and his consort as an act of defilement of the Muslim holy place. Local Hindus declared that the symbols of Rama, the great deity much revered in North India, had not been placed there by human agency but by the action of the god himself.

The reason for this divine action was plain for believers: the temple at Ayodhya was the birthplace of Rama. Because of the special sanctity this gave it for Hindus, it was, according to the Hindu version of events, singled out by Babar, the first of the Mughal emperors in 1526, and turned into a mosque to celebrate the victory of Islam over the idolatrous Hindus. Little is known of the attitude of the Hindu population toward the mosque, which was given Babar's name by the local inhabitants, but since it was in an area that remained in control of Muslim rulers until the nineteenth century, presumably they were not in a position to protest too violently. The situation changed, however, when, as noted above, modern politics gave religious identity a new importance and a new role. Local Hindu politicians, appealing to both piety and anti-Muslim sentiment, joined with local religious leaders in the 1960s to demand that the mosque be restored as a temple so that they could worship in what they regarded as the birthplace of Rama. The appearance of the idols in the temple, by human or divine agency, led to clashes between the two communities, and an appeal was made in 1970 to the courts to permit Hindu worship in the building. The magistrate responded by ordering the doors of the mosque, or temple, depending upon one's point of view, to be locked pending clarification of the facts. Then on 1 February 1986, a group of Hindus petitioned the court at Faizabad, the district capital, to restore the temple to them and to unlock the doors so they could worship there. The judge did not adjudicate the question of restoring the temple. Instead he reported that he had not been able to find any judicial document that supported the locking of the door of the mosque, and therefore the lock should be removed. The local police said that doing so would not lead to violence.[7]

There was, in fact, little violence in Ayodhya itself, but the report of the opening of the mosque for Hindu worship added to the uneasiness and fears that had been created already by the Shah Bano decision. And also, it must be emphasized, the unlocking of the Babri Mosque led to rejoicing on the part of many Hindus, especially those usually identified as Hindu revivalists. On one level, this was pleasure at the return of a sacred site to its proper function; on another, it was gloating over what was regarded as a defeat for Muslims. By mid-February communal rioting broke out in various parts of North India, adding to the sense shared by many careful Indian observers that this new violence, added to the violence in Punjab between Sikhs and Hindus, showed that religion was threatening to destroy the fragile unity of India. Editorial after editorial echoed the somber question of one editor: "Has the nation's sensitivity been dulled to a point where most people seem to be getting conditioned to live (or die) with the fatal virus of communalism?"[8] Two incidents that illustrated the working of that virus, which occurred in the spring of 1986, will be briefly noted. One, in Delhi, seemed to be directly connected with the Shah Bano decision and the Babri Mosque. The other was in Kashmir, where the two legal decisions do not appear to have played a direct part, except insofar as they added to a climate of distrust. Both places were familiar settings for communal violence.

Delhi and Kashmir. Indian newspapers, both by law and by good sense, are guarded in reporting religious violence in order not to increase tension and ill will, and one often has to read between the lines to get a sense of what actually happened. On 15 February the Delhi papers reported that there had been widespread rioting in the walled city the day before. This was an indication that the trouble was related to Hindu-Muslim tensions, since it was easy to start a riot in the old city, with its narrow, winding, dead-end streets, and with its dense population of poor Muslims as well as Hindus, both with bitter memories of the violence of Partition (the division of British India in 1947, when millions of Muslims and Hindus were killed). Without quite saying so, many newspapers implied that trouble had been started by Muslims. Black flags condemning the decision of the Faizabad court in unlocking the Babri Mosque were seen everywhere, it was reported, and the Imam, in his Friday sermon in the great mosque, the Jama Masjid, was said to have denounced the decision. Thousands of worshippers as they left the mosque, according to one reliable newspaper, went on a rampage, stoning the police, stopping buses, breaking windows. So far the Muslims seem to be getting the blame, but then there is a curious sentence in the account: "The violence did not seem directed against members of any particular community."[9] This refers to the activity of the class that was mentioned above as one of the constant elements of communal riots—the *goondas* who are for hire for the loot that they can pick up and for the pleasure that comes from violence. It may very well have been the Muslim leaders who started the riots by inflaming their followers, but other politicians were ready to operate in the conflict situation for their own ends. What the actors seemed to have in common as a target for attack, in this as in other communal riots, was the police. It is sometimes said that this happens because the police stand for law and order against the lawlessness of the mobs, but a more cynical explanation that is often put forward in India is that the police are a third force of violence and corruption.

Kashmir was the other area where communal violence broke out in 1986. These riots are part of the general picture of religion and politics in India, but also a reminder, since they did not seem to be closely connected with the passions aroused by the Shah Bano case or the Babri Mosque affair, that one cannot assume that riots happening in India at the same time are directly connected, even though the protagonists may be Hindus and Muslims. What they tend to have in common are the elements enumerated at the beginning, such as the rights of groups versus the individual, the perception of discrimination by a minority, the demand that the culture of the majority should be the national culture and the legitimization of violence by religious appeal, especially to young men.

Unlike in Delhi and other areas prone to religious violence, the majority in Kashmir is Muslim, and while elsewhere it is the Muslims who suffer most, no matter who starts the trouble, in Kashmir it was the Hindu minority. They are now a small minority, only about 70,000 in a population of 6 million, but there were 300,000 in 1947. Most of them left for other parts of India through the years, and those who remain complain of discrimination against them by the Muslim majority. They are, however, a curious minority, for the state had been ruled for nearly two hundred years by Hindu chieftains, and the Kashmiri Hindus—almost all of whom were Brahmin—had enjoyed extraordinary power in the management of the state. The Kashmiri Muslims resented them then, and even more when they gained a measure of political freedom. This was particularly because they felt their control of their state was eroded by the imposition on them of an unpopular administration by a Delhi government that was perceived as Hindu and anti-Muslim. The result was that at the end of February 1986 bitter riots directed at the Hindu minority broke out, especially in the area of Anantnag, where a number of prosperous Hindu families were living. Explanations of why the rioting had begun covered familiar ground: stories that Hindu women had been raped in Jammu, the Hindu part of the state, which were untrue; that the Babri Mosque had been turned into a temple, which was partly true; and that the Shiv Sena, a Hindu organization dedicated to defending religion, had boasted of the victory at Babri mosque, which was true.

Muslim Women's Bill

The evidence of rising discontent among the Muslims convinced Gandhi's administration that some action had to be taken, not only to ensure the continued support of Muslim voters but to prevent further outbreaks of violence. The step that the government believed would restore Muslim confidence was to introduce a bill in Parliament that effectively abrogated the precedent set by the Supreme Court's award of maintenance to Shah Bano. This had been done under the provisions of Section 125 of the Criminal Procedure Code, which required husbands to support their divorced wives, but the bill abrogated this as far as Muslims were concerned by stating that the clause did not apply to Muslim marriages. Arif Khan, the minister who a short time before had won the prime minister's approval for his defense of the Court decision, resigned his office, no doubt feeling betrayed by the sudden shift on the part of the prime minister.

The proposed legislation, formally known as the Muslim Women (Protection of Rights on Divorce) Bill, while it took away the right of a divorced Muslim wife to receive maintenance from her husband, provided for her support by saying that it would be the duty, in the first instance, of the woman's family and relatives to support her, and, if they were unable to do so, then she could appeal to the *waqf*, the charitable trusts maintained for pious purposes. In defense of the bill, the prime minister said it would further the secularism that was at the heart of India's strength by ensuring religious communities that they were not deprived of anything that they felt was basic to them. There was no hint in his speech that he was aware that his party before Independence had made its stand on common laws and common citizenship, and that a denial of the relevance of religious affiliation to nationalism had been central to its ideology.

The controversy over the Muslim Women's Bill displayed in a remarkable fashion one of the most important aspects of Indian society, namely, the very high quality of literary journalism. Daily newspapers and popular weekly magazines, of which there are an astonishing number, published numerous analytical articles that were far more scholarly and penetrating in their discussion of the role of religion in society than would have been their counterparts elsewhere in the English-speaking world. This was not because Indians are more religious, but because there was a recognition on the part of both editors and readers that fundamental issues were being raised about the dynamics of Indian society, and that the future direction of Indian society was at stake.

Attacks on the bill came swiftly and from many quarters. For many liberals, both Muslim and Hindu, the bill represented a capitulation to the forces of Islamic obscurantism, a return, as they were fond of saying, to the thirteenth century. At the same time, Hindu revivalists denounced the bill as weakening Indian unity by pandering to Muslim separatism and encouraging Muslims to put membership in their religious community over the claims of the nation. It especially angered Muslims, whether liberal or conservative, that the Hindus stressed the injustice that was being done to Muslim women by the bill, but one of the most telling responses to this line of argument came from a non-Muslim, Madhu Kishwar, editor of *Manushi*, the most outspoken feminist journal in India.

Kishwar saw this new concern for Muslim women on the part of Hindus as a thinly veiled way to express hostility and contempt for Muslims. Not only were the conservative and orthodox offended, but liberal Muslims who might have opposed the bill felt that by doing so they were making common cause with Hindu bigotry. She made an interesting comparison with the fact that in the nineteenth century the favorite symbol used by the British for the backward state of Hindu society was the plight of Hindu women. Such customs as the burning of widows, child marriage and female infanticide were used, she argued, as proof that Indians could not run their own society in a civilized manner. Today, she said, Hindus cite the treatment of Muslim women as proof that Muslims are backward and that Islam is a barbaric religion.[10] That Kishwar was not far off the mark is suggested by a series of lengthy articles by Arun Shourie, an erudite and skilled journalist, which attempted to show that while there was much oppression of women under Islamic law, the Quran, rightly interpreted, would make possible the removal of the injustices under which they suffered.[11] Shourie's tone was generous and sympathetic, but he was answered with biting scorn by Rafiq Zakaria, a Muslim and a scholar of Islam. His criticism was precisely along Kishwar's line: that behind Shourie's seeming concern for reform of Islam was a Hindu contempt for it.[12] Possibly Rajiv Gandhi and his advisers were shrewder than their many critics gave them credit for being, and they recognized the dangers of not attempting a reconciliation with conservative Islamic leaders. Something of this kind of thinking may have been in his mind when he told a delegation of women who were opposed to the bill that they should not hold Western ideas about equality between the sexes.[13]

Two hundred women who had apparently not accepted the prime minister's contention that belief in equality between the sexes was an un-Indian idea chained themselves to the gate of Parliament to protest what they called a black bill meant to appease the fundamentalist forces. The bill, however, became law on 6 May, despite the fact that perhaps no other piece of legislation since 1947 had aroused such widespread and impressive opposition. Most of the English-language press, including papers that normally supported the government, opposed it. So did women's organizations. So did Muslim lawyers and intellectuals like A. G. Noorani and Daniel Latifi and virtually all of those who were referred to in Parliament as "the so-called intelligentsia." The government's public defense of its case was remarkably poor, consisting largely of the reiteration by the law minister and others that one had to give the minorities what they demanded. Quite apart from the question of whether the law was harmful to women's interests, this insistence on meeting minority demands, even though they ran counter to the general interest of the country, suggests an acknowledgment that India is not a conventional nation-state, with laws and customs common to all.

There was another note, however, that ran through the speeches of the government's supporters during the last day of the debate: a reference to "our" laws over against "theirs." Arun Nehru, the minister of internal security, and one of the most powerful figures in Gandhi's administration, made this distinction, probably quite unconsciously, when he spoke of "our wishes," which included a common legal code, against "the minority community's wishes," implying that he spoke for India while "they" spoke for their community, which was separate from India.[14] "Hindu chauvinism with a liberal face" was the way one commentator described the positions like those of Arun Nehru and Arun Shourie: "They want the Sikhs and Muslims not to create any trouble and they want them to fall in line." But that is not what happens, he went on to say, when a minority feels the majority is trampling on its religious identity. "It rejects the mainstream and creates as much trouble as it can.... This was what has happened to the Sikhs and could well happen to the Muslims eventually."[15]

Analysts, both Indian and Western, of Indian politics are inclined to speak of the Muslim problem and the Sikh problem, obscuring the singular importance of the religious commitment of the majority community. This is peculiarly the case when the "we" of political rhetoric collapses their religious and political commitments into a single entity, thereby excluding the "other" from participation in the national identity. It is probably fair to say that the opponents of the bill, however self-serving they might be, seemed to understand more clearly than did the government the implications for the future of the state of recognizing and defining the claims of a religious minority in the way this was done in the Muslim Women's Bill.

The Sikhs

It was suggested at the beginning of this chapter that in 1986 religion and politics found their most fateful juncture for India in relation to the Muslim community, but another religious community, the Sikhs, shared the headlines, although not the thoughtful pages of commentary and analysis. With a dreadful monotony, the headlines throughout the year chronicled the killings of bus passengers in Punjab, the murder of politicians and editors and, no less dreadful, the violence of the police against suspected terrorists. (This is how they were always designated in the national press and by the government. In their own literature, they were known as freedom fighters or martyrs.) Most of the accounts, except for the identification of the terrorists as Sikhs, give little if any explanation of the religious component of the violence that has destabilized Punjab for the past six or seven years. The political aspects of the Punjab situation—factions jockeying for power, politicians settling old scores in devious and corrupt ways, the formation of alliances without principles—are all commonplace enough, even if of a stupefying complexity. What was not commonplace in India was the extraordinary level of violence, not just on the part of the terrorists, but also on the part of the government. "Operation Bluestar," the code name for the army action against the Golden Temple in 1984, killed hundreds more people than did the terrorists, many of whom were perhaps guilty only of being Sikhs, just as those whom the terrorists killed were guilty only of being Hindu.

All of this can be, and often is, analyzed without reference to the role of the Sikh religion, but to do so misses much of the inner dynamics and logic of the situation in Punjab. Just as significant, there is scarcely ever, at least in the national press, much analysis of the role of the majority religious community, the Hindus, in relation to the Sikhs. This is one of the ironies of history, for in the popular imagination of both Hindus and Sikhs there is an image of the formation of Sikhism resulting from its struggle with the Mughal emperors, especially Aurangzeb, who is pictured as the embodiment of Muslim fanaticism. Sikhism, it is stressed, was transformed from a peaceful, pietistic sect into a militant community, fighting battles in which quarter was neither asked for nor given, against a powerful government intent on destroying the faithful remnant of believers in the teaching of Guru Nanak. The irony is, of course, that the so-called Sikh terrorists of the 1980s would write these sentences, substituting the Government of India for the Mughals and Hindu fanaticism for Muslim fanaticism.

In the 1980s a group of Sikhs—mainly young men, marginal in many ways to Sikh society as well as to the larger society of India—see themselves as a saving remnant of the kind that fought the Muslim emperors at Delhi, only now the warfare is against the Hindu central government of India. Nothing is more irrelevant than to say they are only a tiny faction, or that most educated, prosperous Sikhs do not agree with them, for saving remnants are by definition few in numbers and marginal to their society. The answer of the violent faction is that of course the majority is not with them. Dulled to true religion, they have accepted the arguments and the way of life of the enemies of the faith, and by doing so have themselves become enemies of the faith. "Choose ye this day whom ye will serve; as for me and my house we will serve the Lord" is not a saying from the Sikh scriptures, but it summarizes well enough the message, equally simple-minded and self-validating, of Sant Jarnail Singh Bhindranwale, the young religious enthusiast who became the center of the storm of violence in Punjab.

Bhindranwale's brief career and the events that followed after his death in the army action against his followers in the Golden Temple in

Amritsar in 1984 are a paradigm of the way in which an alliance between religion and politics can lead to violence. His family were poor farmers from an area near Amritsar known as the Majha region that had not shared in the prosperity that characterizes much of Punjab. Its people have a reputation for their devotion to Sikhism, and Bhindranwale was sent as a little boy to a religious school in the area, the Damdami Taksal, where the emphasis is on the Sikh scriptures and the traditions and beliefs of the community. The founder of the school was one of the heroes of Sikhism, Deep Singh, who, in the eighteenth century died defending the Golden Temple against desecration by the Afghan invader, Ahmad Shah Abdali. The legend of his martyrdom is instructive for understanding the ethos in which Bhindranwale and other young Sikhs were brought up. His head was cut off, but he continued for a time to fight against the Afghans with his head in one hand and his sword in the other. Pictures and stories of such martyrdoms are common, and while it is not a cult of violence for its own sake that was inculcated at the Damdami Taksal, the message that runs through such teaching is that to destroy the enemies of the community is a necessary act, and that the courage to fight and the willingness to die are essential qualities of the devotee of the Guru.

This point must be emphasized, because in India and elsewhere there is a tendency to argue that the violence and the murders done in the name of the Sikh community cannot be the work of religious men. From a more factual point of view, Khuswant Singh, one of the best known Sikh writers, argues that the terrorists are either politically motivated or gangsters.[16] This may be so, but they are undeniably Sikhs, and the fact that they are gangsters in the eyes of the law does not prevent them being, in their own perceptions of themselves and, more importantly, in the eyes of many members of the Sikh community, defenders of the faith. Long ago it was decided in the Christian Church that the validity of the sacraments did not depend upon the personal morality of the performing priest. In the same way the violence—even the gangsterism—of the terrorist Sikhs does not invalidate their acts in defense of truth. Pacifism is no more a virtue among Sikhs of Bhindranwale's persuasion than it was among the ancient Israelites as they drove out the Canaanites and others who were not of the household of faith, nor of the soldiers of Cromwell's rebel armies. We have grown accustomed to accepting the idea that warfare is the monopoly of the state, and we forget that for a believing community, whether the Sikhs or the PLO, its highest duty is to preserve itself by whatever means it can. In the 1930s a young Sikh, Bhagat Singh, was hanged by the Government of India for crimes not unlike those in which Sikhs are now engaging in Punjab, and he was praised by Indian nationalists, including

Mahatma Gandhi, for his courage and patriotism in acting against the British.

Bhindranwale became a popular preacher and later the head of the Damdami Taksal. This was at the time that Indira Gandhi lost the election in 1977 but was seeking new allies for a return to power. In Punjab her opponents were the members of the Akali Dal party, once the spokesmen for Sikh demands for Sikh autonomy, but by then fairly conservative. Mrs. Gandhi's people chose Bhindranwale as their ally against the Akali Dal, which he regarded as lacking in enthusiasm for the restoration of Sikhism to its original purity and for Sikh political rights. This gave him and his followers more prominence and influence within the Sikh community and forced the Akalis to more radical positions in order to maintain their credibility as spokesmen for the community.[17]

What followed was according to the familiar paradigm of what happens when politicians attempt to use religion for their own ends. Bhindranwale moved to more radical positions and Mrs. Gandhi's party, when it came back to power in 1980, could not attack him without weakening its own position. Little action was taken against him as he defied the government, including by directing murders and robberies. Thus although he and his group in 1980 took possession of the Golden Temple in Amritsar and, according to the government, made it a center for subversion and assassination, no real action was taken against them until 6 June 1984, when the army invaded the temple, killing hundreds—thousands according to many accounts—including Bhindranwale. Or at least the government produced evidence to show that Bhindranwale had been killed. A group of his followers claimed then that he had not been killed, and they maintain now that he is still alive and will lead a new attack on the enemies of the Sikhs. This recalls the belief among the followers of Subhas Chandra Bose, the great Bengali leader who fought against the British in World War II, that he was not killed in an air crash but that he is waiting for the right moment to emerge and lead India to a new day. Faith in a new leader who lives on beyond death prepared for him by his enemies is an ancient and potent religious symbol.

The leadership of the radicals came largely from the All India Sikh Students Federation (AISSF) and students or former students of Bhindranwale's school, the Damdami Taksal. The leaders are far more educated than Bhindranwale and his immediate entourage were, and according to one estimate, 90 percent of the Sikh extremists are college graduates. According to an official of the Golden Temple, many of Bhindranwale's followers had been unemployed, uneducated young men, who had little sense of what they were fighting for, but the new group were genuinely motivated by religion.[18] In many ways, 1986 became a replay of the years before 1984 when the radicals had held the temple before and used it as a symbol of their power and influence. Killings of Hindus, as well as of Sikhs who were regarded as traitors, once more became commonplace, reaching a spectacular climax with the near-assassination of Julio Ribeiro, the head of the Punjab police, inside a highly guarded complex. The investigations showed that the radicals had allies and accomplices among trusted Sikh policemen in the complex.

The spokesmen for the radicals in 1986 differed in one very important respect from their predecessors in the years before 1984: they declared that they were fighting for Khalistan, a separate homeland for the Sikhs. For some observers, this seemed proof that the movement had become wholly political, and that it was being financed and encouraged by Pakistan and the CIA. Religion, it was argued, had ceased to be a decisive factor in the Punjab situation. But in a curious, convoluted way this argument itself often masked a religious dimension, for it was used by some Hindus to attack Muslims in India who were regarded as friendly to Pakistan, or, in a favorite phrase, a potential fifth column. As for the demand for Khalistan itself, while the idea of secession might seem purely political, it surely represented dreams and visions of a homeland for the Sikhs of the kind that had made such powerful emotional appeals to Muslims in India before 1947 and, in very different contexts, to Jews. The Sikh policemen who had been in the plot to kill Ribeiro were, by all accounts, very commonplace, not particularly religious, young men, but they explained their actions by saying that Ribeiro was an enemy of the Sikhs, that he "wanted to finish the sons of Guru Gobind Singh," that is, the followers of the great Sikh leader who had consolidated the Sikhs into a militant religious community. They were joining the Khalistan liberation forces, they said, because life was not as dear to them as the fight against injustice. The same point was made by Bhai Mohkam Singh, a spokesman for the Damdami Taksal when he was asked why a religious organization like his was engaged in politics. "Religion and politics go together in Sikhism," he said, "and cannot be separated."[19]

Conclusion

It is not only Sikhs, of course, who declare that religion and politics cannot be separated; so do Christians, Jews, Muslims, Buddhists, Hindus. All the great religions have a vision of what the world should be, and how human beings should relate to this vision. One of the sillier comments often made is that Hinduism or Islam are not religions but are "ways of life," as if all religions by their very nature are not ways of life. It is because religions are ways of life that they have blueprints for the future, which means that they want a society that is Christian or Islamic or Jewish or Sikh, where they will be able to live the kind of life that permits true fulfillment of religious faith. In the modern world, to want a society that conforms to one's vision of the good life is to want a state to embody that vision, with laws to enforce its pattern against its enemies. It is often said in India, as elsewhere, that those who want their own religious laws and customs to be embodied in the constitution of the state are reactionary and backward, opponents of modernity. This was the frequent charge made against Muslims and Sikhs during 1986, but these groups were not defending the past—they were asserting their claims to the future.

In contemporary India, the most important of those groups asserting a claim to the future is neither the Sikhs nor the Muslims, but the Hindus. Here it is scarcely necessary to stress that the Hindus are not, of course, a monolithic unity, any more than are the Sikhs and the Muslims. Rather there are groups that speak for what they identify as Hindu interests, or, more ambiguously, as Indian interests. Such groups are very frequently spokesmen for the amorphous phenomenon referred to as the "Hindu backlash" against the religious minorities. Stated in its simplest form, this is the belief that although 84 percent of the population in India is Hindu and the dominant cultural legacy is associated with Hinduism, the religious minorities have been given concessions that have weakened the fabric of Indian unity. The groups taking this view vary greatly from each other, and it would be an exaggeration to say that they represent a majority of Hindus. Many observers would agree, however, that in the aggregate they represent a significant demand for the recognition that Indian culture has its roots in the Hindu past and that national unity demands a nationalist ideology based upon it. At one extreme are groups that organize under the name of the Shiv Sena (Army of Shiva), which in Punjab has urged that Hindus must be united in a new militancy against the Sikhs. The old Hindu organization, the Rashtriya Swayamsewak Sangh, or RSS, known for its disciplined cadres pledged to support Hindu dominance, was not publicly very active in the past year. But a new and less openly militant group, the Vishwa Hindu Parishad, has taken a leading part in the campaign to have the Babri Mosque recognized a Hindu shrine. The support for organizations like the Parishad seems to come largely from the Hindu urban middle class, an indication that the movement reflects the aspirations of many members of this class to see a clearer identification of Hinduism with the nation. A more thoughtful expression of the Hindu reaction to the demands of minority religious communities emphasizes the longstanding commitment of Indian political leadership, particularly that represented by Nehru, to the ideal of a secular state, that is, one where all religions were respected but none had a special place. For many members of minority groups, however, this attitude moves inevitably to an identification of national values with Hindu values, as it reaches out to encompass others with the dogma that all religions are true. By sheer weight of numbers, a Hindu understanding of the nature and function of religion appears to become an essential element in nationalist ideology.

No one factor can explain the emergence of religion as a crucial element in politics in India or elsewhere at the end of the twentieth century. Very different processes are at work in Ireland, Iran, Israel and Lebanon, and only lazy thinking finds a solution in such catch phrases as "the resurgence of fundamentalism." Each country and each region has to be looked at in terms of its historical experience and its own vision of the future.

Almost inevitably, in a pluralistic society like India, those groups who have a vision of the good society drawn from the religious sources that define their nature and destiny come in conflict with those who have an understanding of their destinies drawn from the experiences and values of other religions. They also come into conflict with those who have a vision of the good society, based not on one of the religious communities of India, but what, for lack of a better term, can be called the secular or liberal democratic tradition. This has found one of its earliest and most elegant statements in the document that declared it to be a self-evident truth that when a political system denied its people the inalienable rights given them by the Creator, that system had to be attacked. This is a revolutionary and radical idea, opening the way for conflict between those with different readings of the intentions of their Creator.

Modern politics in India provide an arena for such conflict in terms of the conventional mechanisms of democracy—voting blocks, parties and platforms. These platforms, however, often make appeals to voters in the language of religion, with the classic example of this being, of course, Mahatma Gandhi's use of a religious vocabulary to define an ideology of nationalism. When the democratic process appears to be unable to satisfy demands that claim to be rooted in religion, violence is the possible and rational solution. Violence in India in 1986 was not, then, senseless and random. It was a way of changing things, of challenging a recalcitrant order of things. In India, as elsewhere in the world at the end of the twentieth century, religions have legitimized violence as people struggle for what they regard as their just claims upon the future. Frustration and fear may have their roots in identifiable economic and social causes which could be ameliorated by secular remedies within the democratic process, but a religious vision can offer a more readily available solution by legitimizing the violence that is borne of hatred and despair.

To sum up the experience of 1986 in another way: the use of the vocabulary of religion has corrupted political discourse in India and is likely to continue to do so in the immediate future. And, unhappily, this is true not only in India, but wherever the vocabulary and vision of a religion is used to institute a social order that is opposed by groups with equally strong and valid claims upon the future.

Notes

1. S. N. Banerjea, *Speeches and Writings of Hon. Surendranath Banerjea* (n. d.), pp. 228-29.
2. Interview in "Women," p. V, *The Times of India,* 8 March 1986.
3. *The Illustrated Weekly of India,* 5 January 1986, p. 11.
4. Arun Shourie, "The Arif Mohammad Affair," *The Times of India,* 3 March 1986.
5. *India Today,* 31 January 1986, p. 56.
6. Interview with Hossainur Rahman, *The Statesman,* 19 February 1986.
7. Editorial, *The Indian Express,* 18 February 1986.
8. Editorial, *The Hindustan Times,* 29 March 1986.
9. *Indian Express,* 15 February 1986.
10. Madhu Kishwar, "Losing Sight of the Real Issue," *The Times of India,* 8 March 1986, p. IV.
11. Arun Shourie, "The Shariat," *The Illustrated Weekly of India,* 5, 12 and 19 January 1986.
12. Rafiq Zakaria, "In Defence of Shariat," *The Illustrated Weekly of India,* 2 and 9 March 1986.
13. *India Today,* 31 March 1986, p. 60.
14. "Lok Sabha passes Muslim Women Bill," *The Indian Express,* 6 May 1986.
15. Vir Sanghvi, "Hindu Chauvinism with a Liberal Mask," *Sunday Mail,* 6 April 1986.
16. Khushwant Singh, interview in *Expanse,* April 1986.
17. A detailed account of the alliance between Mrs. Gandhi's followers and Bhindranwale is given in Mark Tully and Satish Jacob, *Amritsar: Mrs. Gandhi's Last Battle,* 1985, pp. 52-72.

18. Harminder Singh Nanda, "Why Have the Sikhs Taken to Extremism?" *Expanse*, April 1986.

19. *Ibid.*

4
The Economy

John P. Lewis

Some Basic Characteristics

One must start by trying to put the Indian national economy in perspective. It is, in the first place, a giant system. Measured by population size, India is the second largest country. Its total population (770 million) is two or three times as large as that of the third or fourth giants (the USSR and the United States) and is now rapidly overtaking that of China. In the second place, this massive country is so diverse and has such a brief history of national integrity that it does not stretch matters much to call it a "multinational" system. In its numbers of languages, religions, and ethnic groups as well as its geography, the part of the South Asian subcontinent now under the Indian flag is at least as differentiated as all of Western Europe, and only during the past 200 years, first incrementally under the British, then with the help of Mahatma Gandhi and the Independence movement, has the territory achieved a greater measure of political integration than its European counterpart.

Ever since Independence there have been fears that this variegated country was about to break up. Although the recent bitter troubles in Punjab have revived such concerns, there is a kind of mechanical cohesion in India that probably is secure. The system's Indian-ness is well entrenched in the minds of elites and masses alike. Because the system is divided into a large number of geographic units (in contrast to pre-Bangladesh Pakistan or pre-Civil War United States, both of which were divided into two hostile parts), at any given time a majority of the units is likely to favor national integrity. Furthermore, there is an

---

The author is grateful for their help to John Holsen of the World Bank and Devesh Kapur of the Woodrow Wilson School; but anyerrors are his.

instrument (the Indian Army), effectively loyal to the center, so patently capable of enforcing the will of the majority that it seldom has to act.

Nevertheless the diversity of the Indian states, as well as of the country's castes and classes, occasions a great deal of average internal tension, and the diversity of the states' economic performance obviously affects the national averages. Thus during much of the time since Independence the outputs and incomes of such states as Punjab, Gujarat and Tamil Nadu have grown at rates rivaling those of such economic successes as South Korea and Malaysia. But the records of these front-running states have been buried in the national averages that have reflected also such laggards as Bihar, Orissa and Uttar Pradesh.

A third basic characteristic is that the country is poor. It started poor at Independence, and it is still poor. The slow growth of incomes and continuing pervasiveness of poverty since Independence are, of course, clearly the result of the development record I shall be sketching. But it also reflects the economic level at which independent India started as well as the lumbering, diversified massiveness of the system.

According to conventional comparative national income data of the sort shown by the World Bank in its annual World Development Reports (WDR), Indian gross national product (GNP) per capita in 1984 was $260 (1984 dollars). This compared with $310 for China. It was twice as high as per capita income in Bangladesh but lower than income in Pakistan ($360) and in many sub-Saharan African countries in the WDR's low-income category. It is true that these simple per capita dollar comparisons understate certain advantages that India, like the other giant, China, enjoys compared with the low-income African countries, such as a greater relative supply of many kinds of trained professional and paraprofessional personnel. But the fact remains that in absolute numbers, India has far more very poor people (what the World Bank sometimes has called "the absolute poor") than all of the sub-Saharan African countries combined.

The Indian economy's fourth basic characteristic has to do with organization. It is a mixed economy. Since 1951 it has been committed to central planning, but this, like "indicative planning" in France, or indeed, planning regimes in most developing countries and now in such socialist countries as Yugoslavia, Hungary and (increasingly) China, does not exclude a partially self-adjusting market. Indian commodity, labor and other factor markets are semiregulated, semifree. Indian exports face various hurdles in the international market, and the Indian national market, while it has a high measure of protection, offers selective, regulated access to imports of commodities, services, commercial capital and direct investment.

As to the ownership and management of enterprises, while national policy has favored an expanding public sector (especially in heavy industry) through a series of five-year plans, the balance of investment is tilting toward the private side in the current (seventh) five-year plan. There have always been, in fact, a number of mixed or joint public-private (or public-cooperative-private) enterprises. Agriculture, despite a few feints at state farming or "joint cooperative farming" in the 1950s, has remained overwhelmingly private and has been carried out mostly on small (although by no means equally small), owner-operated farms.

Finally, the Indian economy is framed and governed by a democratic polity. This is not a perfect democracy—certainly it does not feature high measures of economic and social equality—but it is a serious one. It is and, except for the two-year aberration of the 1975-1977 Emergency, has been a constitutional democracy. Along with a variety of elites, the common man has more than a ceremonial voice in this governance. Moreover, he has a fairly robust set of institutions and procedures protecting him against arbitrary injuries, whether by government or by private actors.

Given all this, despite the incumbency of Communist state governments from time to time (West Bengal has had one nominally Communist without interruption since 1977, for example), revolution never has been a close thing in independent India. However bold the planning, changes in economic policies and conditions are always incremental. The question usually is whether policies are moving with enough speed and decisiveness to be reasonably responsive to the country's appetites for growth, for a larger measure of social justice and, at the same time, for progress toward economic self-reliance.

Indian fiscal years run from 1 April to 31 March. If this chapter has a precise chronological focus, it is on 31 March 1987: What was the condition of the Indian economy, and what were some of the challenges it faced, as it passed from 1986/87 to 1987/88? To get to the present, however, one must sketch the economy's recent past—during, let us say, the 1980s. Moreover, it adds meaning to the story first to identify a few highlights of the economic—and the economic-policy—experience of the three decades preceding.

The Development Record

An overarching point in the Indian case is that development predominantly has been a purposeful, public-policy endeavor. Before Independence and since, few Indians have questioned the need for government to play an interventionist role in behalf of development. As we shall see, there has been and continues to be much debate over how heavy, detailed and direct the government's role should be. But in a country where even fair and open agricultural trading is done in "regulated markets" presided over by government functionaries, advocates of literal laissez faire are comparatively scarce—even in the business community and the conservative press.

With this said, four aspects of India's development experience in its first three decades (1950-1980) can be described briefly: agriculture; overall growth, industrialization and trade; poverty alleviation; and development-enhancing institutions.

Agriculture

The first really serious Indian economic planning was done, not for India's First Five-Year Plan (1951-1956), but for the Second Plan (1956-1961). Agriculture was not at the top of the planners' list. Retrospectively, one can say that it should have been; agriculture was still the sector that occupied the most Indian workers and supported most of the population. But industrialization was the glamorous issue. By comparison agriculture did not appear to have much potential for dynamic change, although in the aftermath of some exceptionally good monsoons during the early 1950s, it seemed to be performing quite well. More than this, during much of the 1950s a kind of stalemate was created among a variety of policy factors bearing on agricultural performance.

For one thing, Indian technical expertise in agriculture was traditionally preoccupied with avoiding disasters (i.e., droughts and famines), not with maximizing normal agricultural output. Thus the irrigation system gave a thin spread of water to as many clients as possible, and plant breeding focused on drought-resistant, not high-yielding, varieties. Another factor was the Community Development Movement (CD), begun with Prime Minister Nehru's personal blessing at the start of the 1950s. Critics increasingly felt that in its effort to promote overall improvement of village life, CD slighted agriculture and that as the CD model was applied across India, it lost, in mass reproduction, its potential for engaging local participation and energies.

Meanwhile many social scientists assessing rural change were convinced that major advances in agricultural production would have to await the restructuring of rural institutions, in particular the kind of radical land reforms that the rural elites were able largely to forestall. Many policy analysts, moreover, were convinced that Indian peasants were not motivated by the same drives that animated Western economic behavior and saw little point in paying to them the incentive prices that would agitate more politically active city dwellers. In the face of these trends and perceptions, conventional proproduction advocates did not have the political and bureaucratic strength to change policies or the technologies to create production breakthroughs.

An agricultural revolution ensued, however. It was driven in the first place by necessity. As the 1950s unfolded, the weather averaged out, population grew faster than the planners' forecasts, and India suffered a widening food deficit. Then psychologically and politically the priority accorded to agriculture took a further quantum jump in the two back-to-back droughts of 1965/66 and 1966/67. Meanwhile, informed by research and experience, decisionmakers' perceptions of Indian farmers shifted; the latter were seen to be, after all, economic optimizers.

In response to the need there was a drive both within the government and on the part of the international aid agencies to augment agricultural inputs and infrastructure and, in order to maximize the immediate impact and then the spread effect, to concentrate these supplies first in the best agricultural districts. The assembling of these new policies was given indispensable leadership by the appointment in mid-1964 of India's most effective minister of food and agriculture, C. Subramaniam, who in three years transformed "the new agricultural strategy" into an established program.

But the pivotal element in the "Green Revolution" of the 1960s—the element that Subramaniam and the officials and scientists he brought to the fore spotted quickly and exploited boldly—was the new high-yielding varieties technology that, emanating from international origins, was quickly transplanted into an Indian agricultural research system that was in sufficiently good although uneven shape to receive it. The new technology promised explosive increases of short-stalk and short-gestation wheats and rices if they were fed plenty of fertilizer and controlled amounts of water.

Although the scope and impact of the Green Revolution were often exaggerated, the change in Indian agriculture was profound and irreversible. By the late 1970s (1978/79) rice production was 55 percent higher than it had been at the beginning of the 1960s (1960/61), and wheat output was well over three times the earlier level. Ten years earlier India had appeared to face a future of endless food deficits. By the late 1970s it was on average self-reliant in food production, without the access of the poor to food having worsened (it had improved shamefully little). The country built a buffer stock of food grains in the neighborhood of 20 million tons, that is, about one-sixth of its annual production.

Indian crop yields were still very low by international standards and much room remained for improvement. Yet the shape and scale of agricultural production had been permanently altered. A very substantial and effective system of agricultural research was operating as was a large agricultural inputs industry. There had been one other notable change: India, for better or worse, had acquired a farm lobby. Family farmers, particularly of the medium and larger sizes, had found their political voices sufficiently, so that the government's Agricultural Prices Commission, established in the mid-1960s to protect cultivators against politicians' inclinations in behalf of their urban constituents, now found itself opposing the efforts of state leaders to guarantee the farmers unreasonably high prices.

Industry, Investments, and Controls

The industrial strategy adopted in the Second Five-Year Plan in 1956 was a model for other developing countries at that time. Its central objective was to raise the country's investment rate and therefore as soon as possible its saving rate from something on the order of 5 percent of GNP to something closer to 12-15 percent. If, as was widely hypothesized, it took $3.00 worth of investment to achieve a lasting increase of $1.00 in income and output, such a savings rate would assure a growth rate of 4-5 percent in GNP. Or, if population was increasing about 1.5 percent annually (as, at the time, was thought to be the case), 12-15 percent savings would buy per capita growth of 2.5 percent or 3 percent.

To get such expansion the planners looked primarily to industrialization. For the time being this would take a lot of imports of things the economy did not yet produce. But the planners were pessimistic about the global economy's appetite for their exports. Therefore if they were bent on self-reliance—as the Indians emphatically were—they would need to achieve as much import substitution as possible as soon as possible. This meant producing not only most of their own consumer requirements but intermediate components and inputs, and the basic products and commodities from which intermediates were made (e.g., steel as well as cotton). It meant producing the machines that were needed, even the machines to make machines. The chief Indian planner at the time, P. C. Mahalanobis, had a further rationale for pushing capital goods. If one produced capital goods that were good only for producing further capital goods, it tended to lock the economy into the kind of low-consumption, high-savings pattern needed for accelerating growth. At any rate, given the technologies available, many of the items on the economy's broad industrial agenda were capital-intensive. Hence the import-substitution strategy turned out to be capital-intensive—even in a capital-poor system.

Shortages of capital as well as of foreign exchange, therefore, were endemic to the strategy, and at the time it was only natural for much of the needed rationing to be done by direct controls rather than by price. The economy had inherited a whole apparatus of controls used by the British during the war, and in a government that liked to call itself "socialist" or "socialistic" there was little admiration for the magic of the market. Thus from the mid-1950s into the 1960s quantitative restrictions on and banned lists of imports, detailed official allocations of foreign exchange, investment licensing, materials allocation and a broad array of price controls enveloped the economy. The web was self-augmenting. "Working" the system and exploiting the scarcity rents it generated became a new specialized industry, not only for bureaucrats, but for private practitioners, the most skillful and experienced of which tended to be in the employ of the larger commercial and business houses.

In its import-substitution strategy India was, as noted, something of a model for other developing countries. But because of its size and the head start it had in some industrial sectors, it was able to carry import-substituting, capital-intensive, controls-managed industrialization further than most other countries. Thus it also felt the drawbacks of the approach more heavily than most. It is worth emphasizing that the industrial policy choices that had been made were not all misbegotten. Within limits import substitution can, like export promotion, provide a wholesome avenue toward self-reliance. Moreover, Indians piled up learning experiences across a broad array of industries, many of which produced outputs that in due course were useful.

The industrial scene, however, was ridden with inefficiencies. Without market guidance the capacities built did not match the pattern of demands. Many were too small or used outmoded or otherwise inappropriate technologies. Firms were largely undisciplined by internal and especially import competition. And the control system itself laid a heavy burden of unproductive wheel spinning and worse on the whole economy.

These are the lessons that have been progressively learned since the early 1960s. They have been learned most strikingly by Indians themselves, on the one hand by such incisive academic analysts as Jagdish Bhagwati and T. N. Srinivasan and, more recently, Isher Ahluwalia, on the other, by a growing number of the country's more perceptive economic officials, politicians and policy advisers. Strong external voices, including those of the World Bank and the U.S. Agency for International Development (USAID), joined the chorus favoring liberalization in the mid-1960s, and since that time in India as well as outside, the conventional technocratic wisdom has increasingly tilted toward giving open markets more scope. But when a controls system reaches the size it had in India by the mid-1960s, its inertia is enormous. The interests that have a stake in its continuation are numerous and powerful.

Thus the status and prospect for industrial reform remain embattled issues down to this day. One measure of their persisting importance carries us back to the growth theories of the early planners. It will be remembered that they saw the attainment of a 12-15 percent savings rate as a critical but difficult goal. The fact is that a savings rate of 20 percent had already been achieved by the end of the 1970s. Yet gross domestic product (GDP) during that decade grew only about 3.6 percent annually, or, per capita, not more than 1.5 percent a year. This meant that the productivity of capital was far below the expectations of the 1950s. The "incremental capital-output ratio" had ballooned to nearly twice the mythic 3:1 assumed in earlier theorizing, and it probably does not oversimplify matters greatly to attribute this to the entrenched inefficiencies of a controls-fettered economy.

Poverty Alleviation

Officially, independent India has had a soft spot in its heart for the poor from the beginning. One of Mahatma Gandhi's abiding concerns was to end the injustices suffered by untouchables and other disadvantaged groups, just as improved equity was a major objective of Nehru's socialism. Community development was meant to reach the weaker classes, and Mahalanobis' Second Plan, recognizing that the concentration of scarce capital on capital-intensive industrialization would not provide jobs for all who needed them, included a secondary, labor-intensive aspect addressed to that need. The plan itself tended rather wishfully to rely on traditional cottage industries for this purpose. At the same time, however, Indians were among the leading theorizers about the potential that rural public works had for supplementing poor people's employment and incomes. In the early 1960s India was one of the first developing countries to give explicit statistical and analytical attention to income distribution and to ways for meeting the poor's minimum needs.

Nevertheless it is true that in India as in many developing countries during much of the 1960s, as development policy makers focused on agricultural production and increasingly on industrial and trade strategy and on the population problem, the poverty issue—and the closely allied employment issue—tended to get pushed aside. The turn of the decade brought their rediscovery—in India itself, in much of the rest of the third world, in the fora of the United Nations and in both the bilateral and multilateral wings of the development assistance community. A surge of revised thinking was headlined in India by Indira Gandhi's successful 1971 election slogan ("Garibi Hatao"—Abolish Poverty). The common assessment was that, as a single-track development strategy, promoting growth and waiting for the benefits to "trickle down" to the poor were not good enough. There was need for direct attacks on what Robert McNamara, president of the World Bank, called "the absolute poverty" of the third world's lower 40 percent in ways that would meet the basic needs of the poor without placing a counterproductive drag on growth.

Relatively speaking, Indian income distribution (if one relies on the rather scant, wobbly and outdated comparative data on this subject) is not quite as unequal as that of many developing countries. Indeed, India does not compare too unfavorably with the United States. The World Bank reports that the lowest quintile had a higher share in India (7.0 percent) than in the United States (5.3 percent). On the other hand, in the years the WDR table reflects (1975/76 for India, 1980 for the United States) India had a greater inequality at the upper end of the distribution; its highest quintile claimed 49 percent of total household income compared with 40 percent in the United States. Given India's average poverty, however, in absolute terms the number of Indians counted as poor (the country's poverty line is defined in nutritional terms) remained very high throughout the 1970s.

Some antipoverty progress was recorded, however. Advances in food production increased the poor's access to food, particularly through the urban public distribution system ("fair price shops"). A number of new direct antipoverty programs were launched—among them programs for small and marginal farmers and drought-prone areas, the Integrated Rural Development Program (IRDP) and Employment Guarantee Scheme (EGS) in the state of Maharashtra and some national analogues. By itself the proliferation of new programs was nothing new. Indian officialdom always has had a great capacity for spawning new schemes. The difference was that some of those started in the 1970s were quickly scaled up to significant size and were pursued with considerable seriousness even through the political turbulence of that decade. One must take pains, therefore, to see what has happened to them during the 1980s as this story is brought down to the present.

Institution Building

As one sizes up some of the main strengths and problems that the development experience of the preceding thirty years bequeathed to the Indian economy of the 1980s, it is important not to overlook the institutional endowment. India by now has a very large array, not only of public and private enterprises and of governmental ministries, bureaus and agencies devoted to development, but of public, private and mixed not-for-profit institutions wholly or partly dedicated to development promotion. The endowment is not just a matter of numbers however. Any census of development-related institutions undeniably would include many very weak units. The endowment instead consists disproportionately of the minority of better institutions. Many of these are genuinely outstanding. One virtue of the abundance of run-of-the-mill organizations from which these leaders stand forward is that who emerges as outstanding is not always fore-ordained. There is a good deal of rivalry among institutions. Some rise, others decline, and there is considerable facility in the system for identifying such shifts.

It is hard to exaggerate the continuing reinforcement that this institutional array provides to the economy's prospects. In this regard, India's outlook is considerably more promising than that of its next-door neighbor, Pakistan. To date Pakistan's growth has been faster than India's, but the fact that the institutional infrastructure Pakistan has built is considerably weaker than India's may not augur well for the smaller economy's performance over the longer haul.

Institution building overlaps a great deal with "human resource development" or what are often called "the social sectors." From this perspective also there has been much that was ordinary—or spotty—in the development effort's first thirty years. For example, although India had a woman as chief of government during many of those years and has an impressive array of feminist reformers, the fact that, unlike nearly all other countries, India has a majority of males demonstrates how deeply discrimination against females is still embedded in the society. Nevertheless, by the end of the 1970s, although there were great variations among the states, all of the social-sector programs—education, literacy, population and health—were far beyond the lip-service stage.

The Current Economy

For much of the world, including many third world countries, the 1980s have been a rough decade economically. But these years on balance have been the best the Indian economy has seen since the headiness of the 1950s wore off. It is hard to avoid exaggeration in the glib journalistic labels that get attached to distant places. India used to be called a basket case. Now the fashion has swung to the opposite extreme. Suddenly India, like China, has become not just a demographic but a performing giant. People are calling the two of them "NICs" (Newly Industrializing Countries)—the most advanced of the developing-country categories—right alongside the likes of Brazil and Mexico, despite the oddity that India's and China's incomes per capita are an order of magnitude lower.

In part this current lionizing of the two Asian giants is calculated. It is a way, in an era of embarrassingly scarce official development assistance, to rationalize aid cutoffs to these hulking countries, where even the thinnest aid flows can soak up much of what otherwise would be available for needier Africans. But much of the present euphoria is not contrived. For example, Professor Peter Drucker, who included an extravagantly favorable assessment of the Indian economy in an article in the Spring 1986 issue of *Foreign Affairs,* has no anti-aid ax to grind. Rather, he is simply one of those interesting and creative commentators, part of whose stock and trade it is to give their audiences surprises. Good economic news about India was so unexpected that, almost inevitably, it has been exaggerated in the telling.

The fact is that Indian growth has not suddenly lurched up to a world-class rate. Nor have the system's inequities been radically reduced. Many problems remain and changes have been incremental. But many of the changes have been positive, and they add up to a distinct (if not mind-boggling) change of pace—and to a greater measure of confidence. In the media all of this has been packaged in and around the image of the young new prime minister, Rajiv Gandhi. Here again, there has been potential for exaggeration. Mr. Gandhi is an attractive leader, but he is neither a wizard nor a supergrade manager. He is credited with reforms his mother already had largely put in place after she returned to power in 1980. But by early 1987 his honeymoon was over. There was disarray in his administration and the seriousness of Rajiv's new economics was being called into question.

In the remainder of this chapter I shall first outline some major recent economic developments and then review critical issues for the economy. These include the strength of trade and liberalization reform and the country's posture toward new technologies; agricultural and rural development questions; the pivotal issues of internal and external resources, including aid and direct foreign investment; and, finally, some general questions of economic management.

Recent Developments

Not long ago the brilliant and remarkably sensible Indian policy economist Raj Krishna—recently deceased and sorely missed—coined a phrase, the "Hindu rate of growth," to describe India's economic predicament. No matter what the aspirations, strategies and initiatives, the Indian economy seemed to settle inexorably into an average uphill trudge of about 3.5 percent per annum.

This has changed significantly since 1980. During the Sixth Plan period (1980-1985) real GDP had a trend growth rate of a little better than 4.5 percent, and the rate promises to be about 5 percent during the Seventh Plan, now in progress. This may not look like a major acceleration, but consider the translation into per capita terms. Annual population growth, compared with its level of at least 2.2 percent during the periods Raj Krishna had in mind, had subsided to about 2 percent during the Sixth Plan. Thus growth in real GDP per capita went from 1.3 percent to, say, 2.6 percent—it has *doubled* in the 1980s compared with the two previous decades. This has meant improvements in welfare that are highly perceptible to many Indians.

Agriculture, particularly foodgrain and oilseed production (which had been lagging), performed admirably during the Sixth Plan period, growing 4.5 percent annually and exhibiting increased resistance to bad weather. Extending the trend of the 1970s, foodgrain stocks reached a peak of 29 million tons in June 1985, following especially fine weather in the preceding year. Previously some of the worst constraints on Indian growth had been a variety of infrastructural and materials bottlenecks—particularly in the coal, electricity, transport, cement and steel sectors. These supply bottlenecks have been freed up or at least greatly relaxed in the 1980s, and domestic oil production (mainly from the "Bombay High" offshore) has surged.

Manufacturing, on the other hand, fell well short of Sixth Plan targets. In any sort of balanced planning its output was projected to grow twice as fast as that of agriculture. Yet during the Sixth Plan, manufacturers' production managed to increase at an average annual rate of only 4.3 percent. The sector continued to be tangled in the effects of the controls regimes already discussed. In many cases costs were high, efficiency was low, competition was weak and, although many external markets were generally depressed, India's share in them weakened.

The country's collective gains in goods production in the 1980s have been augmented by somewhat faster growth in a mixed bag of services. Taken together, all of this falls far short of a rousing acceleration. But, as indicated, the pick-up becomes more significant when it is (1) translated into per capita terms and (2) compared with parallel development elsewhere in the third world.

Another reason for India's positive economic image in this decade is that the country has avoided getting mired in external debt. By the end of the Sixth Plan the country's debt service ratio (total current interest and amortization on foreign debts as a percentage of total current receipts from abroad) had risen only to a quite manageable 15 percent, and its credit rating was high in international financial markets. This good showing was attributable to several causes. First, during the late 1970s, India, like other countries of the region (although not nearly to the same relative extent as Pakistan), received a flow of remittances from nationals working in the Middle East. Second, it was producing much more of the oil it uses. In 1985/86 domestic petroleum production (30 million tons) was well over four times what it had been in 1970/71 and accounted for two-thirds of total supplies, compared with only a little over one-third in the earlier year.

The third reason for India's sound financial position, however, was simply good financial management. Happily this was not just cautious management. Historically the government of India has been financially prudent to a fault. In particular, whenever the balance of payments tightened, officials were inclined to raise import controls and back away from whatever liberalization had been in train. At the beginning of the 1980s when Mrs. Gandhi had just returned to office and the payments position had worsened in the wake of the second oil shock, the government did not repeat this pattern. Instead it launched a liberalization program that is still unfolding and accepted a large loan from the IMF to cover its temporary balance of payments deficits. Even with the servicing of the IMF loan (in 1984 India refused the second, follow on, IMF credit it had been expected to accept) the government planned to hold the country's debt service ratio under 20 percent.

At the same time the country achieved improved internal financial discipline. The government increased tax collections while lowering rates, improving enforcement and dampening monetary expansion. Wholesale price inflation since 1980/81 has been held to single-digit levels, indeed to an average of less than 7 percent annually.

There is a downside to the financial management story. The country's payment deficit has widened ominously—because of a sluggish export performance that has worsened in the past two or three years. This is the most obviously alarming aspect of the recent record, one that will be examined below.

On the other hand, the Indian government claims that the recent record contains one other major piece of good news: during the 1980s, it says, India has registered a reduced incidence of poverty. Quite a bit is made of this in the Seventh Five-Year Plan document discussed below. The estimate turns on a comparison of two National Sample Surveys, one of 1977/78 and the other of 1983/84, and (say a number of skeptics) on some challengeable statistical reinterpretations. Whatever the resolution of this technical debate, the general acceleration of the economy, more particularly of agriculture, and the enhanced supplies in the public food distribution system are consistent with real income gains for many of the poorer classes.

Also several of the direct antipoverty programs that were started in the 1970s are being implemented quite vigorously, although there is a great scope for doing more (see below). The Integrated Rural Development Program (IRDP), which is aimed mainly at landless laborers and during the later years of the Sixth Plan became increasingly concentrated on scheduled castes and tribes, has been improved by reducing the number of beneficiaries, but its quantitative target is back to 4 million households for the balance of the Seventh Plan. Similarly, the rural employment programs are being sustained at substantial levels—the Maharashtra and other state programs, the National Rural Employment Program and a Rural Landless Employment Guarantee Program created during the later years of the Sixth Plan. In 1984/85 the latter two programs, for example, together generated about 600 million man-days of work. This is not a trivial number. Yet it represents less than 3 million man-*years* of employment. Some experienced observers find the new rural public works activities being run rather more effectively than in the past. However, such efforts (for which the scope is by no means exhausted) pose some serious organizational problems over the longer run.

The Seventh Five-Year Plan and the Policy Process

It is important to include an explicit word about the Seventh Five-Year Plan, which covers the second half of the 1980s. Five-year plans still count for quite a bit in India. Within the government, annual budgets have more immediate effects. With the public sector's share of investment beginning to decline, it is recognized that the plans are statements of recommendations and guidelines, not commands, and by now everyone understands that good plans are not a guarantee of good implementation. Nevertheless, able documentation does make a difference, and the Seventh Plan, like the Sixth before it, is a very good document. It projects progressive but attainable objectives to be achieved by a balanced, comprehensive, coherent program. Its themes—e.g., liberalization, technological modernization, equity, follow-through in agriculture—are distinct; the argument is lucid, the analysis clear, the tone pragmatic. Throughout independent India's history the average quality of the government's economic papers has been outstanding. Thus it is high praise to say that, as vehicles for official data, objectives, analysis and decisions, the current batch of papers—along with the Seventh Plan, such departmental papers as the Ministry of Finance's Economic Survey, the continuing flow of materials from the Reserve Bank and the cluster of liberalization-related special studies mentioned below—may be the best yet.

Substantively, the Seventh Plan is also praiseworthy. It addresses in a neither overly complacent nor overly alarmist way most of the issues taken up in the balance of this chapter. It stretches the planning horizon to the year 2000 and sets a challenging yet, with great effort, feasible set of targets for the end of the century: Real income per capita is projected to rise about 60 percent in fifteen years, or a little better than 3 percent annually. The population, estimated to number 970 million in 2000, is, as the World Bank puts it, "to be served by a diversified and self-sufficient agriculture, a dynamic and outward-looking industrial sector," together with appropriately enhanced power, transport and communications systems. By the year 2000, universal primary schooling and other educational instruments are expected to have eliminated illiteracy. "Together with increased food consumption, better sanitation and health facilities, assured drinking water supplies and controls on air and water pollution are expected to lead to significant increase of life expectancy. The birth rate is expected to fall by 33 percent to 23.1 percent in the year 2000."

But the plan makes no pretense that these goals will be achieved easily. They will be attained only if the government's intervening policies—for example, those concerning industrial and trade liberalization, to which I turn next—are conducive. Moreover, it should be pointed out that the Planning Commission no longer plays as pivotal a role in the economic policy game as it did up to the end of the Nehru era and for some time thereafter.

In terms of month-to-month and year-to-year decision making the Planning Commission is important because it presides over the allocation of development budgets to the states. But typically economic policy decisions at the agency and ministry level have been centered in the Finance Ministry—in the Department of Economic Affairs, in the senior secretaries of the ministry and, when he is strong and builds continuity as did Minister V. P. Singh until he was moved in late January 1987, in the minister of finance himself. In Rajiv Gandhi's administration as in that of his mother, moreover, a great deal of policy influence has lodged as well with one or two senior professional economists in the prime minister's office. The process has become even more personalized and sometimes obscure under Rajiv. An advisory committee of distinguished academic economists (more left-leaning than the full-time technocrats) evidently wields considerable influence at times. At the same time, there is continuous persuasive input not only from some of the prime minister's more market-oriented business contemporaries but from the veteran civil servant, economist, banker, diplomat and state governor, L. K. Jha.

Questions and Challenges Ahead

There are two principal clusters of issues that will give shape to the development strategy India pursues into and through the 1990s. The clusters overlap, each includes several elements and the two are equally important. But at this point I will follow conventional wisdom by giving pride of place to the industry-trade-technology-liberalization complex of questions. This, as the Seventh Plan rightly notes, is where the country must look for radically improved performance if it is going to make good its medium- and long-term goals. But then, second, I will turn to the agriculture-rural-poverty set of issues, arguing that India's agricultural success is by no means sufficient and that there is a great further scope for increasing employment and income benefits for the poor through improved agriculture-industry relations. In addition, I will look at two cross-cutting concerns: first, questions about resources, both internal and external; second, challenges in the realm of economic management.

Industry, Trade, Technology and Liberalization

The government of India has racked up an accumulating record of industrial and trade liberalization during the past several years. As noted, this round of liberalization began at the start of this decade and proceeded piecemeal for several years. During the past three years, however, the agenda of regulatory relaxation has become more comprehensive. Some industries have been exempted entirely from capacity licensing, and others have been allowed to renew or enlarge licensed capacities freely. Through so-called broad-banding more flexibility is allowed in the use of installed capacities for alternative products.

Restraints on the textile industry have been relaxed. Various administrative modifications are claimed to have reduced waiting times for clearances. The small but potentially formidable computer software industry has been accorded limited access to imported software in exchange for expanded obligations to export labor. Some export incentives have been increased and trade policy seems to be moving toward greater substitution of tariffs for quantitative restrictions on imports. The number of companies subject to restraints imposed under the Monopolies and Restrictive Trade Practices Act (MRTP) has been reduced, and MRTP and foreign equity companies still subject to regulation are permitted more flexible operations. There also have been some major moves in the realm of tax reform, as discussed below.

In its pronouncements the government certainly no longer tiptoes around the subject of liberalization. It is the official line, articulated not only in such general documents as the Seventh Plan but in a rather remarkable concentration of special high-powered government committee studies released during 1985 and 1986. Headed by distinguished officials and economists, the studies have dealt with trade policies, the move from physical to financial controls, the "black economy," the monetary system and long-term fiscal policy.

With all this behavioral and documentary evidence, one may wonder why there should be uncertainty about whether the Rajiv Gandhi liberalization push is still underway or is fading. Several reasons may be cited.

First, the liberalization commitment in India is by no means absolute. The government is not prepared to go for broke and sweep away all controls at a stroke. It prefers to proceed incrementally and, while relaxing controls, to keep the controls apparatus in place, ready for reapplication on short notice. Philosophically, as I have noted, the government is not about to opt for full-blown laissez faire. While it is keenly interested in making more effective use of self-regulating markets as instruments of social control, it is not collectively convinced that a single-track strategy of outward orientation suits India in the 1980s and 1990s as well as it did such smaller economies as Taiwan and South Korea in the 1960s and 1970s. With OECD growth slowed, the global market's absorptive capacity for developing countries' manufactured exports may be limited. Import liberalization that gets ahead of export expansion plainly can create balance-of-payments problems. Moreover, there is some backlash in official circles against what are taken to be excessively shrill and simplistic preachments from international agencies and pundits.

Second, there is heavy interest-group and political resistance within the country to the liberalization agenda. Leftward-leaning intellectuals, who are instinctively interventionists, dislike it, and old-line Congress socialists are affronted by it, as, of course, are all of those reaping scarcity rents from the controls system. During 1986 and the first months of 1987 pressures from these quarters forced government controllers into some hesitations and delays.

Third, there is little doubt that a good deal of foot dragging is going on at middle and lower levels of the bureaucracy. One hears fascinating accounts of how, while senior officials, advisers—indeed, the prime minister himself—are broadening liberalization commitment and decisions, functionaries at the implementation level—people who do or do not dispense the licenses, remove the price controls, etc.—are, not uncommonly, standing pat or sabotaging in one way or another the policy changes. The evidence is anecdotal, but it is too widespread to be ignored.

My own net assessment is that, while it will remain partial and halting, the liberalization movement is alive. Its near-term prospects, however, depend a good deal on the subject to which I return at the very end of this chapter—namely, the increasingly puzzling circumstances surrounding the prime minister, his style and his inner direction. Meanwhile the country faces a set of trade and industrial challenges that are far from resolved.

1. *Insufficient growth to meet employment goals?* The overall 5 percent annual growth in national output and income projected in the Seventh Plan has an appealingly sensible outlook—it is not unrealistically ambitious. The trouble is that (with a modest increase in average output per worker and a shift of the increment in output away from agriculture and toward industry) 5 percent may not do enough to dent the economy's employment problem and, by putting the poor to work, raise their productivity. (India's "employment problem" is another face of its poverty problem. The government has almost given up on tabulating unemployment, especially in the countryside—because the poor can seldom afford to remain literally idle. But what can be done to improve the condition of the *underemployed* poor—namely, put them to more productive work—remains a stubborn and critical issue.)

Given the high saving and investment rates already achieved and those the plan now contemplates, it is unlikely that growth can be speeded by further accelerating capital formation. Rather, the productivity of capital—the output gains associated with given investments—needs to be raised beyond Seventh Plan expectations. Some of this could be done by funding somewhat bolder public budgets in behalf of more (worthwhile) labor-intensive, capital-stretching public works. Beyond this, Indian industry in general still needs a lot more efficiency therapy, just as the liberalizing reformers have been arguing. Throughout industry the emphasis must be on getting more output—and more jobs—out of given inputs of capital.

2. *Competition, efficiency and comparative advantage.* No other mechanism can begin to rival that of more open, lustier competition for inducing the country's scarce capital to yield more output and employment mileage. This means livelier internal competition, with the big houses (the quasi-monopolies), on the one hand, stripped of their inside-track advantages for working the controls system and, on the other hand, freed to battle fairly in a broader array of markets. Competition also emphatically means *imports* competition with imports spilling over tariff walls in sufficient volume to keep pressure on indigenous enterprises which have been liberated from the hothouse conditions provided by quantitative import barriers. Competition will promote productive and distributive efficiency as to the cost effectiveness with which particular products are produced and marketed. It will also encourage allocative efficiency; competition, especially from abroad, is needed increasingly to discipline the economy's make-or-buy choices along comparative advantage lines.

3. *Needed: A coherent technological policy.* What is needed here is a particularly tricky piece of ongoing policy design, because the technological policy of an economy as large, as poor and yet as sophisticated as the Indian is inherently complex. If one does not keep the required overall balance in view, the policy will appear contradictory. Plainly, the country needs to pursue comparative advantage along labor-intensive lines. But it also must keep pace with the way competing productive systems are evolving elsewhere around the world. For this purpose it needs to keep importing technologies, not just as ideas, but in some cases as new ideas embodied in goods and in foreign firms making direct investments in India. Besides being technically tricky, these are issues shot through with emotion. Although there is much Indian public discourse on these subjects, technological policy is a field in which policy makers have a great deal of trail breaking yet to do.

At the same time, much is astir in the realm of technological transfer and investment. As will be noted below, direct foreign investment is nowhere near large enough to provide a major answer to India's balance of payments problems. Yet, as *The Asian Wall Street Journal* has been reporting, for example, a veritable migration of exploratory American collaborations is underway from the Silicon Valley and elsewhere to Bangalore, India's burgeoning center of high-tech industries. Moreover, the government is taking increasing interest in attracting back the experience and enterprise as well as the savings of nonresident Indians

(NRIs), tens of thousands of whom are pursuing technically sophisticated careers in North America and Europe. And many of these NRIs are beginning to plan and implement innovative investments. But, as *The Asian Wall Street Journal* also has been at pains to detail, much of this technological transfer stands in grave danger of being aborted by the inadequacies of such basic requirements as the Indian telephone system.

4. *Corruption.* It still is almost impolite for a friendly foreigner to apply this word to the Indian scene. In doing so I do not necessarily imply that governmental corruption in India has become any worse than it has been in recent decades in many US states. But it is foolish not to admit that a substantial level of corruption has come to characterize a wide array of official dealings in India, that the incidence no longer just involves petty transactions to petty officials, that in the early 1980s the condition was widely perceived to be much worse than it had been twenty years earlier and that it has gravely affected the morale of officials and the confidence of the public.

The reason for including this subject in a list of trade and industrial policy issues is that much the most promising cure for corruption is liberalization. There would appear to be very little chance at this juncture for re-creating in India the kind of dedicated patriotic mindset that, in the case of the independence generation, inoculated a large portion of senior officials and politicians against venality. But what can be and is being done is progressively to reduce the sources of and incentives for public malfeasance. Tax reform as a diminisher of the "black economy" has such an effect. So do all facets of liberalization that reduce or eliminate the scarcity rents generated by the controls system. The largest further opportunity for promoting probity in India may be the same reform—namely, public funding of election campaigns—that has the same potential in the United States.

5. *Exports.* The most immediate and urgent unresolved issue for the Indian economy is exports. At the end of fiscal year 1986/87 the trade gap looked slightly less threatening than it was a year earlier. Imports had actually fallen a bit, to about Rs. 180 billion, having been held in check by declining oil prices, while exports were up, surprisingly, in excess of 10 percent. But the latter was the result of a collection of ad-hoc factors that, like the oil price sag, could not be projected to the years ahead, and still the trade deficit was some Rs. 70 billion, or between 5 and 6 billion dollars. To narrow the deficit to a sustainable size and to achieve the income growth (including the needed growth in imports) that the Seventh Five-Year Plan projects will require making good the plan's targeted annual export growth of nearly 7 percent.

This is a tall order. There is a lively, if muted, debate within the Government of India and among its various official and unofficial advisers as to how much of the goal could and should be accomplished by an exchange rate adjustment. The rupee's real exchange rate (adjusted for the comparative inflations of India and its trading partners) jumped some 15 percent in the two years following the 1979 oil shock and did not quickly fall, as it did after the 1973 oil shock. During the first half of the 1980s Indian export prices, measured in US dollar equivalents, lost competitiveness against those of such other countries as Argentina, Colombia, Brazil, Mexico, South Korea, Malaysia, the Philippines and Pakistan. On the other hand, since mid-1985 the rupee, which is tied to a currency basket featuring the dollar, has been riding down with the latter—even outstripping it somewhat—and thereby experiencing a quiet, creeping devaluation, which may, indeed, already have had some positive effect on export sales.

What the situation probably calls for is not the provision of further specific (commodity by commodity and user class by user class) export incentives. These already have so multiplied—and the proliferation continues—as to threaten to snarl implementation in a profusion of clearances. Nor has there been a lack of marketing initiatives by the government. What has indeed been damaging, as will be noted when I return to reflections about the pivotal role of the prime minister, has been the lack of strong and sustained ministerial leadership in the export sector. Nevertheless, given the magnitude of the export challenge, it would appear there is further scope for improving the macroeconomic environment for exports.

The Agriculture-Rural Development-Poverty Complex

It would be a sad mistake for India to relax its agricultural development effort on the theory that the country is over the hump in that department. As noted, average yields are still low. The agricultural research system, water management and dryland farming all contain great scope for further gains in output. If the country desubsidizes the supply of fertilizer and other inputs to cereals producers (as it should), its foodgrains surpluses may well prove to be noncompetitive in the international market. There may be a case, therefore, for policy and incentives designed to shift the product mix toward higher value crops—both for export and for an internal market that demands higher value food and other supplies as per capita incomes pick up.

The main issue for our purposes is simply to avoid relaxation. What Indian officials have written in such documents as the Seventh Plan and the 1985/86 Economic Survey as well as what they say in conversation would suggest that they are on guard against such a letdown. It is important that aid donors be similarly minded. The components of a continued strong pro-agriculture strategy—research, extension, inputs, cost-price adjustments, marketing, etc.—do not need to be spelled out here. What should be emphasized instead are two broader considerations that might be incorporated in the design of a dynamic rural/agricultural strategy for the 1990s.

The first is the need and potential for further developing constructive, complementary, agriculture-industry relations. Food and agricultural production, while it has stepped up to a higher plateau, has flattened in the middle 1980s. So has agriculture's demand for such inputs as fertilizer, and indeed, for capital goods and consumption goods generally—all of this because the nonagricultural economy's performance has remained sluggish. A scenario for more buoyant interactive expansion needs to be spelled out and promoted.

Of particular concern in this regard is the development of stronger agricultural-industrial linkages in decentralized (e.g., town-centered) settings in ways that are technically progressive and cost-effective and yet allow workers to migrate out of agriculture without migrating very far geographically. I will return to this matter under the heading of economic management below.

The second issue worth emphasizing is the opportunity that growing agricultural productivity affords to increase direct nutrition supplements for India's still woefully numerous groups of extremely poor and disadvantaged people. As suggested already, the obstacles to this kind of improvement in antipoverty programs may be more organizational than financial. They too will be touched on under the economic management heading.

Resources Issues

The internal resource issue of greatest interest at present is taxation. The freshness and vigor of the government's approach to tax problems was signaled by the "black economy" report issued in May 1985. Estimating that between two-thirds and three-quarters of taxable income was not being declared and that, overall, black income might account for 18-30 percent of GDP at factor costs, the report blamed the "awesome" variety and complexity of the controls system, high and complicated tax schedules, and slack administration. The government's follow-through with respect to taxation has been striking. It has simplified the tariff schedule, begun a major reform of excise taxes that moves toward a system of modified value-added taxation, moderated the corporate tax, simplified and lowered personal income and wealth tax schedules and radically stepped up tax enforcement. The result in 1986 was all that any finance minister could ask for. With lower rates, collections stepped up smartly.

Even if this pattern of improved tax yields persists fully, however (some of it may represent one-time increases), it does not promise a jump in public saving. Current account government spending is high and rising and, although it certainly needs disciplining, antipoverty spending and social sector outlays may need to rise further. In short, domestic fiscal reform will promote cleaner, more wholesome and socially constructive government, but it does not promise significantly to alter the savings/investment balance. Tax and public expenditure reform are unlikely to take the pressure off India's export needs or its requirements for funding net imports by transfers from abroad.

The country's receipts of external resources remain critical. A year ago the government was taking great satisfaction from the sparing way it had been borrowing commercial finance abroad and from the fact that it had been able to do the borrowing on relatively favorable terms. But now the decline in international oil prices has passed, and the remaining size of the trade deficit has increased anxieties about the scale and terms of prospective nonconcessional borrowing the country needs. India will have to borrow more than it bargained for. In fact, recent estimates, even with hopeful assumptions about trade, aid and deposits on nonresident savings, suggest the country will need some $9 billion of foreign commercial loans during the Seventh Plan period. Its credit ratings can be expected to slump and, perhaps more critical, the government, with its deeply ingrained financial prudence, is very likely to reverse import liberalization.

Americans immediately think of direct foreign investment (DFI) as a solution to such a resource gap. Foreign investment is being given more favorable billing by the Rajiv Gandhi administration, but it clearly cannot be a very large part of the answer to the foreign exchange problem. Primarily, this is just a matter of magnitudes. From 1981/82 through 1986/87 DFI accounted for only 2.2 percent of India's medium- and long-term capital inflow. It produced well under $100 million in each of those years and is projected to average that amount in the Seventh Plan estimates just cited. In short, foreign investment could enjoy the most explosive increase any enthusiast could conjure and still scarcely dent India's quantitative foreign exchange deficit. (This is not to diminish DFI's potential as a vehicle for information and ideas, in particular, new technologies.) There is a further consideration that limits DFI prospects. In the past, foreign firms have found India difficult to enter but a fair and quite profitable place in which to operate. As noted, the government now presents a more amiable face to would-be new entrants. But the *policy* as to admission has not changed: in principle, India does not seek indiscriminately to attract direct foreign investors. They must have something special to offer, and, unless it is quite special in terms of technology or export potential, they may not be able to enter routine consumer goods lines or to stay indefinitely. Thus, while India, with its size and new economic image, will be of increasing interest to foreign investors, it is unlikely to draw a stampede.

All of this makes the prospects for *concessional* flows to India—i.e., official development assistance (ODA)—considerably more critical than they appeared to be a year and a half ago. Throughout the history of foreign economic aid to developing countries India had been, in absolute terms, a major recipient of concessional assistance. Because of the country's size its per capita receipts always have been extremely thin. Yet, at the margin, whether for electric power capacity, or irrigation, or fertilizer, or other nonproject assistance to fund raw materials and spare parts, or foreign exchange for fertilizer plants, or technical assistance in behalf of agricultural research, agricultural universities or institutes of technology, the aid often has been critically useful. Thus it was important to India's development record in the 1970s that, when the United States ceased to be the principal donor early in that decade, the World Bank's soft-loan affiliate, the International Development Association (IDA), took over as the largest donor around which a substantial flow of assistance could be maintained.

Global supplies of ODA have now become more constrained. The needs of sub-Saharan Africa and of such countries as Bangladesh, Nepal and Haiti have become more compelling, and aid has been pulled in other directions politically. As mentioned earlier, these circumstances have fathered the view that it is time for India to be weaned from ODA entirely, or to accept sharp reductions in the IDA and other concessional transfers the country lately has received.

It is not surprising, therefore, that the government's 1986 Economic Survey quoted with approval the conclusion of a task force of the (World Bank and IMF-related) Development Committee, reported in October 1985, that the idea of crowding India and China away from the ODA table was a bad one. It was the unanimous view of the eighteen governments composing this Task Force on Concessional Flows (the United States and eight others from the North, India and eight others from the South) that the needs of the poor still constituted the strongest argument for receiving aid and that India and China, which were particularly well qualified to use aid effectively, should not be penalized for good performance. Instead the Task Force urged all donors to take the (politically difficult but economically easy) step of increasing their planned aid totals.

Thus far the donors' response has been restrained. The United States has radically reduced its bilateral aid to India (lately the program has been in the range of $50 million a year). India, among all Asian ODA recipients, has been the most dependent on multilateral aid—that is to say, on IDA. But the IDA contribution now has been cut to a fraction of what it was in 1980. The figure for 1986 was about $600 million, and $400 million is mooted for 1987. Total ODA to India may not exceed $1.00 per capita this year. The Indians have every reason to complain, but there is little doubt they will be contending with the near disappearance of concessional transfers during the next several years. They may receive a partial offset in the form of nonconcessional or less concessional official transfers from the World Bank and the Asian Development Bank, but these will be a smaller and inferior substitute.

Economic Management

Finally, there are several issues that Indian leaders will deal with in the years ahead either by action or inaction. The two first addressed do not stand out as obvious problems in a quick inspection of the economy, but each is quite vital. Both, broadly speaking, are managerial issues.

First, there is the question, touched on earlier, of whether government can shape the country's pattern of settlements so that more economic activity can be gathered in towns large enough to afford economies of scale without becoming so big as to incur all of the penalties of agglomeration. Can such town centering at the same time facilitate agriculture-industry interchange and provide close-at-hand nonagricultural employment for ex-agriculturalists?

There is a second issue of political/administrative decentralization with which the Indian leadership knows it must wrestle more effectively. A system as large as the Indian almost inevitably requires major geographic subdivisions and, of course, India has such units in its states. But under the British and since Independence it also has had a quite highly centralized political-bureaucratic system, which in many respects has grown top-heavy in power, patronage and decisionmaking. There is now a committee reconsidering the shape and dynamics of center-state relations. As greater reliance is placed on the market it should be increasingly feasible to delegate functions to the state level without destroying the coherence of national economic policy.

There is an even more critical and difficult aspect of needed decentralization—that within states. Further agricultural progress, improved rural employment programs and more effective social sector work at the grass roots all require livelier local participation. But this will not happen until local people have more voice in the decisions that affect them. While awareness of this need is pushing many reformers in the direction of greater reliance on pro bono nongovernmental organizations (NGOs) and local private businesses, the reformers shy away from the obvious. What India urgently needs is vastly more active, responsible and pervasive local self-government. Seeking this is a recipe for a good deal of rather messy turbulence. But healthy and enduring market-guided development probably cannot succeed as well in any other political framework.

Management at the Top

In first draft last January this chapter ended with a brief note regretting Prime Minister Gandhi's penchant for firing ministers. Only Finance, the draft said, had been spared revolving door leadership, and it was very difficult under these circumstances to give a strong sustained lead to such things, for example, as export promotion.

Days after that draft was finished Vishwanath Pratap Singh was bumped from Finance—to Defense. The foreign secretary had been fired. In April V. P. Singh was bumped out of the government altogether. Moreover, what has been emerging is not just that the prime minister has a costly quirk as a personnel manager, or even, more generally, a propensity for snap decisions. The year 1987 has brought forward a complex of partly substantive matters that, turning around the person of Rajiv Gandhi, call into question the economic prospects that have been unfolding in India.

It seems clear that V. P. Singh (the country's most effective economic minister in many years) is out partly because he was pressing investigations of possible venality that were getting uncomfortably near to businesses, businessmen and politicians close to the prime minister. With Singh out, Rajiv as acting finance minister has presented a budget that has back-pedaled somewhat on liberalization. He has taken refuge in leftist rhetoric and availed himself of one of his mother's oldest gambits, namely, to overwhelm allegations of administrative favoritism and clandestine commissions with charges of foreign (i.e., CIA) meddling. Most alarmingly, for its economic consequences, the prime minister has presented a budget that greatly increases defense outlays by 35 percent and, according to estimates in the *Economic and Political Weekly,* devotes between 8 and 9 percent of the national income to defense and security purposes.

It is in the light of all this that one, while still hopeful, must hesitate over India's economic prospects. Much of the momentum and some of the new self-confidence of the 1980s still remains in the system. In mid-April the perceptive *Far Eastern Economic Review* remarked, "Despite increasingly vocal protests by local capital-goods producers, the government's broad commitment to modernization continues to show itself in regulatory reforms and administrative streamlining."

But the balance is now so close between the continued forward thrust of liberalism and pragmatic proequity reforms, on the one hand, and retrogressive rent-keeping socialist sloganeering, on the other, that, to my disappointment as an Indophile, I am loath to bet very heavily one way or the other.

5
Society

Joseph W. Elder

The year 1986 was marked by the eruption of numerous tensions in Indian society. President Zail Singh, in his address to the first session of Parliament on 20 February 1986, declared that communalism, reinforced by religious fundamentalism and fanaticism, continued to pose a threat to India's unity. During the following months, communal violence broke out in Punjab, Gujarat, Kashmir, West Bengal, Karnataka, Goa and Tamil Nadu, underscoring President Singh's declaration.

While headlines reporting India's communal violence attracted the world's attention in 1986, other less-evident social dynamics were also at work. The Seventh Five-Year Plan was launched, aimed at the eradication of poverty and the building of a modern economy. Foodgrain production reached an all-time high of 150 million tons, as did levels of personal savings. A major new report on India's education called for a fourfold increase in state spending on schools and teachers between 1980 and 1990, and greater emphasis on vocational and job-skills training. And a variety of citizens' groups and individuals worked in both rural and urban areas to improve the lot of the poorest of the poor and to raise India's levels of "distributive justice."

In many ways, India in 1986 was an extension of India in 1985 and 1984. Groups competing for social status, economic advantage, territorial control, or political influence frequently clashed with each other or with the civil authorities. When such clashes became violent, or when damage began to be inflicted on property or human life, the authorities all too frequently suspended civil liberties and called on the police (and often also the military) to restore order. Typically, within a few days the police would regain control of the streets or the countryside, the military would withdraw to their barracks, and life would resume a show of normalcy. But the underlying issues would often remain unaddressed and unresolved. Tensions would continue to simmer, awaiting a time when they might surface again.

But the 1986 situation in India was not merely one of groups of citizens in competition with each other becoming impatient with the national structures of dispute-settlement and taking their conflicts to the streets. Time and again, one of the disputants in the 1986 disturbances *was the government itself.* The government would enact (or fail to enact) some policy. An aggrieved group would generate disturbances in protest of the government's actions (or inactions). In quelling the disturbances, the government would be not only restoring order but also imposing its will as a partisan to the dispute. This was a situation for which the founders of India had not made specific provisions in the Indian constitution.

Constitutionally Prescribed Goals of Indian Society

In 1947, when India became independent, some of the most prominent architects of India's freedom movement held markedly different views of what India's future society should look like. Mahatma Gandhi endorsed a land of self-sufficient villages in which the prosperous would share their wealth with their poorer neighbors, and grassroots village councils would promote the welfare of all through example and moral suasion. Gandhi was suspicious of centrally designed plans and doubted if reform could be genuinely effected by government legislation. Dr. B. R. Ambedkar, a highly educated leader of India's "untouchables," was also skeptical of legislation but mistrusted moral suasion even more. As chairman of the constitutional drafting committee, he insisted that India's constitution should unequivocally abolish "untouchability" and forbid its practice in any form. Furthermore, India's laws and courts should also undermine (and eventually destroy) the whole of India's system of hereditary castes and their undergirding religious ideologies. Jawaharlal Nehru, India's first prime minister, felt India should move self-consciously toward a socialist, urban, industrialized society united in its commitment to "humanism and the scientific spirit."

Over the next two years the framers of India's constitution faced the problem of trying to weave together these (and other) visions of India's future society into a single document. In the end, they adopted a series of provisions under which citizens could try to shape their own—and India's—future. These provisions included: (1) voting rights for all men and women over the age of twenty-one; (2) specified property rights for women (as well as for men); (3) freedom of religion within a secular state; (4) the identification of fourteen languages of India and the recognition of the right of any language group to develop and conserve its own language.

In addition to defining the political, economic, religious and language rights of India's citizens, the constitution contained provisions mandating certain future changes in India. These provisions included: (5) the designation of Hindi as the official language of India (to start fifteen years after the enactment of the constitution) and the retention of English as an official language until then; (6) the reservation (initially for ten years) of proportional ratios of *seats in the national parliament and the state assemblies* for elected members of the scheduled castes and tribes (variously referred to also as "untouchables," "ex-untouchables" and "harijans"); (7) the reservation of proportional ratios of *state and central government jobs* (as well as admissions to medical, engineering and other schools) for members of the scheduled castes and tribes and (8) the possible reservation of proportional ratios of state and central government jobs *for members of any "backward classes"* underrepresented in such government jobs, thereby providing a potential mechanism for improving the lot of any disadvantaged categories of citizens, regardless of their caste or tribe.

Many of the events that occurred in Indian society during 1986 are more understandable when seen within the context of India's constitution. On one hand, the constitution outlines the rules whereby individuals and groups in India may attempt to achieve their personal or collective goals, for example, through the ballot box, representative politics and courts of law. On the other hand, the constitution mandates certain changes—changes regarding language policies, reserved seats in elected assemblies, reserved jobs in the central and state services, admissions to educational institutions and so forth. The purpose of these mandated changes may be to correct historic injustices and provide preferential treatment for formerly underprivileged groups. But preferential treatment favoring some is seen to require discriminatory treatment against others. Again and again, those mandated changes written into the constitution by India's founders placed the Indian government on a collision course with groups of its own citizens.

Some 1986 events in India can be seen as the outcomes of individuals and groups trying to achieve their personal and collective goals within the context of India's constitutional provisions. Other 1986 events in India can be seen as outcomes of the Indian government's efforts to implement constitutionally mandated changes in the face of citizens' attempts to hasten, subvert or resist those changes. In 1986 both of these processes generated tensions that pushed to the breaking point the willingness of different groups in India to tolerate one another, the ability of law-enforcement agencies to maintain (or restore) the peace with impartiality and minimum violence and the confidence of some of India's citizenry in the ability of their country to continue functioning effectively within the parameters of a democratic constitution.

Population and Demography

When the architects of India's freedom movement were framing India's constitution, none of them formulated a national population policy. The seventh schedule of the Constitution lists "economic and social planning" on the list of matters to be dealt with by both the central government and the state governments. But it makes no mention of population policy as having any part in that "economic and social planning." Gandhi's teachings regarding population limitation recommended that married couples avoid sexual intercourse except when they wanted children. India's minister of health in the early 1950s was an advocate of Gandhi's teachings. Not until the later 1950s did India's government acknowledge a national concern for population limitation. Even then, India was one of the earliest countries in the world to declare its unequivocal support for such a national policy—earlier by several years than even the People's Republic of China. Since the 1960s the Government of India has publicly advocated family planning as one of its high priorities. And family-planning posters, clinics, camps, etc. have appeared all over India. But—except for a brief period during India's 1975-1977 Emergency when some compulsory sterilizations were performed—family planning and population limitation have been left up to individuals' choices. In a country where infant mortality is still very high and one's old-age security rests with one's grown-up children, few incentives exist to limit one's offspring until three or four of them have survived childhood. Hence, leaving family planning up to individual choice has not resulted in a dramatic decrease in India's birth rate.

In mid-July 1986 India's estimated population was 783,940,000, making it the second most populous country in the world (behind China, with an estimated population of 1,045,537,000 in mid-July 1986). Table 5.1 compares some of India's 1986 population and demographic characteristics with those of other selected countries.

In terms of population density, population growth, infant mortality, life expectancy and literacy, India compares well with most of its immediate neighbors. Only China and Sri Lanka consistently show more favorable demographic characteristics than India. India also fares well when compared with large, developing countries in Africa (i.e.,

Table 5.1

India — Demographic Characteristics, 1986

	1986 persons per arable sq. km.	Annual pop. growth (%)	Infant mortality per 1000	Life expectancy	Literacy (%)
INDIA	477	2.1	116	55	36
PAKISTAN	316	2.6	119	50	24
BANGLADESH	1,097	2.7	119	53	29
NEPAL	757	2.5	143	46	20
SRI LANKA	1,040	1.8	37	68	87
CHINA	990	0.8	na	68	75
NIGERIA	475	2.6	157	48	28
BRAZIL	420	2.5	92	63	76
USA	135	0.9	11	74	99

Nigeria) and South America (i.e., Brazil). India's comparatively favorable demographic characteristics may result from a combination of factors: the relative abundance of arable land in India, a slow rate of population growth prior to World War I, government and private investments in public health and educational facilities during the colonial period, India's growing middle class and so forth. The fact that India might be capable of improving its demographic characteristics even further is illustrated by China. For many years China's characteristics resembled India's. Then China underwent a political revolution. China subsequently altered some of its demographic characteristics radically through its widespread public-health programs, its mass literacy campaigns and its stringent population-control measures.

Between 1947 and 1981, India's population doubled. By the year 2011, India's population will probably double again. During the twenty-first century, India's population size will probably surpass China's. Part of the rapid growth in India's population size will have to do with the relative youthfulness of India's current population. The age breakdown of India's population in 1981 is shown in Table 5.2.

The fact that about half of India's population still have most—or all—of their reproductive years ahead of them suggests that India's population is going to increase steadily for several decades. Currently an estimated 125 million couples enter the fertility age-group every decade. Before the end of the century that figure is expected to rise to between 170 and 180 million. India's family planners have noted that the 1981 census shows fewer children in the 0-4 year age-group (83.7 million) than in the 5-9 year group (93.6 million) or in the 10-14 age

Table 5.2
Age Breakdown of India's Population, 1981

Under age 15	40%
Ages 15-29	26%
Ages 30-44	17%
Ages 45-59	11%
Age 60 and over	6%

group (85.7 million). This provides some hope that by the turn of the century the number of couples entering the fertility age-group will begin to decline.

National averages tend to conceal variabilities within nations, and such is the case for India. The overall density of India's population in 1981 was 208 persons per square kilometer (counting both arable and nonarable square kilometers). However, the population density varied considerably from state to state, as shown in Table 5.3.

Although there is rarely a one-to-one relationship between population densities and social policies, it may not be coincidental that both Kerala and West Bengal (the two highest-density states) have elected and reelected Marxist ministries during the past several elections. Their Marxist ministries have promised centrally planned economic growth, reductions in income disparities, widespread access to education and health facilities, and greater benefits for the poorest sectors of the population. To many of those in the most crowded states of India, private ownership and market forces have appeared to contribute to the perpetuation—rather than the solution—of social problems. Furthermore, their Marxist ministries, through their networks of organizations, have been able in certain instances to improve the lot of many of the voters. Population density alone does not explain voting patterns. But population density may be one of several factors that help explain the politics of Kerala and West Bengal.

In 1986 the Government of India continued to rely on voluntary family planning to slow down its rate of population growth, with clearly limited impact. (The government-enforced sterilizations of the 1975-1977 Emergency period generated such resentment that no subsequent government has attempted to reinstate them.) India's 1971 Medical Termination of Pregnancy Act legalized abortions. Family-planning clinics throughout the country, with their inverted red triangle symbol, preach the virtues of small families and distribute subsidized family-planning equipment. And parents who already have several children are encouraged to undergo voluntary sterilization. Nevertheless, the

Table 5.3

Indian Population Density by State, 1981
(persons per square kilometer)

High-Density States		Medium Low-Density States	
Kerala	654	Maharashtra	204
West Bengal	615	Tripura	196
		Andhra Pradesh	195
Medium High-Density States		Karnataka	194
Bihar	402	Gujarat	174
Uttar Pradesh	377	Orissa	169
Tamil Nadu	372	Madhya Pradesh	118
Punjab	333	Rajasthan	100
Haryana	292		
Assam	253	**Low-Density States**	
		Himachal Pradesh	77
		Manipur	64
		Meghalaya	60
		Nagaland	47
		Sikkim	45
		Jammu and Kashmir	27

statistics do not yet show the widespread adoption of family-planning practices. Census figures reveal that India's annual rate of population growth, which stood at 2.2 percent throughout the 1970s, has declined only to an estimated 2.1 percent in the 1980s. The Sixth Five-Year Plan (1980-1985) aimed at covering 36 percent of India's couples with contraception of some kind. By 1985, however, only 32 percent of India's couples used contraceptives. Furthermore, the rate of contraception adoption was slower than that of many developing countries. For example, between 1980 and 1985 the number of eligible couples in India using contraceptives rose from 22 percent to 32 percent. During a similar five-year period Mexico experienced an increase from 13 percent to 40 percent, the Philippines from 19 percent to 37 percent, and Colombia from 31 percent to 46 percent. As a result, India continues to average about 24 million births each year (equivalent to the population of the state of California).

Considerable differences exist in family-planning adoption among the different states of India. According to Health Ministry statistics, nearly half the fertility-level population in two of the more prosperous states, Maharashtra and Punjab, have adopted some form of contraception. In fact, among demographers the adoption of family-planning practices has sometimes been seen as a measure of prosperity. By contrast, in the Hindi heartlands of Rajasthan, Uttar Pradesh, Madhya Pradesh and the Bihar only between 13 percent and 17 percent of the relevant populations have adopted any form of contraception. Various reasonable guesses can be offered for why this is so: the widespread poverty in these areas (nearly one-third of the rural population have no land), the conservative outlook characterizing this area, the relatively high proportions of Muslims (who, as a minority group conscious of their small number in relation to the Hindu majority, have shown little interest in family planning) and the relative lack of funding and energy expended by these states on their family-planning programs.

Two major shifts have occurred in birth control practices among women in the last decade. The number of women using the pill has sharply increased (from 5.5 million in 1983/84 to 9.3 million in 1984/85). And the number of women undergoing tubectomies has also increased (from approximately 1.0 million in 1979 to 3.8 million in 1984). The effects of increased tubectomies on India's overall population size, however, are offset by the fact that the majority of women requesting tubectomies have already undergone an average of 3.7 births. The popularity among men of vasectomies has declined precipitously from a high of over 6.1 million in 1977 to less than 1.0 million in 1986.

India's family planning programs have shifted their emphasis over the decades. In the 1970s the main slogan was the descriptive "Two or three children are enough!" In the 1980s the theme is: delay the first child, space the second child, and eliminate the third child altogether. The emphasis is now on imperatives rather than descriptives, with different contraceptive strategies called for at different stages in one's married life.

Rural Life, Urban Life and Patterns of Migration

For years India has been viewed as a land of villages. The 1981 census indicates this view is still basically correct. Furthermore, the ratio between the rural and urban populations has changed little since Independence, as seen in Table 5.4.

Urbanization is a worldwide trend and is often seen as automatically accompanying industrialization and economic "development." India's slow rate of urbanization, therefore, is viewed by some as an anomaly. Table 5.5 provides some international comparisons. Two reasons are

Table 5.4

Rural-Urban Breakdown of India's Population, 1951–1981 (percent)

	1951	1961	1971	1981
Rural	82.7	82.8	80.1	76.7
Urban	17.3	17.2	19.9	23.3

Table 5.5

Urbanization — A Comparative Measurement

	India	USSR	USA	China
Number of cities with populations over 500,000	36	50	65	78

often cited for India's slow rate of urbanization: (1) India's relatively slow rate of industrialization (virtually 71 percent of India's labor force still work in agriculture); and (2) India's relatively inhospitable and expensive urban environments. Rural migrants into cities are apt to find themselves crowded into impoverished slums or even living on the sidewalks. Given the harsh realities of city life, many migrants prefer to leave their wives and children in their villages while they themselves earn what they can and live where they may in the cities. When their sons become old enough to migrate to the cities, the fathers frequently "retire" back to the village, leaving their sons to earn what they can and live where they may in the cities. This helps account for the fact that in many cities more than half the population grew up outside the city and migrated to the city in search of work.

When India's national leaders were drafting the constitution, they shared no clear-cut policy regarding migration or rural-urban development. Gandhi strongly opposed cities, seeing them to be centers of accumulated political power, wealth and exploitation. He advocated the return of city-dwellers to their ancestral villages, where they could take up the lives of farmers and craftspersons, enjoy the spiritual closeness to the land, and participate in the simple activities of rural communities. Nehru was more willing to endorse cities. As a socialist and a "modernist," he hoped that the growth of urban industries would provide jobs for surplus farm workers in India, just as urban employment had provided jobs for surplus farm workers in Europe and the United States. India's other national leaders similarly lacked any general consensus regarding rural or urban policies.

One outcome of these differences of opinion among India's leaders was that India's constitution made no pronouncements regarding urban migration or rural-urban development. Market forces, presumably, would take care of industrial development, urban growth and labor migration. Not until the late 1950s did planners begin to develop strategies for dealing with India's increasing urban problems. By then, some of the problems seemed almost hopeless.

Today some Indians have begun to question whether or not the largest Indian cities like Calcutta and Bombay are any longer "livable." Bombay is one of the most congested cities in the world, with a population density four times that of New York City, at approximately 385,000 people per square kilometer. Bombay averages 650 new arrivals every day. Over 50 percent of the city's population (nearly 4.5 million of Bombay's 8.2 million people) live in slums or on pavements. Bombay's overcrowded Dharavi, which covers 80 hectares and houses half a million people, has been called the largest slum in Asia. In 1981 the then-chief minister of the state of Maharashtra, A. R. Antulay, ordered the demolition of some of Bombay's slums, the deportation of 100,000 slum dwellers beyond the city limits, and the eviction from the state of any slum dwellers who were not Maharashtrian. Antulay's actions aroused so much outrage that the People's Union for Civil Liberties filed a writ petition. The Supreme Court ultimately issued an interim order staying all large-scale demolitions. And Bombay's slums continue to grow.

Calcutta is little better. About two-thirds of Calcutta's population (9.2 million) live in makeshift or mud and thatched roof buildings. One-third of the approximately 3.3 million people living in Calcutta's core area are crammed into dwellings with less than thirty square feet per dweller. Calcutta's streets are jammed with lorries, cars, buses, hand-carts and 20,000 hand-pulled rickshaws. Only one bridge spans the Hooghly River between Calcutta and Howrah, and hundreds of thousands of vehicles and pedestrians must cross that one bridge every day. Calcutta's urban decay has reached the point where in 1985 the city's telephone authorities announced that 55,000 telephone lines were lying "dead" and could not possibly be restored in less than two years. Despite the fact that no less a figure than Rajiv Gandhi has referred to Calcutta as a "dying city," Calcutta maintains traditions of creativity seldom found elsewhere in India. Over 700 magazines devoted to pure literature are published in Calcutta every year. Bengali films made in Calcutta regularly win the president's annual Gold Medal. And the citizens of Calcutta continue to flock to evening literary discourses, concerts and theater rehearsals that, for some, more than offset the spreading squalor of Calcutta.

Table 5.6

Indian Household Income by Quintile (percent)

1	2	3	4	5 (highest)
7.0	9.2	13.9	20.5	49.4

Bombay and Calcutta may demonstrate the most dramatic consequences of urban overcrowding with its accompanying breakdown of amenities, public services and personal safety. In India, as elsewhere, tensions that might dissipate under less oppressive conditions can, and often do, erupt in crowded slums and market places, where people may be forced to live in close proximity to groups toward whom they may feel hostility, and where rumors circulate freely and with little chance for verification. It is not accidental that some of the most severe tensions to erupt in India in 1986 did so in India's cities.

Despite Hinduism's age-old dictum against crossing the dark waters, Indians in the 1980s continue to travel abroad in significant numbers, drawn primarily by occupational opportunities. Approximately 11 million Indians currently reside outside of India. The largest number (approximately 3.8 million) live in neighboring Nepal, where their presence is not always appreciated by the government of Nepal. Other large contingents of Indians currently work in the Persian Gulf states, where their incomes provide a significant increment to India's foreign-currency earnings. Many Indians have migrated to the United Kingdom and Canada, where their presence has sometimes triggered social unrest and political pressures. And over 400,000 Indians have emigrated to the United States, where many of them have adapted comfortably to the lives of middle-class American professionals.

The Middle Classes

The majority of Indian citizens live with little or no financial surplus. The lowest 40 percent of India's population share only 16.2 percent of India's household income (see Table 5.6). By almost any criteria, they can be considered "very poor." As a matter of fact, the Indian government's statistics say that 37 percent of India's population currently fall below the poverty level. (Those same sources predict that five years from now only 26 percent of the population will still fall below the poverty level.)

At the top end of the income quintiles are India's new middle classes. They are estimated to number about 100 million (more than the entire population of many countries). Their demands for consumer items are nearly insatiable. The sales of motorcycles, scooters and mopeds have increased by a factor of five during the last decade. The sales of refrigerators have quadrupled. The sales of synthetic clothing have tripled. And the sales of even such expensive items as cars have more than doubled. India is now one of the world's largest markets for television sets (2 million sets—including 800,000 color sets—were sold in 1985). And the demand for expensive VCRs exceeds the supply. A $100 million beauty industry of shampoos, lipsticks, deodorants and moisturizers caters to the fancies of the middle classes. Home-appliance stores in India's cities offer wide selections of washing machines, vacuum cleaners, mixer-grinders, electric cookers, hot water heaters and air conditioners. And urban supermarkets exhibit shelves full of processed foods, detergents and bathroom supplies.

Middle-class consumerism has stimulated a wide range of entrepreneurial activities. Bajaj Auto, Lohia Machines and Vespa Car may soon be the biggest scooter manufacturers in the world. Within the near future, eight car manufacturing companies may be operating in India. A spate of high-quality magazines, complete with glossy photographs and English-language articles, have appeared, financed in large part by a growing advertising industry.

India's new middle classes want to build homes and buy apartments. In Delhi alone 2,000 cooperative societies wait to be assigned land by the Delhi Development Authority so that they can start building living units. One of the anomalies of any large city in India is the sight of lavish homes and architecturally planned housing colonies rising amidst the squalor of urban slums. In the largest cities, five-star hotels, built ostensibly for foreign tourists, have become settings for the lavish wedding receptions of the new middle classes. And the middle classes have moved into the stock market. During the past decade, private holdings of company stocks have increased tenfold, and the number of investors has risen from 1.5 million to 7 million.

One of the first priorities of these middle classes is a top-quality education for their children. This has encouraged educational entrepreneurship from nurseries and preschools to "public schools," "convents" and private colleges. During the past decade, the number of engineering colleges in India has doubled, while universities and colleges have added evening classes and correspondence courses to try to meet the rising demands of the new middle classes for their childrens' education, including English-medium education. Today, especially in non-Hindi speaking sections of India, many English-medium schools or English language sections of mother-tongue schools are besieged by parents at the beginning of each academic year trying to get their children admitted into the English-medium educational tracks. Many middle-class parents believe that control of the English language will give their children more assured access to future employment and advancement opportunities anywhere in India...or perhaps even in Britain, Canada or the United States.

Many of the tensions that erupted in India in 1986 had little to do with India's middle classes. In fact, in many instances the middle classes held themselves aloof from the fray and commented disparagingly on the "fanaticism" and "ignorance" of the demonstrators and street politicians. However, when middle-class children's education became an issue, the middle classes, too, joined the demonstrations. In 1986 this was most apparent in Gujarat, where the "backward classes" movement threatened to restrict middle-class children's access to engineering, medical, veterinary and polytechnic institutions. Middle-class students' organizations and middle-class parent-student support groups held rallies and press conferences, pressured politicians, blocked roads, closed down trade establishments and otherwise brought normal activities to a halt throughout much of Gujarat in their ultimately successful efforts to halt the "backward classes" movement and protect their own children's access to higher education.

Education and Educational Policies

The literacy rate in India during the post-Independence period has risen from 16.7 percent in 1951 to 36.2 percent in 1981. These percentages, however, conceal the fact that during this same period the actual numbers of illiterates rose from 300 million to 437 million. Marked differences exist between male and female literacy rates. In 1981, 46.9 percent of the men were literate and 24.8 percent of the women were literate. The differences between male and female literacy rates were higher in rural areas (40.8 percent and 18.0 percent) than in urban areas (65.8 percent and 47.8 percent). Historic legacies play a role in the sharp differences in literacy rates between different states. Kerala's legacy of vigorous religious—and missionary—related education is reflected in the highest current literacy rate of 70.4 percent. Rajasthan's legacy of minimum public investment in education during the days of the princely states is reflected in the lowest current literacy rate of 24.2 percent, with an especially low literacy rate for women (5.5 percent). According to World Bank estimates, by the year 2000 India may have the largest concentration of illiterates in the world (i.e., about 55 percent of the

Table 5.7
School Enrollment in India, 1981

School Level	Percentage of School-age Population	Millions
Primary	80	100
Secondary	25	13
Tertiary	4	5

world's illiterate population between the ages of fifteen and nineteen).

In 1950 the architects of India's constitution declared (Article 45) that by 1960 India's states should have free, compulsory education for all children through age fourteen. By 1980 India was spending only about 3 percent of its gross national product on education (in contrast to many countries that spend between 6 percent and 8 percent). And, as Table 5.7 shows, India's goal of free, compulsory education for all children through age fourteen had not yet been realized, even though twenty years had passed beyond the proposed deadline.

Because India's constitution places most educational matters under the jurisdiction of the state governments, there is considerable variation between states in the proportions of their budgets and the amounts of their resources spent for education. By 1981 the states that had come closest to attaining the goal of universal primary education were Kerala, Tamil Nadu, Maharashtra, Karnataka and Gujarat. The states that were furthest from this goal were Rajasthan, Harayana, Punjab, Uttar Pradesh, Bihar and Madhya Pradesh.

The Indian public has sometimes placed on Indian higher education the responsibility for two phenomena identified as national problems. One of these phenomena is the "overproduction" of college graduates (and the consequent phenomenon of the "educated unemployed"). India's relatively sluggish economic growth has meant that the annual cohorts of students graduating from universities have exceeded the new jobs available. Horror stories abound of bachelor's and master's degree holders becoming ticket-collectors, rickshaw drivers or pursuers of additional certificates and diplomas in hopes of someday getting a job they feel is commensurate with their qualifications. A second phenomenon identified as a problem is the "brain drain" of college and university graduates leaving India to find employment elsewhere in the world. During the 1970s and 1980s tens of thousands of well-trained Indians found employment in the Persian Gulf countries. Additional tens of thousands emigrated to Britain, Canada or the United States, where visa preference is given to those with advanced degrees in medicine, engineering and so forth. The Nobel prize awards to Hargobind Khorana of the University of Wisconsin and Subrahmanyan Chandrasekhar of the University of Chicago have highlighted India's "brain drain" to the United States.

As part of his interest in industrial policy and its related social issues, Prime Minister Rajiv Gandhi has made educational reform a major goal of his government. In 1985, at his request, the report of a wide-ranging study of Indian education, entitled *Challenge of Education—Policy Perspective*, was presented to Parliament. In addition to proposing a restructuring of India's whole educational system, the report recommended a fourfold increase in state spending for education between 1980 and 1990. Such increased spending would enable 2.25 million more teachers to be hired (in addition to the 2.0 million teachers already on state payrolls). *Challenge of Education* called for funding pace-setting model schools in every district in the country to demonstrate what can be done with good curricula and good instruction. At the higher levels, *Challenge of Education* recommended shifting from more liberal arts colleges to more vocational training in secondary schools and technical institutes. The report also pointed out that approximately 80 percent of educational spending went into teachers' and administrators' salaries, and relatively little went for classroom equipment and teaching aids.

Challenge of Education is not the first high-level review of education in India. Twenty years ago *Education and National Development: Report of the Education Commission 1964-66* presented an equally far-reaching analysis of shortcomings in India's educational system and provided a series of positive recommendations. However, in the end *Education and National Development* produced few concrete improvements. Unless considerably more follow-up effort is expended on *Challenge of Education* than was expended on *Education and National Development*, the 1986 shortcomings in India's educational system may continue for many years to come.

Kinship and Caste

The architects of India's independence sometimes referred to their dreams of a "casteless, classless society." Many of them believed that India's caste system, with its status-rankings based on birth rather than personal achievement, and with its deeply rooted hierarchies and inequalities, ran counter to the basic tenets of democracy. Some analysts even predicted that, after India achieved its independence, its castes and caste loyalties would subvert—and eventually destroy—any semblance of democratic decision-making.

Observers watched with interest in 1951 and 1952 as India went to the polls for its first postindependence national elections. To the astonishment of some (and the reassurance of many), the elections came off smoothly, on the whole. During that and subsequent elections, observers noted that in India the processes of democratic electioneering and the dynamics of competing castes seemed to mesh rather comfortably. Just as ethnic and occupational divisions provide pressure groups and voting banks in the West, so caste and kin divisions provide pressure groups and voting banks in India. Rather than obstructing or subverting democratic decision-making in India, castes and caste associations were seen often to enhance and invigorate the democratic processes.

Most citizens of India belong to one or another caste group. Such groups, bearing distinctive names, appear as extended lineages, acknowledging their kinship with each other and tracing their ancestries back to a common set of actual or mythical forefathers. An individual's caste group typically defines the outer limits of families from whom one selects a bride or groom for one's own sons or daughters. One's caste group also typically defines the outer limits of families with whom one can, without compunction, share food and shelter. Castes vary in size from a few hundred households to tens of thousands of households.

In most Indian languages, the term for "caste" is *jati,* which refers to a "group into which one is born." Different animal species are referred to as *jati;* thus, there is a goat *jati,* a cow *jati,* a water buffalo *jati,* etc. Genders are defined as *jatis* (for example, there is a female *jati* and a male *jati*). The principle underscored here is that one *is* a member of a *jati;* even if one were to try to conceal the fact, one would always *be* a member of that *jati.* The closest parallel one might find to a *jati* in the United States would be some tightly-knit ethnic community (perhaps Jewish immigrants from a particular location in Europe, or Amish living in a rural county). The distinctive features of such a group would be a sense of tightly knit kinship and shared responsibility within the group, a reluctance to have much social intercourse with persons not belonging to the group and a prohibition against marrying outside the group.

One of the most frequent misconceptions in the West about India's caste system is that all castes are hereditarily linked to specific occupations. Caste names reflect a variety of different bases for categorization. Most caste names are merely designations with no particular meaning (much as are family names in the West). Thus, for example, the large majority of the thousands of caste names appearing on the government lists of scheduled castes are simply appellations (e.g., Ajila, Baiswar, Chero). Some caste names reflect a region of origin (e.g., Adi Andhra, Adi Dravida, Adi Karnataka). Some caste names reflect occupations (e.g., Barhai=carpenter, Bhangi=sweeper, Chettiar=merchant, Julaha=weaver). Some caste names are (or were) honorific titles (e.g., Patel, Shah, Rajput). Some caste names reflect doctrinal affiliations (e.g., the distinctions between Smartha and Shri Vaishnava Brahmins).

As the caste names suggest, there have probably been a wide variety of "origins" for particular castes or *jatis.* Floods, famines and wars led groups of relatives to migrate from one section of India to another. Kin groups of peddlers and traders decided to establish outposts in new locations. Family feuds caused relatives to separate. Economic and political alliances enabled certain groups to unite. Wealth, or receiving titled rank from some local ruler, permitted some groups to "move up" above their relatives. Poverty, or social disgrace, led some groups to break away or be ostracized by their relatives. Tribal groups moved down from the hills and settled among the people of the plains. Invading armies left their legacies of soldiers and officials who preferred not to return home. The typical social processes of avoidance and integration were underscored in India by a widespread belief that food that is cooked acquires the ritual pollution of the cooker. Therefore, one must be careful to eat only food that is cooked by a member of one's own *jati* (or possibly a member of a higher *jati*)—never by a member of a lower *jati,* otherwise one might become ritually "polluted." Were this to happen, it might lead to social ostracism by one's own *jati*—and the consequent need either to split away and establish a new *jati,* or to pay compensation to one's kinfolk in order to be reintegrated into one's original *jati.*

India's *jati* system is believed by many to be embedded in a variety of widely shared myths of origin. The "Hymn of the Primeval Man" in the *Rig Veda* (the ancient Vedic scripture) describes the emergence of four hierarchical categories (*varnas*) of humans from different parts of the sacrificed primeval man's body: the Brahmin (priest) from his mouth; the Kshatriya (warrior/administrator) from his arms; the Vaishya (artisan/farmer) from his thighs and the Shudra (servant) from his feet. Subsequent myths explain the proliferation of additional categories of humans through the dynamics of miscegenation (e.g., Brahmin females impregnated by Shudra males give birth to "Chandala" offspring). One contemporary relevance of these myths of origin is that even today people sometimes try to negotiate their own *jati*'s status upward within the mythical original *varna* hierarchy. Techniques for negotiating one's *jati*'s status upward include: acquiring wealth and power, adopting stricter standards of ritual purity (e.g., barring widow remarriage), abandoning activities considered by some to be ritually polluting (such as eating meat, handling carcasses, etc.), finding a priestly sponsor who will grant ritual status in return for financial patronage, discovering a more noble line, and so forth.

Although the myths of caste origin are typically Hindu, non-Hindu Indians (including Jains, Buddhists, Christians, Muslims and Sikhs) frequently find themselves members of *jatis*. Even if they reject the beliefs regarding pollution in cooked food, they often subscribe as rigorously as Hindus to the customs of intra-*jati* marriages.

"Scheduled castes and tribes" are another contemporary phenomenon derived from the widely shared myths of caste origin. Over the centuries of India's history, certain castes and tribes, especially in southern India, were treated as being beyond the pale of normal social intercourse. These castes and tribes came to be labeled "untouchables." Such castes and tribes were often barred from places of high-caste worship, prevented from using certain wells and roads, required to live outside the villages or towns (or in the least desirable quarters within the villages and towns) and forced to perform a village's or town's most unpleasant occupations.

In 1936, to comply with provisions of the Government of India Act of 1935, the British Government drew up a list (i.e., schedule) of all of India's "untouchables." The 1936 "schedule" has undergone several subsequent revisions (the most important of which has been the inclusion of Sikh scheduled castes). Today the official list of "scheduled castes and tribes" includes about 15 percent of India's population. It is on the basis of this list that the Indian constitution's provisions for the scheduled castes and tribes have been enacted.

The constitutional provisions of *reserved seats* in education and employment for members of the scheduled castes and tribes were initially designed to continue for ten years. Parliament has subsequently extended the provisions for three additional ten-year periods. During that time thousands of members of scheduled castes and tribes have stood for elections to the national parliament or state assemblies, and hundreds of them have been elected to office. One of the best-known scheduled caste politicians to emerge from within these electoral arrangements was Jagjivan Ram, who died on 6 July 1986. Born an "untouchable" in a village in Bihar in 1908, he became president of the All-India Depressed Classes League at an early age. Following Independence, Jagjivan Ram was a stalwart supporter of the Congress party and a frequent member of its cabinet. After the 1977 Janata party victory, he served as deputy prime minister and was a serious contender to be prime minister.

His life reflected the possibilities inherent in India's constitutional provisions for the scheduled castes.

The British Government's 1936 "schedule" of "untouchable" castes and tribes (and its subsequent revisions) and the Indian constitution's stipulations regarding scheduled castes and tribes have, on the whole, worked fairly smoothly. Individuals or groups can be rather readily identified as being (or not being) on the "schedule." However, the Indian constitution's stipulations regarding who is (or who is not) a member of the "backward classes" are entirely unclear. In the absence of any official clarification from the central government, the matter of determining who is and who is not a member of a "backward class" has been left to state governments, appointed commissions or individual claimants. Some have argued that objective measures of "backwardness" should be used, e.g., a group's average level of income or education. Others have argued that "backwardness" should be based on a group's low status or inferior treatment. Almost all have agreed that, whatever criteria are used, they should apply to groups (i.e., "classes") and not to individuals. Since the most easily recognized groups in India are caste groups, this has meant, in effect, that "backward classes" have been identified as "backward castes." In a number of states, politicians have tried to assign particular castes with large populations to their state's list of "backward classes," recognizing the vote-getting potential of such moves. In effect, this has generated a distinction between "backward castes" (those castes considered historically disadvantaged according to some criteria) and "forward castes" (those castes *not* considered historically disadvantaged). Efforts to extend "backward class" benefits to more and more castes led to the state of Tamil Nadu raising its reservations quota to 68 percent, the state of Bihar identifying 78 percent of its citizens as members of "backward classes" and the state of Karnataka declaring that 92 percent of its population belonged to the "backward classes."

Tensions arising from considerations such as these came to a head in Gujarat in 1985 and 1986. In the 1950s and 1960s political power in Gujarat had belonged to the landed Patel castes, who comprised about 22 percent of Gujarat's population. But land reforms eroded the Patels' power base, and by the mid-1970s the Patels found themselves being pushed aside by the Kshatriya castes (who comprise about 40 percent of Gujarat's population). When Madhavsingh Solanki (a Kshatriya) became chief minister for the Congress (I) party in 1980, he did not include a single Patel in his first cabinet.

In 1981 the Rane Commission on backward classes submitted its report to the Solanki government. The report declared unequivocally that family income and occupation—not caste—should be the sole criteria for "backwardness." The Solanki government tabled the report. Then, in January 1985, the Solanki government announced that if the Congress Party were returned to office in the coming election, it would raise the total reservation figures from 31 percent to 49 percent (an increase of 18 percent). These figures would apply to such things as admissions to engineering, agricultural, veterinary and polytechnic institutions. Sporadic clashes ensued between the "backward castes"—including Muslims and Dalits (members of scheduled castes)—and the "forward castes"—including the Patels, student organizations and parent-student support groups. It was clear to these groups that an 18 percent increase for the "backward castes" meant an 18 percent *decrease* for the "forward castes." In cities such as Ahmedabad what began as intercaste clashes along class lines ignited Hindu-Muslim riots as well and eventually a war between the people and the police. By the time the rioting ended, the army had been brought in, scores were dead, and hundreds were injured. As *The Times of India* said, "Seldom before have so many kinds of antagonisms exploded at one time in one place...similarly, while we have not been unfamiliar either with police revolts or with police excesses, the two have seldom gone together. In Ahmedabad they have."

Following the elections, Solanki announced that the increase in reserved quotas would be postponed until there was a national consensus on the issue. Even then, peace was long in coming to Gujarat, and intercaste tensions continued throughout 1986. The "backward classes" issue generated similar intercaste tensions and conflicts in other parts of India during 1986.

After forty years of India's independence, one finds little evidence of significant moves toward either a "casteless" or a "classless" society. To be sure, concerns over pollution through eating other castes' cooking are gradually giving way—for men more than for women, and in cities more than in villages. And a few self-supporting young adults in urban centers are choosing their own fiancés and having intercaste "love marriages." But for the great bulk of India's population, "caste" means "kin." And to engage in activities that would needlessly alienate one's kin seems both costly and foolhardy. As a child, one learns the rules of life from older members of one's caste. As an adult, one arranges one's children's marriages with the sons and daughters of one's caste relatives. In one's old age, one is cared for by younger members of one's caste. And in the end one's body is carried to the cremation grounds on the shoulders of one's caste fellows. Until alternative institutions appear in India to provide for these human needs, one can expect India's caste system to continue to flourish.

Language and Ethnic Identity

When India became independent in 1947, virtually all of its leaders agreed that the English language of India's colonial past should be replaced by some language indigenous to India. With this intention, the Constituent Assembly wrote into India's constitution the provision that Hindi (spoken by about one-third of India's population) would become the official language of India starting fifteen years after the enactment of the constitution, and English would be retained as an additional official language until then. It was not long before the implications of this arrangement became clearer—and more sinister—to the two-thirds of India's population who did not speak Hindi. They feared that if Hindi ever became the sole official language, they and their non-Hindi-speaking descendants would be forever linguistically disadvantaged. As the government in Delhi proceeded with the gradual implementation of Hindi as the language of official communication, anti-Hindi sentiment began to surface throughout the country, particularly in the Tamil-speaking portions of the South. Strikes, protest marches, property damage and even self-immolations finally led to a major change. In 1967 India's Official Languages (Amendment) Bill indefinitely extended the status of English as an additional official language. In state elections held that same year, the pro-Tamil Dravida Munnetra Kazhagam (DMK) party captured power in Tamil Nadu. During the campaign, the DMK had stressed the distinct identity of the Tamil language and had insisted that English be retained indefinitely as an official language in order to protect South India from "North Indian domination." One of the DMK's first acts after winning the election was to abolish Hindi instruction in the state's schools. The DMK also terminated the National Cadet Corps in the state schools on the grounds that the Corps' commands were given in Hindi. Following these anti-Hindi gestures, the DMK settled down to its major tasks of administering the state of Tamil Nadu.

The year 1986 saw an unexpected resurfacing of anti-Hindi sentiment in South India. Students and others in Tamil Nadu heard that the central government in New Delhi was sending out a circular to its branches in the various states instructing them to observe a "Hindi week" beginning on 16 September. During that week, central government officials were to write all letters (and even addresses on envelopes) in Hindi. If any officials lacked a working knowledge of Hindi, they should at least sign their names in Hindi to all government documents. The existence of the New Delhi circular triggered a chain of anti-Hindi activities in Tamil Nadu. Protest marchers filled the streets, shouting slogans, obstructing traffic and tarring any Hindi signs they found.

Schools and colleges were closed. Angry Tamils now felt that, if the New Delhi government continued "surreptitiously" to try to undermine English, only a constitutional amendment guaranteeing the indefinite use of English could protect the majority of Indians from "Hindi domination." In December over 3,000 DMK volunteers were arrested in various parts of Tamil Nadu when they burned the official-language excerpts from the Indian constitution. The year 1987 began with tensions still high and new boundaries drawn regarding the future roles of Hindi and English as India's official languages.

Women and Women's Rights

At the close of 1986 the Indian government reported that some 1,666 women had been murdered in the preceding twenty-two months—murdered under circumstances suggesting each was a "dowry death." Seventy-three of these "dowry deaths" had occurred in New Delhi. Another 633 had occurred in India's most populous state, Uttar Pradesh. What is a "dowry death," and what are its causes?

Throughout much of India, at the time of a marriage, the bride's family provides the groom's family with a substantial gift or dowry. The exact contents of the dowry are prearranged before the marriage—often through long drawn-out negotiations. A poor family might provide a little cash, jewelry and bedding. A rich family might provide a car, a VCR, a refrigerator, some real estate and lucrative investments. Sometimes during the marriage celebrations the dowry is exchanged in the presence of the wedding guests so that everyone can witness that the transaction actually occurred. Government efforts to discourage ruinous dowries, or even to make dowry-giving illegal (e.g., the 1961 Dowry Prohibition Act), have proved to be futile.

When the bride's relatives are not able to provide the complete dowry at the time of the marriage, they sometimes promise to pay the dowry in installments. If they then delay, or if they appear likely to break their promise, the bride may be harassed by her husband, her mother-in-law or other members of her husband's family in order to bring pressure on her relatives. In exceptional cases, the harassment may turn to torture. And in even more exceptional cases, the torture may turn to murder. When murder occurs, the bride usually burns to death "accidentally" in a kitchen. Within the past decade, the media and the police in India have become increasingly aware of these "dowry deaths." Cases have been brought to trial, and offenders have received heavy punishments. Key to some of these trials have been members of India's women's movement. Such women have insisted that police investigate suspicious cases, that evidence be recorded and that probable cases of dowry deaths be brought to trial.

India's contemporary women's movement grows out of 150 years of social reform in India. In the early nineteenth century male intellectuals like Raja Ram Mohan Roy and Ishwar Chandra Vidyasagar attacked such practices as *sati* (the immolation of widows on their husband's funeral pyres), polygamy and child marriage. They demanded property rights and education for women and campaigned for legislation permitting widows to remarry. By the end of the nineteenth century women had emerged as leaders of the women's movement. Swarnakumari (of the distinguished Tagore family) opened a Ladies' Theosophy Society in 1882. Women such as Pandita Ramabai, a Sanskrit scholar, initiated several organizations and set up institutes and homes for distressed and stigmatized women. In 1889 ten women were invited to participate in the annual meeting of the Indian National Congress. When Mahatma Gandhi returned from South Africa and joined the Indian National Congress, he encouraged women to link their everyday lives with the nationalist cause. With his support, prominent women such as Sarojini Naidu and Kamladevi Chattopadhyaya entered the public arena.

In the 1920s and 1930s women participated in the noncooperation and civil disobedience movements against the British, and many of them served jail sentences. The All India Women's Conference became the major vehicle for the women's movement, shifting from welfare requests to demands for full political and legal equality for women in virtually all arenas. When India finally became independent, the Congress movement implemented many of the All India Women's Conference demands, including passing legislation prohibiting polygamy, liberalizing divorce and granting equal inheritance rights to women.

During the 1960s women's issues were taken up by radical student groups as well as by grassroots movements among tribals and dalits (scheduled castes). India's women's movement was also influenced by the women's movement in the West, the International Women's Year (1975), various reports on the status of women prepared for the July 1975 UN World Conference on Women in Mexico City and the declaration of the International Women's Decade.

In Ahmedabad in 1972 Ela Bhatt, a lawyer and daughter of a judge, registered the Self-Employed Women's Association (SEWA) as an independent bargaining unit under the auspices of the 120,000-member Textile Labor Association. In the years since then SEWA has offered hope to thousands of Ahmedabad's women (many of whom are from tribal or low-caste backgrounds) who work at the lowliest occupations in the informal sector of the economy. These women support themselves and their families by selling vegetables, milking cows, stitching rags into shirts and bedcovers, hammering household aricles from used metal and pulling heavily loaded handcarts. SEWA has helped them by providing day-care centers, legal protection against police harassment, vocational and household management training and cooperative banking services that enable them to free themselves from the grip of moneylenders. In 1977 Ela Bhatt was selected for the prestigious Magsaysay Award (the Asian equivalent of the Nobel Prize). And today branches of SEWA exist in other cities such as Bhopal, Lucknow, Mithila, Bhagalpur and Delhi.

Toward the end of the 1970s women from radical and progressive backgrounds formed autonomous women's groups such as Stree Sangarsh (in Delhi), Forum Against Rape, later renamed Forum Against Oppression of Women (in Bombay) and Pennuramai Iyakkam (in Madras). And feminist publications such as the bimonthly *Manushi* (Hindi and English) were attracting a wide readership. The agenda dealt with by these groups and publications includes patriarchy, the sexual and economic exploitation of women, women's equal access to education, divorce laws, women's property rights, women writers and women in the political arena. These autonomous women's groups focus more than their predecessors on special issues needing to be addressed in their local settings and less on broad pronouncements of women's rights. Until recently, autonomous women's groups were found almost exclusively in India's major cities like Bombay and Delhi. More recently they have begun to appear in smaller cities and towns all over India.

In the mid-1980s two court cases placed women's rights in the Indian forefront. Shah Bano, a Muslim divorcée in Madhya Pradesh, sued her ex-husband for maintenance. The Madhya Pradesh High Court ruled that her husband had to pay her maintenance, based on Section 125 of the Criminal Procedure Code regarding maintenance of close relatives who are indigent. Shah Bano's husband, Mohammed Ahmed Khan, took the case to the Supreme Court of India, insisting that, as a Muslim, he was not obliged to pay maintenance beyond a period of three months and ten days (the tradition under Islamic law). In 1985 the Supreme Court upheld the Madhya Pradesh High Court's decision and ruled that Mohammad Ahmed Khan had to support his ex-wife under Section 125 of the Criminal Procedure Code, which applied to all persons regardless of their religious affiliation. This Supreme Court decision was hailed by feminists as a major step for protecting women and providing them with economic security.

The second court case, also decided by the Supreme Court in 1985, declared that all gifts made over to a woman at the time of her marriage remain her absolute private property till her death. Neither her husband nor anyone else has a right to those gifts unless sanctioned by the woman. The court based its decision on the ancient concept of *stridhan* (woman's wealth). In doing so, it negated an earlier judgment by the Punjab and Haryana High Courts that *stridhan* becomes the joint property of both husband and wife after a wife enters her husband's home. As in the Shah Bano case, feminists praised the High Court's decision. Madhu Kishwar, editor of the feminist journal *Manushi*, stated, "It's the best judgment the Supreme Court has given in a long time." The Supreme Court's decision considerably strengthens the hand of the wife in any dowry dispute with her husband or husband's family.

Nongovernmental Efforts at Social Reform

Although contemporary analyses of Indian society tend to focus on the policies of the central and state governments, much of the vitality of Indian life has been, and continues to be, found in nongovernmental activities, often far removed from the centers of political power.

Individuals like Mother Theresa, the 1979 Nobel Peace Prize winner, define and carry out those tasks they feel need to be done, where they need to be done—with or without the assistance of government. Public activists like Ashok Advani take upon themselves the problems of Bombay's environment and prefer to try to solve them through private movements rather than through the arena of competitive politics. And Baba Amte, the winner of the 1985 Magsaysay Award, carries on his work among lepers in the hinterlands of Maharashtra and Madhya Pradesh. The public service of individuals like these is sometimes supported by privately funded organizations such as the Ashoka Society that seek to foster grassroots responses to India's social and economic problems as well as to encourage supportive networks of development entrepreneurs.

India has no shortage of nongovernmental groups concerned about social issues. One of the more visible products of such a group was the New Delhi Centre for Science and Environment's "citizen's report" entitled *The State of India's Environment 1982*. This report, written by a variety of different groups and individuals, not only provides figures on India's levels of pollution, soil loss and destruction of forests, but also explains what those figures imply for the present and future lives of India's citizens. The report includes a discussion of the Chipko Andolan (the movement to hug trees), perhaps the best-known grassroots ecological movement in India, where hill-dwellers in Uttarakhand have devised a series of direct-action techniques to prevent contractors from cutting down the local trees.

Seva Mandir in Rajasthan, organized by Dr. M. S. Mehta and some dedicated urbanites, focuses on adult literacy in the rural areas surrounding Udaipur, as does Literacy House near Lucknow in Uttar Pradesh. Sulabh Sauchalya, founded by a Gandhian from Bihar, distributes and maintains standardized sanitary latrines and human-waste disposal systems. Anand Niketan Ashram in Gujarat, founded by Hari Vallabh, oversees some four hundred villages, including village cooperatives, irrigation systems, local courts and life schools. The integrated community health project in Jamkhed, Maharashtra, launched by Magsaysay awardees Rajnijkant and Mabelle Arole, works on preventive medical strategies involving community participation and responsibility. ASTRA, a voluntary group of faculty members from the Indian Institute of Science, experiments in Karnataka with appropriate technology, including low-cost construction materials, community bio-gas, and solar energy. The Kerala Sastra Sahitya Parishad prepared a book entitled *Resources of Kerala* and held workshops to familiarize people with the book. It has trained village groups to gather data on the ecological impact of nearby factories and development projects and to press for environmental responsibility. And a broadly based citizens' group, under the leadership of the Sankat Mochan Mahant of Varanasi, has launched a movement to clean up the water flowing in the Ganges River. This movement has won the cooperation of various chambers of commerce in cities bordering the Ganges, and its activities have been noted even by Prime Minister Rajiv Gandhi.

The quiet, meagerly funded nongovernmental efforts at social reform cited above may seem unworthy of serious attention when looking at all the events that occurred in Indian society in 1986. Nevertheless, in many ways they probably represent the types of worthy activities India's general public have for years endorsed and supported. And in the long run they—and activities similar to them—may provide the direction whereby Indian society will eventually address its various problems.

Conclusion

India's 1986 headlines tended to present the more dramatic (and violent) struggles between groups trying to achieve their ends within the contexts of India's major institutional structures or addressing their grievances against a government apparently unable (or unwilling) to deal effectively with a host of problems. At times various levels of the government itself (municipal, state and national) managed to protect human life and restore the peace. At other times various levels of the government themselves became embroiled in these struggles. Sometimes they dealt effectively with the issues. More often they managed to defer or postpone any major consideration of the problems. Few clear societal patterns or directions emerge from the complex events of 1986.

It may well be that, when one looks back on 1986 with the perspective of time, the more important events will have been the less dramatic ones—a court decision here, a citizens' action there, a technique of group mediation somewhere else—that moved India forward toward some of its long-range ideals.

6
Culture

Girish Karnad

Introduction

It is impossible to generalize about anything Indian without risking distortion of some basic truth. Centuries coexist across the vast span of the country as well as within the confines of a home. Regions have eccentric histories of their own which seem insignificant in the national context and yet affect local cultural life profoundly. Burning controversies involve issues often incomprehensible to immediate neighbors.

Even within a regional culture, different art forms contain different historical options. Colonial education discouraged interdependence of native art-forms, persuading each to emulate directly its Western counterpart. Some forms became totally imitative, some accommodated Western ideas, others refused even to take cognizance of the colonial culture. Thus today, Indian music can casually assume a continuous—if erratic—history of over a thousand years of its own but painting has to go back only fifty years to stare into a century-long void. Dance, its origins rooted in Indian courts and temples, can take its identity for granted while theater, which developed in colonial cities, cannot.

In this chapter, therefore, I examine each form separately with no attempt at a general overview. Yet a few themes are seen to recur: tradition versus Westernization, the search for authenticity, the advantages and dangers of state patronage as against those of cultural laissez faire. In some cases, I have ignored the diversity within a field to focus on a single phenomenon. There are, for example, several schools of Indian dance, but I have confined myself to Bharatanatyam, a dance form of Tamil Nadu, not because it is in any sense "more Indian" than the rest but because the historical problems it faced during the course of its development suffice to suggest the sort of situations other schools also had to face. Thus, like Bharatnatyam, Kathak in the North achieved respectability by denouncing the very class of dancing women that had nourished it through the centuries. The often uncanny parallel between histories of different schools also underlines how different regions responded to the common challenge of modernity.

Dance

On 6 January 1986, the arts academy of Kalakshetra, in Madras, completed fifty years. The Golden Jubilee was celebrated with the prime minister, Rajiv Gandhi, presiding over the event. A month later, Rukmini Devi Arundale, founder of Kalakshetra, died at the age of eighty-two. Rukmini Devi's entire life had been devoted to the academy and the style of dancing it had done so much to revitalize and spread—Bharatanatyam.

Indian dancers, critics and scholars usually talk of Bharatanatyam as an ancient dance form, handed down through the centuries with little or no change. Thus Kapila Vatsyayan, dance critic and scholar, has argued that "Bharatanatyam is perhaps the oldest among the contemporary classical dance forms in India...whether the dancer was the *devadasi* [servant of god] of the temple or the court-dancer of the Maratha kings of Tanjore, her technique followed strictly the patterns which had been used for ages."[1] But such statements do little justice to the radical changes made in the very nature of the dance in this century, by institutions such as the Music Academy of Madras and the Kalakshetra.

When Rukmini Devi, encouraged by her English husband, started dancing in 1935, dance in South India was a prerogative of the *devadasis*, women dancers-cum-singers hereditarily associated with the temples. The institution of the *devadasis* had flourished continuously for more than a thousand years in a cultural setup where the power of the court and the glory of the temple were closely interrelated. The temple dancers naturally had an important role to play in all temple rituals, religious festivals and processions. But as women "married to the god" and therefore as those for whom there was no fear of widowhood, they were also able to bring to secular festivities their ability to ward off evil. Dance and music, which were seen as essentially two facets of the same art, figured prominently in the fulfillment of these responsibilities.

In 1853, however, the British annexed the kingdom of Tanjore, the last of the courts to have patronized the *devadasis* and their art. The dance (called "Sadir," "Nautch" or "Dasiattam," the slave's dance) and singing became means of livelihood, and by the turn of the century, the profession had become virtually identified with prostitution. By the late 1920s, an "anti-nautch" movement had gathered enough momentum to demand in the Madras Legislative Council that performances by professional dancing women should be prohibited and the *devadasi* system be abolished. At the same time, the Music Academy of Madras (founded in 1928) had been persuaded by one of its secretaries, E. Krishna Iyer, to try to gain social acceptance for the dance by inviting *devadasis* to dance at the Academy.

Rukmini Devi, unique in being a Brahmin married to an Englishman and connected with the prestigious Theosophical Society, set herself two goals: first, to rescue dance from its disreputable association with the *devadasis;* and then, to purify it of all accretions resulting from this association. Her success on both these fronts was phenomenal. By 1955, the Kalakshetra had eighty students, all from non-*devadasi* castes. The number had swelled to 250 by 1986. By then, the alumni of her school included several dancers from "respectable" families who had gone on to achieve all-India distinction—Mrinalini Sarabhai, Yamini Krishnamurthy, Uma Rao, Leela Samson and Krishnaveni Lakshmanan.

It was in her second achievement, however, the purification of what had become an occupational requirement into a "classical" art form, that Rukmini Devi developed a methodology that was to have seminal impact in other parts of India on other forms of dancing. With the assistance of Sanskrit scholars, musicologists and dance experts, she revamped, polished and extended the repertoire of gestures, physical postures and movements that formed the basic vocabulary of "Sadir." Dance poses sculpted in south Indian temples were studied and matched with the various gestures and steps described in the classical text, *Abhinayadarpana* by Nandikeswara. Traditional Sadir dress was given up in favor of costumes modelled on these sculptures. Musicians of stature such as Papanasam Sivan, Tiger Varadachariar and Mysore Vasudevachar composed new tunes for the songs.

The adoption of the name "Bharatanatyam" was part of the effort to make the dance more respectable. The Music Academy of Madras was goaded by E. Krishna Iyer into renaming Sadir as "Bharatanatyam." Contrary to popular belief, the name has nothing to do with the author of the *Natyasastra.* "Bharatan" is the honorific form of the title of a Brahmin dance teacher—as distinct from "Nattuvan," signifying a teacher of *devadasi* origins—and until the eighteenth century dance instruction was largely a monopoly of the Brahmins. The new name thus was clearly intended to evoke respectable associations and reflected the need of the pro-Sadir group to win the acceptance and support of the powerful Brahmin intelligentsia of Madras. Once that was achieved, Iyer began to underplay the caste reference by arguing that the name was chosen as a homage to Bharata Muni, author of the ancient treatise on dance and drama, the *Natyasastra* (200 B. C.).

Another example of the successful application of the technique of "purifying" temple dancing into a "classical" dance form is Odissi, again often claimed as an ancient art. It is, however, a tribute to the healthy debate generated by Rukmini Devi that today the Odissi dancers feel no need to play down their debt to the *devadasis.* If Bharatanatyam has been criticized for sacrificing the natural sensuousness of the original "Sadir" to technical perfection in an effort to gain "respectability," Odissi draws unselfconsciously and heavily on the eroticism of the temple sculpture in Orissa—and implicitly on the *devadasi's* repertoire.

In March 1986, Anamika Kala Sangam, a cultural organization in Calcutta, organized a three-day dance festival, which included a seminar on tradition and the need for innovation in Indian dance. It is interesting that Mrinalini Sarabhai, a student of Kalakshetra and founder of the Darpana dance academy in Ahmedabad, understood the theme of the seminar as whether traditional dance was capable of "dealing with contemporary problems such as dowry, suicide and ecological pollution."[2] For her the question was whether traditional dance grammar was capable of formulating propositions about burning contemporary problems.

The problem of tradition and experiment was tackled at a more fundamental level by Chandralekha, a Bharatanatyam dancer from Madras but not an alumna of Kalakshetra. She attacked the very philosophy behind classical dance forms. As has already been pointed out, the name, Bharatanatyam, is increasingly used to link the dance to Bharata's *Natyasastra,* in which it is asserted that all performing arts originated in the gods. Chandralekha finds this theory of "divine origin" not just misleading but dangerous. For her it devalues the basic centrality of the human body.

In her theory as well as performances, Chandralekha has sought to integrate Bharatanatyam with yoga as well as the South Indian martial arts, Kalari Payattu. The program notes to her show *Angika* (1985), which brought her instant national recognition, read: "The story of the body in our times can be understood by taking a closer look at the origins and sources of the classical dance forms in India—forms which have been nourished and nurtured over the last two thousand years as the ultimate aesthetic expressions of the human body and its potential."

Reacting to Chandralekha's attack on the "divine origin" theory and the disastrous effect it has had of alienating the dancer from the dancing body, critic Sunil Kothari wryly commented in his review of the Anamika Kala Sangam seminar: "Blasphemous though it may sound, the *Natyasastra* is certainly not the last word on Indian dance any more."

Theater

It is indicative of how differently the same "tradition" is valued in the different arts that while dance is rejecting its "divine origins," theater has just begun to insist upon them. A monograph on traditional Indian threater by Suresh Awasthi, noted theater critic and scholar, is titled, *Drama: the Gift of Gods* (1983). Awasthi argues that Bharata's *Natyasastra* is still the most complete key to the Indian identity of our theater.[3] Earlier, in 1980, Kapila Vatsyayan had made a similar plea in her *Traditional Indian Theater: Multiple Streams.*[4] There she had argued that most of the semiclassical and folk forms, scattered in the remotest corners of India, have nevertheless a common approach to drama and theatric form, ultimately rooted in the *Natyasastra.*

This difference in the ways in which dance and theater confront their common tradition is explained by the very different histories of the two forms. Bharatanatyam traces its roots back to the Hindu temple towns and the ancient institution of temple dancers. On the other hand, what is called "modern Indian theater" originates in three colonial cities: Calcutta, Bombay and Madras. These cities have no pre-British, "Indian"—whether Hindu or Muslim—history, being entirely the creations of the British rule (the East India Company). They were ports developed for colonial maritime trade. It was inevitable then that the Indian populations that contributed to the growth of these cities and participated in their prosperity should be conditioned by their need to work with or under the British. Thus, unlike cities with an "Indian" history, these three cities developed an urban ethos that tried hard to be "Westernized" and therefore consciously—at least outwardly—dissociated itself from the traditional way of life. It was equally inevitable then that when, in the middle of the nineteenth century, this newly emergent bourgeoisie felt the need for entertainment, it looked for guidance to the visiting Victorian theater groups rather than to traditional forms then associated with backwardness.

It should be pointed out here that the term "traditional Indian theater" includes at least two distinct streams: the first, often termed "classical," was the theater in the ancient Indian language of Sanskrit, the language of the educated elite. This theater remained confined to courts and probably temples and displayed a refined, carefully trained sensibility. Sanskrit plays continued to be written till the tenth century or even later, though undoubtedly theatrical productions had ceased long before. The second stream, in which the performance forms used the spoken languages of their locality and region, came into its own after the ninth century, by which time Sanskrit had lost its central position as the language of courtly and intellectual discourse.

Although these forms have changed profoundly through the centuries, and although those that have survived to this day differ radically from each other, certain basic features, common to all, are easily identified. There is no written text. Actors depend on improvisation within limits imposed by convention. Performances are staged in the postharvest season when actors as well as spectators have free time. They are staged in open-air theaters, and since the audiences often number in the thousands, the acting style as well as make-up and costumes are designed for enlarged projection. Acting space is flexible and there are almost no stage properties or scenery. The narrative, invariably a myth already known to the audience, is enacted through dance, music, mimetic gesture and stylized choreography.

"Modern Indian theater" in the nineteenth century deliberately turned its back on this format and imitated the European stage, two features of which were to alter the very understanding of "entertainment" in India. The proscenium brought in "theatrical illusion" and wholesale indulgence in spectacle. The new convention whereby audiences paid in advance to see a show further underlined the idea of "pure entertainment" where the success of a play would be judged entirely by the "run" of the play. If medieval patronage had tended to make arts conservative, laissez-faire made them entirely neutral on ethical and political issues and indifferent to aesthetic considerations. Only the box office mattered.

As a result, although this theater flourished for over seventy-five years, it produced no great drama, no school of acting, no theatrical tradition beyond spectacle. However, it did absorb some features of traditional theater—particularly the use of songs. Every play had to have songs. Often it was the songs that made or broke a play. And by combining classical tunes with the popular, this theater created a new genre of "theater songs" which are popular even today. The coming of sound to films in the 1930s dealt a blow to this theater from which it never recovered. Films could meet the demand for "pure entertainment" on a bigger scale and more cheaply.

With the coming of independence in 1947, the state of Indian culture naturally became a topic of prime public concern and debate. In the mid-1950s, the government of India set up three "akademis" to study, document, encourage and popularize all aspects of Indian culture. The Sangeet Natak Akademi looked after the performing arts, the Lalit Kala Akademi after the fine arts and the Sahitya Akademi after literature. Parallel with these three central akademis but independent of them, akademis began functioning in the states, fully financed by their own state governments. Whatever the criticism levelled against these akademis, they succeeded in bringing to light artistic forms that had been forgotten during the colonial regime. And with that the question of what relevance these traditional forms could have for urban theater became a hotly debated issue.

The December 1985 issue of *Sangeet Natak* (the official organ of the Sangeet Natak Akademi) was on "Traditional Idiom and Contemporary Theater." In one article—significantly entitled "In Defense of the 'Theater of Roots'"—Suresh Awasthi recalled a seminar on theater held in 1961, in which he had read a paper on the relevance of traditional theater to contemporary playwriting. "The idea was then ridiculed; and I was dubbed a revivalist or reactionary by practitioners of the colonial theater.... They maintained that traditional theater had no relevance for contemporary work which with its inspiration in Western theater had to follow its own course."[5] In the same journal, the guest editor, N. C. Jain, theater critic and one-time teacher at the National School of Drama, listed nearly eighteen plays written since 1961, all of which draw upon "the structural or staging techniques of one or more traditional form." "Today the wheel seems to have turned full circle," he concluded. Indeed, the fact that a whole issue of *Sangeet Natak* could be devoted to the interaction between new Indian theater and the traditional forms clearly showed how productive the intervening twenty-five years had been.

By the mid-1980s both the Ford Foundation and the Sangeet Natak Akademi were giving grants to playwrights and theater-workers who wanted to explore the possibility of using traditional theatrical techniques to develop modern stage. One of the productions supported in this way and cited by Awasthi and Jain for its successful synthesis of the traditional and the modern was *Chakravyuha,* written and directed by Ratan Thiyam. At the East West Theater Encounter in Bombay in April 1986, *Chakravyuha* received the longest standing ovation I have ever known a performance to receive in India, from an audience consisting entirely of theater experts.

Thiyam comes from the geographically isolated state of Manipur in northeastern India. Although he has no fixed style, the basic shape of his productions is derived by synthesizing elements of the varied and rich regional rituals and performance forms of Manipur: the eighteenth-century story-telling, the nineteenth-century Sankeertan music and dance involving chanting, drumming, cymbal-playing and intricate movements, the prose narrative of Wari Leeba and the Thang Ta martial arts. These disparate elements are integrated in visual compositions of terrifying impact.

Thiyam has been criticized for using ritual objects for purely aesthetic purpose with no respect for their ritual value.[6] In Manipur, where the search for a local cultural identity is bound up with the return to the pre-Hindu Meitei rituals and lore, the ease with which Thiyam moves between the Meitei and Hindu mythologies—*Chakrauyuha* is based on an incident from the *Mahabharata*—has led to the problem, in Thiyam's words, that "Manipuris find my work alien while outsiders find it very Manipuri."

In 1986, within a few months of Awasthi's appointment as the chairman of the National School of Drama Society, Thiyam was appointed the director of the school. It was almost a public acknowledgment of the fact that the avant garde of 1961 had become now the "establishment."

It would be wrong to give the impression that the work of Thiyam or of his brilliant contemporary from Kerala, Kavalam Narayana Panicker, has had any impact on the professional theater in India. Actually there is very little in Indian urban theater today that would qualify for the adjective "professional." In Maharashtra, groups of mostly "semi-professionals" tour the state staging drawing-room comedies or domestic melodramas in portable three-walled sets. In the city of Calcutta, the situation of the dozen-odd theaters is aesthetically as well as financially depressing.[7]

In the Bengali countryside, however, one witnesses a burst of theatrical activity which at the same time is an interesting variation on the theme of "return to roots." This theater calls itself Jatra (literally "pilgrimage"). The original Jatra almost died of neglect during the British rule. Even after Independence little attention was paid to the revival of the traditional Jatra. In the 1960s, however, with a certain amount of economic prosperity and minimal comforts appearing in rural Bengal, a need for entertainment was felt and Jatra was quickly revived to fill the vacuum. With admirable adaptability, the new managers of Jatra switched themes and format to suit the moods of the times. Mythological and costume dramas dominated the 1950s, whereas the 1960s saw the emergence of social drama. In the 1970s, with the great leftward swing in Bengali politics, Marx, Lenin, Hitler as well as local political figures replaced the mythological and historical heroes. In the 1980s popular turning away from political activism was exactly reflected in the return to costume drama. Microphones, spotlights with color filters, diverse stage properties, Western music and tape recorders were all introduced to make the form attractive. The strategy has continued to yield dividends. The Jatra audience (by 1980) was 110 million and the annual turnover was approximately 510 million rupees. It is more popular today than ever before.

"But then let us not doubt," sighs critic and theater director Rudra Prasad Sengupta, "that it is no longer a folk theater; it is at best a hybrid—an unholy mixture of urban pollution and what Mathew Arnold called 'provincial'.... Yet when the concert starts to play in the presence of a ten-thousand strong audience, nostalgia does creep into the Bengali soul and one wonders what has gone wrong."[8]

The last, heart-wringing question succinctly sums up the unease many feel when faced with a phenomenon like Jatra. When a moribund traditional form revives and succeeds in the marketplace, can we blame it for its corruptions and vulgar alterations? Can a traditional form regain its popularity and yet retain a design perfected in some other historical situation? On the other hand, how many of the forms, subsisting on artificial injection of state money, deserve to be kept alive?

Music

Similar questions have dominated another debate that has been raging for about forty years now—on the merits of film music versus classical music.

The Indian sound film was born fully decked with songs. *Alam Ara,* the first sound film, had ten songs. During the next decade, major film-producing studios hired trained classical musicians to compose music for their films. But with the advent of the Second World War, individual entrepreneurs with fortunes made elsewhere (and often dubiously) entered film production. They were quick to note that a couple of popular stars and half a dozen good songs were enough to ensure the success of a film, and began to buy off the best acting and musical talent available. The studios that could not survive against this "formula" system collapsed. How durable this formula has proved to be can be judged by B. K. Karanjia's description of film production in 1986: "While elsewhere a script is written and valued, and stars and songs are chosen accordingly, here it is the other way round. A star is signed, songs are recorded and only thereafter is a script written!"[9]

Actually for Indians songs and dance have always been a part of the very act of gathering together. Fairs, marriages, funerals, even political meetings, are not complete without them. Once the technique of "play back" (actors miming to songs recorded by professional singers) was perfected in early 1940s and the singing voice did not have to fulfill the additional requirement of belonging to the actor or the actress, what little connection bound the music to specific films disappeared and film songs developed an autonomous existence. Even today records of a film's songs are released in advance of the film so that the audience can come to the film in order to relish songs already familiar.

The nonstop demand for songs forced music composers in the early 1940s to look beyond simple classical melodies to folk songs, traditional melodies and, most importantly, to Western music. In the West they discovered fresh instruments like the xylophone, saxophone, guitar and piano, and fascinating if unfamiliar concepts like color, harmony and orchestration. Goan Christian musicians, trained in Western music, were largely responsible for bringing in the harmonic element. With large budgets available for music, the composers sometimes used an ensemble of as many as seventy instrumentalists. As Bhaskar Chandavarkar wrote in 1980, "Purists have often said the downfall of film music started here!" He quotes music critic Gopal Sharman: "Most serious music lovers in India condemn popular and film music as something hybrid, a mixture of East and West, handled with inadequate understanding of either. Instead of the proper use of a modal melodic system, one often comes across a fumbling attempt to use European harmony."[10]

Over the years, however, awareness has grown that in its own groping fashion, film music was expressing something new. In the view of people like Naushad Ali, himself a successful music director, "film music—a spontaneous, exuberant growth, emerging from an older folk music and adopting itself to a new era and its influences—was the real folk music of modern India."[11]

But Chandavarkar, music director and one time professor of music at the Film and TV Institute of India, has pointed out that the very antithesis is between "classical" and "popular" music is a false one. As for the term "classical," he writes, "the Indian elite borrowed it from the British, but the Indian connotation of the word is not the same as the English one, for in the Indian context, 'classical' music does not belong to any particular period in history.... The terms used in local languages are *shastriya* or *shastrokta,* which literally mean from the scriptures, scientific or as ordered by scriptures, sciences. The terms are attempted synonyms for the English term 'classical'."[12] Chandavarkar goes on to comment that what is considered classical music today had its birth in "the music meant for entertainment of the audience" and therefore would not itself have qualified as the superior kind according to the classification of India's ancient aestheticians.

The most powerful part of Chandavarkar's argument is his listing of nine elements that characterize "classical" Indian music of whatever vintage. He then shows how Indian film songs fulfill all these norms. The two belong to the same mainstream! He also points out that harmonizing of Indian music has a respectable history. The great

Rabindranath Tagore had attempted it. So had Ravi Shankar and the All India Radio Vadya Vrinda (Orchestra) in the 1950s. Indeed in this particular area, the experiments of music composers for films have been most productive in extending the possibilities of Indian music.

The government of Madhya Pradesh state gives annual awards to artists of all-India stature for the contribution they have made in their respective fields. In 1986, in addition to conventional areas like literature, classical music, theater and painting, a new area was singled out for attention—popular music. The award was named after Lata Mangeshkar, who is by far the most successful playback singer in the history of Indian cinema, having sung more than 25,000 film songs. And it was awarded to Jayadev, a music director in Indian films. The choice was certainly a safe one: Jayadev came from a classical background and his music was known for its melodic structuring. But the establishment of the award itself seems to indicate that at long last film music was being given its due as a genre in its own right.

If the genre of film music has to some extent been rehabilitated, the attitude towards classical music, which a large majority of people of people have always considered obscure and elitist, has also been changing. In the last few years classical music suddenly seems to be gathering support particularly among those in their late teens and early twenties. Until the late 1970s the sale of classical music formed about 5 to 7 percent of the total sale of discs and cassettes. During the subsequent five years, it went up to around 15 percent. But in 1985-1986 alone, there has been a 30 percent increase in the sales figures. Organizers of musical concerts agree that classical concerts have a much larger attendance today than two decades ago and that most of the audience is under twenty-five.[13] In 1986, 50 percent of all sales—cassettes and discs—was of classical music. At least in commercial calculation, classical music had almost caught up with popular!

The sudden interest among the young in classical music started in the 1960s with the Beatle, George Harrison, coming to Ravi Shankar to learn the sitar. Since then many organizations and institutions have been working assiduously for promotion of interest in classical music. St. Xavier's College, Bombay, and St. Xavier's in Calcutta hold special classes. The Society for Promotion of Indian Classical Music and Culture among Youth has built a countrywide network since its inception in 1972. Apart from concerts, the society organizes special classes in music and lecture demonstrations.

Several events in the field of music itself have also contributed to this resurgence of interest, such as the boom in *ghazals* (poetic compositions set to music, dealing essentially with the themes of love and suffering but open to interpretation on various levels—secular, religious, mystical or philosophical) initiated by the Pakistani singers Mehendi Hasan and Ghulam Ali. The missionary work done by the handsome young percussionist Zakir Hussain and the imaginative use of mass media by artists like the vocalist Jasraj or the flautist Chaurasia have been very influential as well.

The Fine Arts

The problems confronting Indian dance and music have been mainly of internal origin. Western dance and music have hardly made a dent on the classical Indian scene. Painting and sculpture, on the other hand, are still fighting the overpowering influence of the West. Nineteenth-century Indians were embarrassed by the formal conventions of their traditional painting and happily embraced the photographic realism of Western painting. Ravi Verma and his colleagues reapplied the successful Victorian combination of naturalism and sensuality to paint gods and goddesses as fleshy human beings posing, as in a photograph, against realistic landscapes. Commercially the lithographs proved a sensational success. Every Hindu home hung, or aspired to hang, rows of them in the living room as much as in the room in which the gods were worshipped. Ravi Verma's Victorian aesthetic found immediate universal acceptance, and other arts, like the newly-emergent theater and its successor, the movies, consolidated their position by drawing upon the lithographs for costumes, decor and choreography. This school of painting, perpetuated by bazaar painters, survives to this day as calendar art and is as ubiquitous as the film song.

Indian painting never fully recovered from this damage, for no later painter achieved either Ravi Verma's eminence or posed a challenge to his aesthetics. When, in the late 1920s, serious attempts were made to arrive at an authentic Indian style of painting, it was discovered that no living tradition was left to relate to. As artists like Abanindranath Tagore, Nandalal Bose and Jamini Ray rushed to Japanese art, Mughal miniatures, Ajanta frescoes and folk painting in search of ideas and inspiration, not merely the lower middle classes in the cities and the rural populace but even the educated urban elite, content with the sensual realism of calendars and magazine covers, turned its back on an art form that seemed irrelevant to its social or spiritual concerns. That is how matters lie even today. Without a continous tradition to draw from, unable to find acceptance except as a minority indulgence, modern Indian painting continues isolated in its own culture, helpless to escape the shadow of the West.

Actually, for the excitement of line and color, material and texture, one has to go to the textiles and handicrafts, where traditional patterns and methods have been revived and combined with principles of modern design to produce works of exquisite beauty. Despite the enormous amount of kitsch sold, it is in the marketplace that the best in graphics is also found—on the saris, shawls, towels, carpets, pottery and other handicrafts.

Alternately, one must turn to folk and tribal artifacts, produced by cultures such as Warli, Santhal, Toda or Naga, which have begun to receive serious attention only in recent years. Bharat Bhavan, the multi-art complex inaugurated in Bhopal in 1982, has the largest collections of folk and tribal artifacts in the country. No museum of modern art in India compares with it for sheer visual delight.

Literature

Happily, literature has not become quite as irrelevant to the mainstream of Indian life as painting or sculpture. Yet there is a sense of futility and demoralization even there. In the early decades of this century, national leadership was in the hands of the educated upper classes, who were responsive to fiction and poetry. Writers like Tagore, Sharatchandra and Premchand had visibility on the national scene. The expansion by Mahatma Gandhi of the base of the nationalist movement to enable participation by the masses progressively moved the writer to the periphery of public life. In democratic India, with its universal suffrage, writers feel they have practically ceased to matter. The main reason is that only 17 percent of the population is literate. Then again, even this minority is divided into nearly twenty languages with no communication between them except through English or Hindi. Film and television seem to attract the best of new talent, for they offer money and instant fame. Besides, it is impossible to compete with the two for audience.

It is difficult to think of any literary work published in the last decade that has had national impact. A flip through the November/December 1986 issue of *Indian Literature,* the journal of the Sahitya Akademi, shows that even in regional languages, the situation is depressing. The issue surveys the literary output in Indian languages in 1985. "The most exciting literary event of 1985," exults the survey of Gujarati literature, "was that the prestigious novel *Jher to Pidhan Che Jani Jani* by Manubhai Pancholi "Darshak" (which was first published in part thirty-five years ago) is now complete!" And that is the most enthusiastic opening line in the whole journal. Openings of other surveys range from "The year 1985 rolled out without leaving much of an impression on Maithili readers. It was the bleakest in recent years," to "The year was by no means an outstanding one for Marathi literature." Other literatures sound the same dull, if not disheartened, note. This sluggishness has been characteristic of Indian literature as a whole at least since 1980.

Actually for the last notable event on the literary scene one has to go back to 1960, when the "Dalits" made their appearance—first in Marathi, then in Hindi, Kannada, Gujarati and other languages. A popular dictionary translates the word "Dalit" as "rent, broken, torn, split, trampled, ruined."[14] The term was defiantly applied to themselves by a group of young activists from the "lowest of the low" in the Indian caste hierarchy: the untouchables. For centuries this stratum of society had been denied access to education, indeed to any means of bettering itself socially or economically. Dalit writing therefore immediately attracted attention, for it spoke of a whole range of experiences never written about before—the agonies that had become part of the fabric of daily existence, the humiliations relentlessly piled on in the name of caste, the economic-social-sexual exploitation for which through the ages there has been no redress. The writers were angry, bitter, direct, and shatteringly honest about themselves. (That a militant wing called itself the "Dalit Panthers" clearly shows the sympathy and admiration they felt for black activism in the United States.) Despite some excellent fiction (Baburao Bagool) and poetry (Namdev Dhasal, Yeshwant Manohar, Arjun Dangale, etc.), the real achievement of Marathi Dalit literature has been in autobiography, a form little explored in India. Daya Pawar's *Baluta* (a one-time payment in grain for services rendered through the year), Lakshman Mane's *Upara* (Outsider), P. I. Sonkamble's *Athawaniche Pakshi* (Birds of Memory)—all vividly picture what it means even in today's democratic, secular India to be an untouchable.

But by the 1970s, Dalit literature had begun to repeat itself. Most of the writers continued to react emotively to their experiences, never stepping beyond the caste matrix to analyze their history in a larger sociopolitical context. The writing became predictable.

The most important work to appear from the Dalit background in recent years is neither fiction nor autobiography, but a historical study, *Dasa-shoodranchi Gulamgiri* (The Slavery of the Dasa-Shoodras). Published in 1982, it is written by Sharad Patil, a social activist and political leader who was expelled from the Communist Party of India (Marxist) for insisting that it was futile to talk of class struggle in the Indian context without first taking into consideration the more important factor of caste. If earlier Dalit intellectuals had called for a total rejection of the Indian cultural-philosophical heritage, as well as of Hindu religion itself, for not having allowed the lower castes to participate in their histories, Patil represents a new school of Dalit thinkers who insist that these "deprived" castes and tribes have made a positive contribution to the Indian heritage that needs to be recognized as well as reevaluated. It is sad that no imaginative work from the Dalits has shown the same grasp of the complex political and cultural forces that have shaped their history.

The Arts and the Government

As already noted, one of the first policies adopted officially by independent India was the study, retrieval and encouragement of traditional arts and crafts which had suffered neglect during colonial times. And it must be admitted that in the last forty years the agencies of the state and central governments as well as autonomous organizations financially supported by the government have, against all odds, done creditable work in this field. The akademis have sustained artists and craftsmen with pensions, fellowships, grants-in-aid and often by simply providing their work with visibility. In the 1950s, the All India Radio employed seven thousand classical musicians, thus becoming, in the words of B. S. Keskar, "the greatest patron of Indian music and musicians, greater than all the princely and munificent patronage of former days." Subsidies given by states like Karnataka as well as farsighted policies of the government-financed Film Finance Corporation (later the National Film Development Corporation) made the noncommercial, art-film movement possible in the 1960s and 1970s.

The involvement of the central government with the arts took a quantum leap in 1980 with Prime Minister Indira Gandhi's decision to hold a Festival of India in Britain, followed by similar festivals in the United States and France. According to Mrs. Pupul Jayakar, chairperson of the Festival of India Advisory Committee, the main objective of these festivals was international "public relations." Talking of the success of the festivals, she said: "India was in the limelight for eighteen months. According to the Ministry of External Affairs, the media coverage of the festivals abroad in money terms was over $2 billion!"[15] It is now proposed to hold similar festivals in the USSR, Sweden and Japan.

The need to do something similar within India, to "bring Indian culture to the people and to expose others where Indian culture is still alive," seems to have led to the idea of a National Cultural Festival in New Delhi in November 1986. The initiative again came from the prime minister, "who emphasized the need for awareness and participation at the grass roots level and the need to involve the people in a sense of cultural commonality."[16] The country was divided into seven cultural zones. A budget of about three million rupees was allotted to each zone for this year's festival. The festival, called "Apna Utsav" (Our Own Festival), opened on 9 November. Nearly 6,000 artists from the seven zones were brought to Delhi to perform at seven primary open grounds, each group performing at a site for three days before moving on.

In terms of the attendance and the enthusiasm it generated, the festival was acknowledged a huge success. It was covered in great detail by television, which ensured a national following. Inevitably there were criticisms of bureaucratic muddle and official insensibility to the psychological state of folk artists who had been thrust into the middle of an extravaganza far away from their home. But this is only the first year of the festival and such difficulties could be ironed out in the future. More pertinently, there were questions about the impact such a festival would have on the artists themselves. The grandeur of the spectacle came in for criticism. Organizers of the festival argued that such a scale was essential to make an impact: "to bring people of neighboring states together through arts, dance, music, culinary art, camps, performances, get-togetherness...every possible strategy that the government can employ."[17] But critics asked whether after the inevitable competition to gain attention and applause at these vast shows, the participating artists would not go back convinced that such glamour and extravagance were the essence of culture.

Others questioned the whole purpose of erecting one more new structure to look after culture, and asked whether it would not be more sensible to revitalize existing organizations—such as the akademis—which the government itself had sustained for three decades and which have become inactive from lack of funds. Surprisingly it was Mrs. Jayakar, recently nominated to be the prime minister's cultural adviser, who criticized the creation of the Zonal Cultural Centers: "We have enough institutions. Why are they not functioning? Why are our museums, libraries and archives not maintained properly? I am not in favour of adding institutions!"[18] As N. C. Jain has pointed out, the new institutions, such as the Zonal Centers and the Indira Gandhi National Centre for the Arts, have one feature in common: they are largely administered from the center. Jain expresses concern that this "centralization of cultural activity" leaves "the planning of important policies and important ventures" to a few civil servants.

Of course, traditionally the Indian arts have depended upon official patronage. But, as Suresh Awasthi has pointed out, the patrons did not hope to gain, either in terms of power or materially, from the arts they patronized. The arts were believed to be essential for the spiritual well-being of the patron and his society. But in a modern democratic set-up, patronage means power, power over artists and over institutions, thus subjecting culture to the vagaries of politics and careerism.

Other critics have seen a sense of political insecurity in this harping on culture, and the use of culture to push slogans of "national integration" and the "unity of diversity." Critic Rita Manchanda, quoting a speech by the prime minister ("This cultural centre will not only serve Punjab but also the Zone. We will ensure that this would promote and strengthen the culture of North. We have to remember that Punjab is strengthened culturally as a part of India"), argued that it was no accident that the Zonal Culture Centre in Punjab was inaugurated exactly a year after the assassination of Indira Gandhi and the Sikh carnage in Delhi. The aim, according to Manchanda, was to ensure that "a regional ethos beyond the narrow confines of a state emerged and became a part of a great loyalty to the country based on cultural integration."[19] As the news magazine *India Today* bluntly put it: "Behind the burst of festivity lies a deep fear, hysteria almost, about the holding together of the country."[20]

Nevertheless some critics greeted the concept of a National Cultural Festival with enthusiasm. As Kothari said: "The country is so vast and there is so much to do in the field of culture that any attempt to encourage arts is most welcome, as it helps artists survive and dying arts to find a new lease of life."

Film

One medium that could have done with less attention from the government was the commercial feature-film industry. On 10 October 1986, the film industry in the state of Maharashtra stopped work. For the first time in the seventy-three years since the first Indian feature film was made in the state, the entire industry, from the biggest producers to an estimated 40,000 daily wage earners, went on a strike of indefinite duration. In 1962, there had been a "bandh" (closure) in the film industry that had lasted forty days, but it was limited to the city of Bombay. The strike in 1986 covered the entire state and led to "sympathetic strikes" in other film-producing states as well.

India today produces the largest number of feature films in the world, more than Hollywood or Japan did at their most productive. In 1985/86, 912 films were produced in nearly a dozen languages. Almost half were made in Hindi. Maharashtra accounts for 30 percent of all films produced in India and 90 percent of those in Hindi. Thus, if the strike went on long enough, its impact would be felt over the whole country.

The immediate provocation for the strike was a new sales tax of 4 percent imposed by the government of Maharashtra on all transactions in the film industry. The amount payable to the state would have worked out to little more than twenty million rupees annually. The smallness of the amount and the disproportionately angry response to it clearly showed that it was not the immediate tax as much as the attitude of the government behind it that irked the film industry. Director-lyricist Amit Khanna expressed the real grievance of the industry when he said: "The film industry is like a milch cow to outsiders. Everyone always wants to milk it." As though to prove this, the finance minister of Maharashtra offered the following justification for the new tax: "The state needs money. The cotton monopoly has suffered, we had an unexpected drought.... We need to finance so many projects. Education, irrigation...."[21]

It was not as if the film industry was not already paying heavy taxes. The industry was paying an excise levy of Rs. 35,000 to 40,000 on each print of a new film, a 15 percent sales tax and 4 percent tax on raw stock. There was a 10 percent surcharge which had been levied in 1971 to raise funds for refugees from Bangladesh. The refugees had gone back, but the surcharge continued under a new name: "nutrition" charge! Apart from all this, there was the prohibitive entertainment tax which went up to 177 percent according to the ticket rate. According to the Film Federation of India, on every rupee earned in ticket collection, 24 percent was shared by the producers and distributors, 18 percent went to the theater owners (most of it toward maintenance) and the rest to the government.

At least in the case of the 1986 strike, the industry was quarrelling with the government of the state in which it was located and from which therefore it could demand responsible behavior. Most states have no film industry to worry about—they merely exhibit the films made in Bombay. And for the governments of many such states films have literally been the goose that lays the golden egg. Entertainment tax flows into the state coffers with no responsibility on the part of the governments to worry about the health of the industry.

The very ambiguous attitude of the governments toward the film industry has two different causes. First, cinema is the most influential medium of entertainment and communication today. It does not have the widest audience; radio has that distinction. Radio covers nearly 95 percent of the country's population while cinema is still confined to urban and semi-urban areas. Film's reach is limited by the fact that there are only 14,000 projection halls—including touring tent theaters—in India today. But the government-controlled radio programming is so heavily didactic and unimaginative that the influence of cinema is far more pervasive and deeply felt. Second, film is the only communication medium of its scale entirely financed by private capital, with no help from the government (except in the case of some regional and experimental films). Although it is by no means the only industry to indulge in black money deals, the combination of corrupt practice with glamour and independence helps to make it an object of envy and suspicion.

The film industry's relative independence from governmental control should have enabled it to operate from a position of strength from the beginning, but it did not. Even the 1986 strike ended in bitter recriminations and accusations that the leaders had betrayed the 300,000 workers in the industry. B. K. Karanjia, editor of the film weekly *Screen,* wrote, "The industry seems to be suffering from a guilt complex and an inferiority complex. It has always bowed down to government bullying. How did the entertainment tax reach this level...? Isn't it because the industry has allowed the Government to ride rough shod over their protests...? Other industries have black money too. How have they managed to command the government's respect?"[22]

Karanjia went on to point out that though filmmaking calls itself an industry, it is "a most disorganized one. No market surveys, no costing methods—at best it is run on an *ad hoc* basis. Banks and insurers will not look its way till it gets organised and till then it will have to pay exorbitant interest rates (15 to 60 percent).... The trade bodies are too busy fighting each other to fight a common platform. And as the veteran film historian Feroze Rangoonwalla says, the government has a vested interest in this chaos."

Television and Video

Adding to the woes of the film industry, a new threat has appeared on its horizon—video. Ten years ago Indian films were regularly shown in East Africa, West and South Africa, England, the Middle East and Southeast Asia. (The Soviet Union bought, as it continues to do, Indian films for consumption mainly by its Asian republics.) In a big-budget film, almost 50 percent of the budget was covered by distributors from outside India. By the early 1980s, however, most of these markets had disappeared. Not a single theater exhibits Indian film in England or East Africa anymore. The immigrant Asian population, which had provided the main audience in these countries, now preferred to watch films on video. Video piracy was also rampant in India, with the local authorities showing little enthusiasm for curbing it. The film industry's brush with television scared it, but not for long, as will be seen later.

Whether by piracy or not, video is already showing signs of developing into a serious rival medium. Nari Hira, a nonresident Indian who controls several magazines, launched "Hiba Video" in 1985-1986 in Bombay to make video films, followed by Charuhasan's "Goodwill" in Madras. The fact that G. P. Sippy, Ramanand Sagar and B. R. Chopra, major producers of feature films who have already moved into television programming, are seriously contemplating video film production clearly indicates the panic that is setting in. There are 1,500 video libraries in Bombay and 2,500 in Madras. In Tamil Nadu, customs authorities have cleared about 700,000 video cassette players and video cassette recorders, and today video libraries have an estimated turnover of one billion rupees a year.[23] Besides, there are cable TV services catering to apartment houses, hotel chains and airlines. At the moment "video parlors" offering paid public exhibition of videotapes are illegal. But they defy the law and continue to multiply at a furious pace. Ultimately the government may just have to face facts and legitimize them. The dramatic shift toward video has also been helped by the fact that the cost of equipment and theater construction have already limited the spread of cinema in India. Even today the number of cinema houses is just about half the number Britain had in 1945.

Given the low cost and operational simplicity of the newer models of video equipment, unless television can shake off its urban orientation and prim, middle-class notions of entertainment, video may become the truly "mass" medium of the future. Video film production at present is strongly reminiscent of filmmaking in its infancy. Hira completes a film in a month. His target is to finish a film in twenty days—"like bringing out a magazine." Charuhasan hopes to bring out twenty-five films a year costing 250,000 rupees a film. Actors and actresses are on contract with the production company. New talent is encouraged since it makes for economy.

Television has already overtaken films and is reaching out into areas untouched by cinema. Television was started in India on an experimental basis on 15 September 1959. Regular general service started in August 1965, but television continued to function as a part of the All India Radio for another eleven years until April 1976 when it was given an independent operational structure. Television's arrival was accompanied by fierce debates in the press about whether India with its economic problems benefitted by taking on such a heavy investment or whether it was merely a question of keeping up with the Joneses. The government asserted that India could not afford to be left behind technologically. The question whether India could afford it was met with the assurance that television would be developed for educational purposes, with programs aimed mainly at schools and rural areas.

Given television's avowed educational aim, the most interesting activity of this period was the Satellite Instructional Television Experiment (SITE), conducted for one whole year from 1 August 1975 utilizing the facility offered by NASA's ATS-6 satellite. Specific developmental programs were transmitted from an earth station in Gujarat to the satellite and beamed to 2,400 villages in Andhra Pradesh, Bihar, Orissa, Karnataka, Madhya Pradesh and Rajasthan. The impact of the experiment could not be properly assessed, since most of the software was produced hurriedly to meet the deadlines and there was no proper follow-up study. But Doordarshan—as Indian television is called—was slowly gaining confidence.

Through the 1970s, however, progress was slow. TV viewing remained confined to six cities: Bombay, Srinagar, Calcutta, Madras, Lucknow and Jalandar. Relay transmitters at Amritsar, Pune, Mussorie and Kanpur brought the states of Maharashtra, Jammu and Kashmir, West Bengal, Tamil Nadu, Uttar Pradesh and Punjab under its coverage. In 1982, the decision was made to introduce color—again after heated public controversy. But the real push came with the TV coverage of the prestigious Asian Games in New Delhi in 1982 and subsequently of the Nonaligned Summit. Before the Asian Games only eighteen transmitters had beamed programs to less than 25 percent of the population. In July 1983, the government decided to extend TV coverage to all towns with a population of 100,000 and above, selected border and strategic areas and important national project sites. By 1 January 1987, a total number of 187 transmitters covered 72 percent of India's total population!

In late 1983 Doordarshan took a decisive step that was to alter the entire status of television viewing in India. It accepted the principle that shows may be produced and sponsored by nongovernmental bodies. In association with a private advertising agency, Doordarshan coproduced a soap opera, "Hum Log" (Us), inspired by the Mexican serial "Accompany Me." A sentimental saga of a lower-middle-class family in North India, the serial instantly became a craze. Doordarshan's Audience Research Group estimated that over two billion "viewer hours" were spent in watching the soap opera run its course through 157 twice-weekly episodes. In towns ranging in population from 100,000 to 500,000, the viewership rating was 90 percent. An average of 400 letters a day from the viewers poured in, advising, commenting, criticizing. At one point in the story, when a female character refused to marry the right man, viewers marched to the actress's house to persuade her to change her mind. When the marriage actually took place, the event was celebrated in the streets of Allahabad, Varanasi and Lucknow. India was discovering television addiction.

The impact of the programming change was reflected in a phenomenal increase in the number of television sets in Indian homes. At the start of 1985, there were 5,200,000 television sets in India, which meant a captive audience of 50,000,000. During that year another 2,000,000 sets were sold. By the end of the decade, it is expected that there will be 30,000,000 sets with a viewership of 300,000,000.

Another measure of the change was viewer preferences. According to the Indian Market Research Bureau, in 1976 only three programs were watched by 70 percent of the viewers, all three dependent on Hindi feature films: "Chitrahaar" (a collage of film songs), an interview show with film personalities called "Phool Khilen Hain Gulshan Gulshan" and of course the Hindi feature film on Sunday evenings. In 1985, according to the same survey, even the feature film had slid down to the ninth place in Bombay, eighth in Delhi and fifth in Madras.[24]

The programming shift was a bonanza for advertisers who had only had a limited access to television time before 1983. Revenue increased from eight million rupees in 1976/77 to one billion rupees in 1985/86 and is expected to touch two billion rupees in 1987. Commenting on this increase, the Operations Research Group said: "Doordarshan continues to be a proliferator of consumerism in the country with more than a quarter of all commercials being on toiletries, washing materials, packaged foods, cosmetics and textiles."[25] Doordarshan, now rich and in demand, had come a long way from its early commitment to rural education and a developmental strategy whose basic principle was control of consumption!

The success of "Hum Log" and other serials initially seriously affected box office collections for films. Cinema attendance slumped. Of the 734 films released in 1984, only one—a 3-D film for children—was considered a "super success" by the Trade Guide as against the six "super successes" of 1983. Critics bleakly pointed out that mass desertion of films for television was no new phenomenon, and that the experience of Hollywood should have prepared the Indian film industry for a collapse, delayed here only because Doordarshan had kept program production in its own hands till recently.

But the effect did not last long. Within six months, cinema attendance was booming again. Television did not seem to have undercut the long-standing support for big-budget commercial feature films, except of course on Sunday when a Hindi feature film is shown on television. There has been much speculation on this unexpected turnabout on the part of the audience. It has been argued that the main audience for feature films comes from the lower economic strata in the cities as well as from women of all economic and social classes. And both these groups have definite expectations about a "good evening's entertainment" which have their roots in traditional viewing habits in the countryside as well as in habits formed in the last forty years. These expectations include a sufficiently long duration (at least 140 minutes in the case of a film) and an emotionally intense narrative laced with songs, dances and strong music. In addition, films provide a legitimate excuse for going out, a very real need in the overcrowded urban tenements.

Doordarshan programs, on the other hand, inevitably reflect the white-collar tastes of the civil servants who run the organization, the press critics who influence policy decisions and the large, educated middle class which owns the sets. Certainly sex and violence, which are regularly quoted as the staple of successful formula films, find no place on Indian television.

How long the film industry can afford to remain complacent is another matter. TV viewing has an insidious habit of winning over converts, and it may not be long before the industry again faces the threat. At least the big movie moghuls seem to have decided to play safe by going into producing television software. The most popular soap opera running at the moment, "Buniyad" is produced by G. P. Sippy and directed by his son Ramesh Sippy, a combination that also produced "Sholay," the biggest box-office grosser in the history of Indian cinema. Ramanand Sagar, another producer, has made a serial on the Indian epic, the *Ramayana,* and B. R. Chopra is producing one on another classic, the *Mahabharata.*

Although the long-term impact of television on commercial big-budget films is not yet very clear, its effect on medium and small-budget films has been nothing short of disastrous. The latter were patronized by exactly those classes that prefer to watch television today. Govind Nihalani, whose two earlier films had proved very successful at the box office, had to premiere his two recent films on television. The same fate befell Prakash Jha's "Damul," which won the national award for the best film of 1985, and Jayoo and Nachiket Patwardhan's "Anantayatra." Four films of Shyam Sengal have yet to find distribution. Basu Chatterjee, whose early light-hearted comedies had been welcomed with such relish by the urban middle class, admitted he could not find buyers for his films.

As a result, 1986 found all the stalwarts of the "parallel" cinema—as the nonformula, medium-budget, mainly realistic films are called—producing programs for television. Sandeep Ray (son of Satyajit Ray), Mrinal Sen, Shyam Benegal, Basu Chatterjee, Amol Palekar, Sridhar Kshirsagar and Saeed Mirza each had a serial running on television.

The unhappy aspect of this situation is that all these people had been considered uncompromising radicals in the film world, artists who had refused to accept the "formula" and stood apart, their integrity intact. It is true many of their films had been backed by the National Film Development Corporation, which is fully financed by the government of India. But the corporation is an autonomous body, situated in Bombay, far away from the capital, and its record has been surprisingly liberal. Many of the angry, rebellious, politically critical films made by young filmmakers had the financial support of the NFDC.

Doordarshan, however, is a part of the Ministry of Information and Broadcasting. Although the ministry has asserted that it does not control—or even wish to control—the programming policy of Doordarshan, the case of Jack Anderson's film "Rajiv's India" as well as the Hindi feature film "New Delhi Times," both of which had been announced in 1986 with a great deal of fanfare and then withdrawn from telecasting at the last moment without explanation, indicated that Doordarshan's decisions could be overruled. With only a single channel for national broadcasting and with film-makers elbowing each other for time on it, the government's newfound power to patronize intellectuals and artists was cause enough for uneasiness.

This, however, is a minor worry compared to the profound sociological impact that the sudden intrusion of television could have on a traditional society such as India. As has already been pointed out, cinema has remained a basically urban medium. Its impact on the vast hinterlands, particularly in North India, has been minimal. Even today there are people in India who have never seen anything moving on a screen. But a less extreme illustration will serve to illustrate the problem. Even in areas that are by now used to films as regular entertainment, the communication between the interior of a house and the world outside is carefully controlled. Older members of the family and, in the case of women, adult males censor the flow of information. (Thus many film-makers do not like an "Adult" certificate, for it at once reduces female attendance. Heads of families do not permit their women to see "Adult" films). Whatever happens in the world outside, no book, no object, no source of new information can enter the house without being first monitored by the elders.

Television flattens these hierarchies by exposing all generations, sexes and castes simultaneously to its constant outflow of information, thus nullifying the power of traditional monitoring agencies. A feudal family could thus be thrust into the twenty-first century with nothing to absorb the shock of this violent upheaval. The effect of such a cultural displacement could be more traumatic and its sociological cost higher than that of the physical displacement that has been the root cause of so much restlessness and violence in India in the last four decades. Sir Denis Forman, the chairman of Granada Television, almost understated the case when he said Indian television "is a tremendous phenomenon and the country has turned into a laboratory for communication experts!"

Conclusion

Against this background of traditions stretching back into antiquity and future shocks waiting just around the turn of the century, one could do worse than end with a touching little fable. During the Festival of India in the United States, the Children's Museum in Washington, D.C., invited a man called Nek Chand from Chandigarh to build a garden for them. Nek Chand was a road inspector in the Public Works Department of Punjab state until his retirement in 1984. In 1958, quietly, without any definite plans or even a proper blueprint, he started building a garden. He collected broken bottles, china, scraps, rags and machine parts and with this junk started sculpting fantasy figures to fill the fantasy landscape he was creating. His immediate supervisors encouraged him, but it was only in 1970 that his work was taken note of by the government and he was allotted funds and land. In a twelve-acre plot at the foothills of the Shivalik mountains, Nek Chand continued to create a weird world of birds, women, soldiers, dream figures—made with bits and pieces of metal, glass and wood.

Eight million people a year come to see Nek Chand's garden. Chandigarh, known as the city designed by Le Corbusier, is today also famous as the city with the "Rock Garden."

In 1986, the Washington Building Congress awarded Nek Chand the Superior Craftsman Award. His garden for the Children's Museum will probably be the only permanent legacy of the Festival of India in the United States.

Notes

1. Kapila Vatsyayan, *Indian Classical Dance,* New Delhi, 1974, pp. 15-16. Quoted in Richard Schechner, *Performative Circumstances: From the Avant garde to Ramlila,* Calcutta, 1983, p. 185.
2. Sunil Kothari, *India Today,* 15 April 1986, New Delhi.
3. Suresh Awasthi, *Drama: the Gift of Gods,* Tokyo, 1983.
4. Kapila Vatsyayan, *Traditional Indian Theatre: Multiple Streams,* New Delhi, 1980.

5. Suresh Awasthi, "In Defence of the 'Theatre of Roots'," *Sangeet Natak,* July-December 1985, New Delhi.

6. Likendra Arambam, "Manipuri Theatre: A New Look Upon Tradition," *Sangeet Natak,* July-December 1985, New Delhi.

7. Rudra Prasad Sengupta, "The Hijack of Jatra," *Sangeet Natak,* July-December 1985, New Delhi.

8. *Ibid.*

9. B. K. Karanjia, "For Want of a Leader...," Bombay, 22 November-6 December 1986.

10. Quoted in Bhaskar Chandavarkar, "The Great Film Song Controversy," *Cinema Vision India,* October 1980, Bombay.

11. Erik Barnouw and S. Krisnaswamy, *Indian Film,* New York, 1980, p. 213.

12. Bhaskar Chandavarkar, op. cit.

13. *India Today,* 15 March 1986, New Delhi.

14. *Bhargava's Standard Illustrated Dictionary of Hindi Language,* Varanasi, 1984.

15. *India Today,* 15 October 1986, New Delhi.

16. *Report of the Festival of the National Cultural Festival,* quoted in *India Today,* 15 November 1986.

17. Sunil Kothari, "Unity in Diversity," *The Illustrated Weekly of India,* 9 November 1986, Bombay.

18. *India Today,* 30 November 1986.

19. Rita Manchanda, "Culture: The Great Leap Forward," *The Illustrated Weekly of India,* 9 November 1986, Bombay.

20. *India Today,* 30 November 1986, New Delhi.

21. *Bombay,* 22 October-6 November 1986.

22. B. K. Karanjia, op. cit.

23. *India Today,* 15 September 1986, New Delhi.

24. *India Today* 31 December 1985, New Delhi.

25. *The Times of India,* 11 February 1987, Bombay.

7
Foreign Relations: Elusive Regional Security

Marshall M. Bouton

India encountered growing difficulty in its foreign relations in 1986, especially in its relations with its neighbors. The trend was dramatically illustrated by events in India's most important bilateral relationship, that with Pakistan. In December 1985, an historic breakthrough seemed imminent between the two nations that had fought three wars in less than forty years. India's new Prime Minister Rajiv Gandhi and Pakistan's President Zia-ul Haq agreed in principle not to attack each other's nuclear installations, thus removing a possible cause of renewed conflict. But in January 1987, only thirteen months later, military buildups by both countries along their common border created a war scare not experienced since their last clash in 1971.

More broadly, the orientation of India's foreign policy during 1986 shifted from one of moderate change and openness to one of more familiar themes and caution. The fresh approaches that Rajiv Gandhi brought to India's foreign relations during 1985—a more conciliatory posture toward India's neighbors, an effort to improve relations with the United States, more emphasis on action and less on rhetoric—were suspended if not abandoned by the end of 1986. This shift was evident quite early in the year. On 29 March a noted commentator on foreign affairs, A. S. Abraham, writing in *The Times of India,* described the trend as a "Retreat from Euphoria: Back to Basics in Foreign Policy."

What caused this rather abrupt change in India's foreign relations? The most important factor was the impact of domestic politics on

---

The author wishes to acknowledge the valuable assistance of Owen M. Crowley in the preparation of this chapter.

India's foreign policy. Rajiv Gandhi's growing political difficulties caused him to become more cautious in foreign policy and to attempt to shore up his political support by playing on foreign troubles and threats. For instance, the prime minister began to adopt a harder line in relations with Pakistan after the breakdown of the effort to resolve the Punjab crisis in early 1986. India's ethnic politics and its foreign relations were impinging more and more uncomfortably on each other. The presence of Sri Lankan Tamil refugees (including armed militants) in India's Tamil Nadu state became a more volatile issue in both Indian domestic politics and Indo-Sri Lankan relations.

Other factors which explain the disturbing trends in India's foreign relations during 1986 were international developments—such as the movement towards Sino-Soviet rapprochement or the progress in Pakistan's nuclear program—and apparent disarray in the Indian foreign policy process. The fact that India had three different foreign ministers during 1986, and the tensions between the prime minister and the foreign policy bureaucracy revealed in his public dismissal of his foreign secretary in early 1987, complicated India's response to a deteriorating environment.

Fundamentals of Indian Foreign Policy

The fundamental goals of Indian foreign policy did not change during 1986. These goals are rooted in India's history, especially its colonial past, and in its geopolitical position, and have endured largely unchanged since India achieved independence in 1947. Rajiv Gandhi's proposed new directions were alterations at the margins, not at the core of Indian foreign policy. However, the events of 1986 did raise questions about how India might best seek to attain its foreign policy goals.

The foremost goal of Indian foreign policy is the security of the South Asian subcontinent. India sees its security perimeters as encompassing the entire region. As the largest and most powerful nation in South Asia, India regards itself as the arbiter of regional security. India's relationship with Pakistan is most central to its security concerns because the northwest has historically been the gateway to the Subcontinent and because Pakistan is India's most powerful rival in the region. India's determination to be the regional security manager has led to constant friction with its neighbors, who have frequently looked outside the region for support in their efforts to counter Indian dominance.

A second goal of Indian foreign policy has therefore been to limit and eventually to eliminate the roles and influence of outside powers in South Asia. Thus, India has objected strongly when its neighbors have taken what India insists are bilateral disputes into international fora. It has also objected to its neighbors becoming involved in alliances or security relationships with outside powers and has warned them against permitting foreign bases on their soil. This principle of Indian policy has been a point of contention in India's relations with the United States because of Pakistan's ties with the United States. But India has also been concerned about Nepal's ties with China and, recently, Sri Lanka's ties with Israel.

A closely related third goal of Indian policy has been to maximize India's national self-reliance and independence of action in the international arena. This goal is deeply felt because of India's sense of historical and cultural autonomy and its colonial experience, and is the basis of India's policy of nonalignment. Nonalignment is often confused with neutralism or equidistance between the superpowers, but this is not the Indian interpretation. For India nonalignment means that it does not automatically side with any power but is free to take a position on a given issue according to India's interests. In practice, as we shall discuss below, India has usually taken stands on many issues closer to those of the Soviet Union.

A fourth major element in Indian foreign policy which the others ultimately serve is India's aspiration to eventual great power status. A sense of national "manifest destiny," not clearly formulated or expressed, lies behind many foreign policy calculations. As a continental nation with the world's second largest population, the third largest army, and the tenth largest industrial output, India sees itself as a candidate for global leadership. Partly for this reason India has sought and gained a leadership role in the Third World and international organizations. But it must be emphasized that this aspect of Indian foreign policy is much in the background. Current policy focuses heavily on India's own region.

In part because of the continuity of these goals, an extraordinary consensus underlies Indian foreign policy. Partisan politics and public opinion have little impact on foreign policy except as a limiting factor. Foreign policy is seldom an issue in Indian election campaigns. The prime minister has always dominated Indian foreign policy and policy is formulated and implemented by a small elite. Parliament plays little role. But, foreign policy may be used to affect domestic politics, as happened in 1986.

India and the Region

India's stance toward its regional neighbors, which had been quite accommodative in 1985, became less so in 1986. The harder line was prompted in part by the domestic political ramifications of ethnic conflicts that spilled across India's borders with its neighbors and in part by India's mounting concern over its security interests in the region. A more promising development was that the newly formed South Asian Association for Regional Cooperation (SAARC) played a modest role in helping to manage regional tensions during 1986.

Pakistan

The relationship between India and Pakistan has been the central feature of South Asian international relations since the two nations became independent in 1947. For virtually this entire period the relationship has been one of deep distrust and conflict. The reasons for this are embedded in the history and geopolitics of the Subcontinent. The two nations were created in violence out of the same social and cultural milieu but with competing national ideologies. India was dedicated to a multi-religious secular state, Pakistan to an Islamic state. India has seen Pakistan as the chief obstacle to its regional security, while Pakistan has seen India's regional ambitions as threatening its very existence. As mentioned above, Pakistan has sought to counter Indian dominance by linking up with outside powers—the United States in the 1950s and 1960s, China and the Islamic nations in the 1970s, and the United States again in the 1980s. This intrusion of outside powers has only deepened India's distrust of Pakistan. Finally, the three wars they have fought have instilled a collective memory of conflict in both countries.

The long-standing dispute between India and Pakistan over Kashmir embodies most of the elements of the conflict, although Kashmir itself is no longer central in it. At Independence Pakistan laid claim to Kashmir with its predominantly Muslim population, while India argued that Kashmir's Hindu ruler had acceded to India. For India the inclusion of this Muslim-majority state in the union (the only one) is testimony to India's secularism. For Pakistan Kashmir's exclusion is an affront to the Islamic character of the country. Because of its geographic position, Kashmir is important to the security of both nations. The division of Kashmir which resulted from the first Indo-Pakistani war in 1948 has been the source of periodic armed clashes along the cease-fire line as well as diplomatic sparring in the UN and other fora. The most serious recent clashes occurred in 1985, when Indian and Pakistani forces exchanged fire in the Siachen Glacier region of Kashmir.

The year 1986 began on a more positive note, however. Over the previous two or three years there had been significant improvement in Indo-Pakistani relations despite the difficult regional environment created by the Soviet invasion of Afghanistan. In 1981 Pakistan's President Zia-ul Haq offered to sign a no-war pact with India. After some hesitation the then Indian Prime Minister Indira Gandhi responded with a proposal that the two countries sign a treaty of peace and friendship. In November 1982 Zia-ul Haq and Indira Gandhi met in New Delhi, the first meeting between Indian and Pakistani leaders since the Soviet invasion of Afghanistan, to consider ways of improving relations. In March 1983 India and Pakistan agreed to set up a joint commission and four subcommissions to expand official contacts and cooperation.

Despite ups and downs this warming trend in Indo-Pakistani relations continued over the next two and a half years, accelerating after Rajiv Gandhi came to power and culminating in President Zia's December 1985 visit and the oral agreement not to attack each other's nuclear installations. Zia and Gandhi also agreed that Gandhi would visit Pakistan within the next six months. In January 1986 the finance ministers of the two countries signed an economic cooperation agreement, the defense secretaries discussed how to end clashes in the Siachen Glacier, and the foreign secretaries began to work on translating the Zia-Gandhi no-attack pledge into a written agreement.

But beginning in February-March 1986 the climate changed drastically. India began issuing a series of official statements accusing Pakistan of aiding Sikh terrorists, a drumbeat of criticism that continued throughout the year. The effort to formalize the oral agreement reached by Zia and Gandhi was suspended. India began dropping hints that Rajiv Gandhi would not visit Pakistan as planned and in March Gandhi himself said that Pakistani statements concerning Kashmir and its handling of the Sikh hijackers of an Indian plane had caused him to put off his visit indefinitely. In August the Indian minister of state for external affairs told Parliament that there is "no question of the prime minister visiting Pakistan until Pakistan agrees not to bring third parties into bilateral disputes and not to allow foreign bases on Pakistani soil." In September Rajiv Gandhi harshly criticized Pakistan for its handling of the hijacking in Karachi of an American aircraft carrying many Indian citizens. By October the Indian newspaper, *The Hindustan Times,* editorialized that India should "tell off Pakistan" and the Karachi edition of the Pakistani newspaper, *Dawn,* observed on 15 October that "the bright outlook for Indo-Pak relations has evaporated and the two states have returned to their normal state of acrimony and suspicion."

The sequence of events suggests strongly that one immediate cause of the abrupt change in Indo-Pakistani relations was the collapse of the Punjab Accord in late January 1986. By accusing Pakistan of permitting or even encouraging the cross-border movement of Sikh terrorists, the prime minister perhaps hoped to deflect domestic criticism of himself and his government for not successfully concluding the Punjab negotiations.

Once the trend of the relationship changed, other outstanding issues quickly came to the fore. The major issue in 1986 as earlier in the 1980s was the differing Indian and Pakistani responses to the Afghan situation. India criticized Pakistan strongly for having turned to the United States for support and claimed that the US involvement would only prolong the Soviet presence in Afghanistan and fuel the arms race in South Asia. India also contended that the arms sought by Pakistan were really intended for use against India rather than on the Afghan border. Indian officials pointed specifically to weapons such as Harpoon anti-ship missiles acquired from the US that could not conceivably be used on Pakistan's western border. The issue of US arms supply to Pakistan became even more heated later in the year when it was announced that the US might supply airborne early warning systems to Pakistan, an issue which will be described in more detail below.

Pakistan's advancing effort to develop a nuclear weapons capability added to the tension in India-Pakistan relations in 1986. Press reports during the year that Pakistan had been able to enrich uranium to weapons-grade levels and to perfect triggering devices led to calls in the Indian Parliament and press that India develop its own weapons. (In January 1987 the head of the Pakistan nuclear program told an Indian journalist that Pakistan had actually acquired a nuclear weapons capability.) Although Pakistan maintained that its program was strictly for peaceful purposes, Rajiv Gandhi did tell the Lok Sabha in April that if Pakistan developed a weapon, India would have to think seriously about its own options. And in November he cited Pakistan's nuclear program as a reason for the "slowdown" in the process of normalization between the two countries. Pakistan reiterated during the year its offer to negotiate an agreement (such as a South Asia nuclear weapons-free zone or an inspection regime) with India to prevent the development and/or deployment of nuclear weapons in the two countries. As before, India rejected these proposals on the grounds that with respect to nuclear weapons South Asia could not be considered separately from other areas, such as China or the Indian Ocean.

The cumulative impact of these differences in Indo-Pakistani relations was dramatically demonstrated by the military confrontation that developed between the two countries late in 1986. It began in October with a larger-than-ever Indian military exercise, code-named Operation Brasstacks, on India's border with Pakistan. As the number of troops involved in the exercise increased, Pakistan responded by mobilizing its own forces across the border.

By November, however, Indian and Pakistani leaders had begun to take steps to defuse the rapidly worsening situation. Talks between Rajiv Gandhi and Pakistani Prime Minister Mohammed Khan Junejo at the SAARC meetings in Bangalore resulted in high-level discussions of border problems in December and talks in January which led to the pullback of forces on both sides.

Under the circumstances that prevailed during 1986 it is not surprising that no progress was made on a broader agreement that might help to prevent a confrontation between India and Pakistan in the future. The principal obstacle to such an agreement is the different approaches that the two sides bring to it. Pakistan's proposal for a no-war pact puts first its desire for an Indian guarantee of Pakistan's security. India's proposal for a treaty of peace and friendship puts first India's desire to normalize relations in the political, trade and other areas. India also insists that as part of such an agreement Pakistan commit itself to bilateralism and to no foreign bases on its soil. Pakistan regards these conditions as an infringement on its sovereignty and as an effort by India to institutionalize its dominant role in South Asian security matters.

Sri Lanka

India's relations with another neighbor, Sri Lanka, were also marked by tension and frustration in 1986. The difficulties between India and the island nation on India's southeast coast resulted from the spillover of Sri Lanka's ethnic strife between Tamils and Sinhalese and its effect on Indian domestic politics. Some observers compared the situation to Indo-Pakistani tensions over Punjab, with India being accused by Sri Lanka of harboring and aiding Sri Lankan Tamil forces and India accusing Sri Lanka of discriminating against a key minority and seeking a military rather than political solution. India's own efforts to promote a political solution, hampered by the difficulty of controlling the Tamil militants and by some disarray in India's management of its role in the crisis, were on-again and off-again and finally met with little success. At year's end the stage was set for a renewed escalation of the crisis in 1987.

The essence of the Sri Lanka crisis is the demand of the Sri Lankan Tamils, who comprise 11-12 percent of the Sri Lankan population but are concentrated in the northern and eastern sections of the country, for greater autonomy from Colombo and, among the more radical Tamils, for an independent state. The Sri Lankan Tamils, whose ancestors migrated to the island centuries ago, resent what they regard as efforts by the Sinhalese majority to isolate and weaken their community by limiting their access to education and employment and by restricting the use of the Tamil language. The conflict gathered force during the 1970s and early 1980s and exploded in July 1983 in massive riots in Colombo.

In the four years since the Colombo riots the conflict has become more and more polarized. Although fragmented into several competing groups, the Tamil movement has increasingly committed itself to a separate Tamil state ("eelam"). India has also become inexorably more involved. Over 125,000 Sri Lankan Tamil refugees have fled to India. The major militant groups, including the Liberation Tigers of Tamil Eelam (LTTE) and the Tamil Eelam Liberation Organization (TELO) have established headquarters and training camps across the Palk Strait in the Indian state of Tamil Nadu. Supported by that state's ruling and opposition parties, the militants have operated with considerable impunity. The difficulty that the Indian government has had in controlling the militants was illustrated when in 1985 it had to back down on its decision to expel two militant leaders following an uproar in Tamil Nadu.

Indian efforts to mediate the conflict, which had been low-key since 1983, were stepped up after Rajiv Gandhi came to power. Gandhi enhanced India's credibility by his efforts to win over Sri Lanka's President Junius Jayewardene. India helped arrange a cease-fire in June 1985 and in late 1985 persuaded the Tamil militants and the Tamil United Liberation Front (TULF) representing the moderates to come to the meeting table with the Sri Lankan government. But the distrust between the two sides was too deep, the talks were not successful and the cease-fire broke down.

As 1986 opened, India's attitude toward Colombo hardened. In February the Indian minister for external affairs, B. R. Bhagat, accused the Sri Lankan government of committing genocide against Tamils and gave it a month to reach a political settlement. After Colombo reacted sharply to Bhagat's statement, India announced that it would not participate in the Asia Cup cricket tournament in Colombo at the end of March. On 5 March the Indian deputy external affairs minister told Parliament that India planned to ask Sri Lanka to pay part of the cost of keeping the Sri Lankan Tamil refugees in India. Relations continued to deteriorate in April and May, as the leaders of India's main opposition parties called for economic sanctions against Sri Lanka, President Jayewardene criticized India for its continued assistance to the Tamil separatists, and in May the Sri Lankan military mounted an offensive against Tamil rebel forces on the Jaffna peninsula. On 17 May a leading columnist, A. S. Abraham of *The Times of India,* wrote that India might have to intervene militarily to prevent the slaughter of Tamils. And on 30 May India announced that it was suspending mediation efforts until Sri Lanka offered more satisfactory proposals to end the crisis.

Throughout this diplomatic sparring, Delhi made clear its vehement opposition to any effort by Colombo to internationalize the crisis. In March the Indian external affairs ministry's report for 1985-86 registered "serious concern" at the activities of foreign security and intelligence organizations in Sri Lanka, citing specifically Sri Lanka's growing military links with Pakistan. The external affairs minister expressed India's opposition to a possible Commonwealth initiative on Sri Lanka. In April Rajiv Gandhi observed that various "defense presences" in Sri Lanka, including those of Pakistan and Israel, were of concern to India.

Beginning in June, however, the exchange between India and Sri Lanka on the crisis took a more positive turn. After reviewing what Sri Lanka described as rock-bottom proposals for ending the conflict, the Indian government said they should be more carefully considered by the Sri Lankan Tamils. In July President Jayewardene sent specific proposals to Delhi to be passed on to the Tamil groups which reportedly went further than any previous offers. Although India rejected Jayewardene's request that India "guarantee" implementation of any accord between the Sri Lankan government and the Tamils, India did step up its pressure on the Tamils to negotiate seriously. In August, for instance, the Colombo newspaper, *Lanka Puwath,* reported that three senior Indian ministers had met with the Tamil militants in Madras to urge their support for ongoing negotiations between the TULF and the Sri Lankan government.

But the split between the TULF and the militants continued to frustrate India's effort to mediate the conflict. After two more months of little progress in Colombo, the Tamil Nadu police raided militant camps in the state in advance of a meeting between Prime Minister Gandhi and President Jayewardene at the SAARC summit in the nearby city of Bangalore on 16-18 November. Although the Indian government renewed its endorsement of the Sri Lankan government's proposals and brought LTTE leader Prabakaran to Bangalore during the Gandhi-Jayewardene talks, no agreement resulted. By year's end the momentum in the negotiating efforts was lost and India was once again accusing Sri Lanka of bad faith.

Bangladesh and Nepal

India's relations with its other two principal South Asian neighbors—Bangladesh and Nepal—were less stormy during 1986 than its relations with Pakistan and Sri Lanka. But underlying the correctness of these relations were thorny issues similar in many respects to those affecting India's relations with Pakistan and Sri Lanka. These included the spillover of ethnic conflicts, managing the movement of people and resources across very permeable borders, and differences over the involvement of third parties in these issues. Behind the issues lay the deeper problem of distrust fostered by the asymmetries of size and power between India and its dependent neighbors.

Bangladesh. India's pivotal role in the creation of Bangladesh in 1971 forged a close relationship between the two countries during the first few years of Bangladesh's independence. But after the death in 1975 of Bangladesh's first leader, Sheikh Mujibur Rahman, the natural antipathies between two such unequal states as well as specific problems led to more prickly relations. Relations began to improve somewhat in the late 1970s and early 1980s, and in October 1982, the leader of Bangladesh, Lt. General H. M. Ershad, visited New Delhi for the first summit talks between India and Bangladesh in eight years.

The two most difficult issues in Indo-Bangladesh relations, then as now, were the sharing of Ganges River waters and the migration of Bangladeshis into the adjoining Indian state of Assam. The Ganges River, which enters Bangladesh from India at Bangladesh's northwestern corner, is critical to both economies. Especially during the relatively low-flow summer months, the Ganges waters are vital to agriculture and to inland navigation in Bangladesh and to the use of Calcutta port in India. An Indian dam near the border at Farraka diverts the Ganges waters into India.

Since the late 1970s India and Bangladesh have agreed to a series of interim water distribution arrangements while they have sought a more permanent solution to the dispute. India has proposed that the Ganges flow be augmented by linking the Ganges with the relatively untapped Brahmaputra River through a canal across the northern part of Bangladesh. Bangladesh rejects this proposal because of the unacceptable diversion of agricultural land it would require. Bangladesh has instead proposed augmenting the Ganges flow by storing excess winter flow in northern India and/or Nepal. India has responded that the political and financial costs of Bangladesh's proposal are too high.

Rajiv Gandhi has adopted a relatively conciliatory posture on the river waters dispute. In October 1985 Gandhi and Ershad agreed to continue the interim agreement on dry-season sharing through 1989. At a meeting of the Indian and Bangladeshi irrigation ministers in August 1986, India agreed for the first time to tripartite talks on the river waters issue involving Nepal. But at year's end the issue seemed no closer to solution than it had been in 1985.

The second major issue in Indo-Bangladeshi relations in recent years has been the migration of Bangladeshi nationals into Assam where they compete with native Assamese for land, employment and education. This influx has produced a strong political backlash in Assam and was the principal cause of violent unrest in Assam in the early 1980s. Rajiv Gandhi attempted a resolution of the problem through an accord with the Assamese militants in August 1985. But the continuing flow of migrants in 1986 as well as other difficulties in the accord and its implementation have kept the Assam crisis brewing. India has proposed to build a fence along the length of the India-Bangladesh border to stop the migration but has done little to implement this proposal, perhaps out of the realization that the fence would not be very effective.

Tensions along the border between Bangladesh and India's Tripura state were another irritant in the relationship during 1986. In April Indian and Bangladeshi troops exchanged fire along a disputed section of the border at Muhari Char. More significant was the movement of dissident Chakma tribals from the Chittagong Hill Tracts district of Bangladesh into Tripura. Over 20,000 of the Buddhist tribals, fleeing clashes between armed tribal militants and Bangladeshi government forces caused by the government's effort to bring Muslim settlers into the area, were reported to have sought refuge in India. Bangladesh agreed in August 1986 to repatriate the refugees, but continuing clashes between the tribals and the government caused even more tribals to flee into India.

Nepal. Few specific issues arose between India and Nepal in 1986. But the relationship remained somewhat strained by the enduring conflict between India's determination to maintain Nepal as a secure buffer between itself and China and Nepal's effort to achieve greater autonomy from India. Totally landlocked and dependent on India for trade and transit, Nepal has sought for many years to resist Indian domination. But the interpenetration of the Nepalese and Indian economies and India's ability to interfere in Nepali politics have made this quest difficult.

The key issue in Indo-Nepali relations has been the 1950 treaty of peace and friendship between the two countries which requires them to consult with each other in the event of a threat to the security of either. Nepal regards other provisions of the treaty, such as those dealing with citizenship and national treatment, as discriminatory. Nepal has also sought to modify its special security relationship with India by proposing that Nepal be made a "zone of peace."

Cross-border movement is another problem in Indo-Nepali relations which became more salient in 1986. An estimated 500,000 Nepalis cross the border into India each year to find work. Many settle permanently. But they are not able to acquire Indian citizenship and the economic benefits it confers. In 1986 ethnic Nepalis in the Darjeeling area of West Bengal state formed the Gurkha National Liberation Front (GNLF) to agitate for the political rights of Nepalis in India, including a separate state of Gurkhaland. While the government of Nepal did not become publicly involved, this development created a potential new source of tension in Indo-Nepali relations. In September, for instance, the chief minister of West Bengal state asked the central government to tighten border security in order to prevent Nepalis from crossing the frontier to join GNLF demonstrations.

Regional Cooperation

Considering the tensions and setbacks in India's relations with its regional neighbors during 1986, the continued gradual progress toward a framework for regional cooperation in South Asia was surprising and welcome. The South Asian Association for Regional Cooperation (SAARC) is an initiative toward which India remained fundamentally ambivalent, but the opportunities provided by the second SAARC summit in November 1986 to deal with bilateral problems demonstrated one of the advantages of the association.

The original proposal to create a cooperative framework in South Asia was made by President Ziaur Rahman of Bangladesh in 1980. The idea did not gain acceptance very quickly, even though South Asia was the last major world region not to have a regional association. The smaller states welcomed the proposal but India and Pakistan were initially suspicious. India feared that a regional framework would be used by the smaller states to gang up on it. Pakistan feared that India would use any framework to assert its dominance in this region. Both countries were eventually persuaded to join in a series of meetings at the foreign secretary level, beginning in 1981, to design a program of regional cooperation. In August 1983 the foreign ministers of the seven countries (including Bhutan and the Maldives as well as the five examined in this chapter) met to approve a framework for cooperation in nine fields: agriculture, rural development, planning, health, education, transportation, telecommunications, sports, and culture (a tenth field, women and development, was added in 1986). After additional preparatory meetings, SAARC was formally established at a summit meeting in Dhaka in December 1985.

The SAARC program is mainly technical and nonpolitical. At India's behest, two principles of operation were adopted. First, all decisions would be unanimous. Second, SAARC would not deal with bilateral and contentious issues. Both principles were obviously intended to prevent the smaller states from embarrassing India in SAARC. However, this has not prevented SAARC from being used indirectly to deal with bilateral issues, as when Gandhi met separately with Jayewardene and Junejo on the occasion of the 1986 SAARC summit. In fact, had the 1986 summit not occurred, it is difficult to imagine how the three leaders could have justified the meeting to their countrymen at a time of high tension. The constructive outcomes of these "side meetings," especially the Gandhi-Junejo meeting at Bangalore, illustrate the usefulness of a forum which brings South Asian leaders together periodically.

The development of SAARC will be gradual and limited in scope for the foreseeable future. But the much expanded contacts among working-level officials and scholars which are now the essence of the SAARC process will in time have a constructive effect on perceptions in the region. Ultimately, however, the success of SAARC will depend most upon improvement of India's political relations with its neighbors.

India and China

After several years of slow but steady improvement, Sino-Indian relations took a marked turn for the worse in 1986. This was most evident in renewed confrontation over the highly sensitive border issue between the two countries. By early spring 1987 tensions had escalated into a military buildup on the disputed northeastern border and some observers were comparing the deterioration in Sino-Indian relations to the events that preceded the 1962 war between the two countries.

The renewed crisis in Sino-Indian relations had its origin in the 1962 war. In that conflict Chinese troops captured disputed territory in both the northwestern region known as Aksai Chin and the northeastern region now known in India as Arunachal Pradesh. In the northeast the Chinese eventually pulled back their troops to the Chinese side of the boundary claimed by India, the MacMahon line, although they continued to claim a large amount of territory on the Indian side of the MacMahon line. The fact that the MacMahon line was never demarcated on the ground left further room for dispute.

The Indian military humiliation in 1962 forged a deep and bitter hostility toward China in India, and gave the conflict with China a place in Indian attitudes and policies second only to that with Pakistan. At least until recently, the force of Indian public opinion vis-a-vis China has clearly limited Indian flexibility on the border issue. Indeed, Sino-Indian relations remained frozen for almost fifteen years while India continued to strengthen its military forces on the border with China.

China's opening to the West in the mid-1970s produced a mild thaw in Sino-Indian relations, beginning with Prime Minister Indira Gandhi's decision in 1976 to raise diplomatic relations to the ambassadorial level. The Chinese and Indian approaches to further normalization were different, however. China wanted to set aside the border dispute and concentrate on improving other ties. India wanted to focus first on the border question. By 1981 India and China were able to agree to begin talks on the border while simultaneously developing relations in other areas. In the border talks, however, India and China still could not agree how to proceed. China wanted to move toward a package deal in which India would accept China's claim in the northwest in exchange for China accepting India's claim in the northeast. India rejected such a compromise at the outset and insisted on a "sector-by-sector" approach. This basic difference persisted until the sixth session of the talks in November 1985 when the Chinese negotiators agreed to a sector-by-sector approach.

The change in the Chinese position apparently masked a deeper change of mind with respect to the border dispute with India. At the 1985 session, the Chinese pushed their claim to territory in the northeast for the first time in several years. The harder Chinese line was further signalled by Chinese "intrusions" across the MacMahon line at Sumdurong Chu in June 1986, a month before the seventh round of the border talks was due to open in Beijing. The border talks took place on 21-23 July as scheduled but accomplished nothing.

At first the Indian government seemed to be caught off guard by these developments. In July and August officials of India's external affairs ministry made contradictory statements to Parliament concerning Chinese military activities in the northeast, including the reported construction of a helipad on the Indian side of the MacMahon line. By September, however, India was seeking to dampen the Indian public reaction to the Chinese activities and was emphasizing the use of political channels to deal with border incidents.

Two months later the Indian government took a dramatic step that further heightened the tension with China. In December the Indian Parliament passed a bill changing Arunachal Pradesh from a union territory into a full fledged state. China vigorously protested this move as evidence of India's intransigence on the border issue. Later that month, India reported that Chinese troops were not withdrawing from the positions along the border that would normally be abandoned in winter. In the spring of 1987 both sides greatly strengthened their military deployments on the northeastern border, raising fears of a new border war.

Various observers offered different interpretations for the dramatic worsening of the Sino-Indian border dispute. Indian analysts agreed that China was taking a tougher position on the border question and reinforcing the seriousness of its claim to territory in the northeast. They speculated that China had decided it did not want to settle the border dispute after all or at least wanted to raise the price that India would have to pay for a settlement. One reason offered for such a change in Chinese attitudes was the recent improvement in Sino-Soviet relations which would have strengthened the Chinese hand vis-a-vis India.

India's own hard line was also seen by some observers as a test of the limits of the improvement in Sino-Soviet relations, perhaps even an effort to derail it. That the Indian decision to grant statehood to Arunachal Pradesh followed soon after Soviet leader Gorbachev's visit to New Delhi, during which he refused to side with India against China, is perhaps a coincidence and perhaps not. Finally, it was suggested that Rajiv Gandhi might have been seeking to bolster his domestic political position by rallying Indian public opinion around a threat from China. As 1986 ended, however, the real reasons for the renewed Sino-Indian border confrontation remained obscure.

Sino-Indian relations in 1986 were troubled also by developments in China's ties with Pakistan and India's ties with Vietnam. These triangular relationships, which illustrate well the principle in international relations that "the enemy of my enemy is my friend", have long been irritants in the India-China relationship. China has provided military and economic assistance to Pakistan since the late 1960s, while India's early support of the Vietnamese-backed Heng Samrin regime in Kampuchea angered China. In 1986 a new nuclear cooperation agreement between China and Pakistan was strongly protested by India, and India's role in attempting to find a diplomatic solution to the Kampuchean situation was not welcomed by China.

Behind all the geopolitical maneuvering between India and China, it must be emphasized, is not just calculation of short-term advantages, but also a sense of long-term rivalry. That rivalry, which was submerged in the early and mid-1980s, now seems to be prominent again.

India and the Superpowers

During 1986 India continued its policy of remaining basically independent of either superpower while seeking maximum advantage in its relations with both. In practice, this has meant a closer relationship with the Soviet Union than with the United States, based primarily on the greater convergence of Indian and Soviet interests on the Subcontinent. While the fundamentals of India's relationship with the Soviet Union were unchanged in 1986, some uncertainty about the future, and perhaps even some anxiety in Indian thinking, were introduced by developments in Sino-Soviet relations and their possible implications for Soviet support of India's security interests. At the same time, efforts to improve Indo-US relations were endangered by persistent disagreements on US security policy in South Asia. As a result, India's prized maneuverability between the superpowers seemed to have narrowed.

Relations with the Soviet Union

The central event of Indo-Soviet relations in 1986 was the November visit to India of Soviet leader Mikhail Gorbachev. The importance of India to the Soviet Union was reflected in the fact that this was Gorbachev's first state visit outside the Soviet bloc. The importance of the Soviet Union to India was indicated by the unprecedented welcome extended to the general secretary and by the ten hours of talks between Gorbachev and Rajiv Gandhi (including three and a half hours of private talks). The affinity of Indian and Soviet views on global issues such as disarmament were reaffirmed in the so-called Delhi Declaration. While no new arms supply deals were announced, the Soviets offered a $1.3 billion credit to expand the economic ties between the two countries.

At the same time the visit demonstrated the limits of Indo-Soviet relations. Mr. Gorbachev failed to persuade Rajiv Gandhi to endorse his call for an Asian-Pacific security conference. India, sensitized by Gorbachev's July 1986 speech at Vladivostok which seemed to give greater importance to China and Japan than to India, failed to obtain clear assurances that the Soviet Union would assist India in a conflict with Pakistan or China. Gorbachev's advice that India should improve its relations with its two adversaries reportedly unnerved many Indian officials, especially in view of the rising tensions described above. In general, however, India in 1986 continued to look upon the Soviet Union as, in Rajiv Gandhi's words, "an old, tried and trusted friend."

India's close relationship with the Soviet Union has been largely a function of India's regional security concerns and of international developments which thrust the two nations together. The relationship began to develop in the mid-1950s in the context of the newly established security ties between the United States and Pakistan under the SEATO and CENTO pacts, the appeal of the socialist path to development to Indian planners (including Nehru), and Soviet willingness to assist India's flagship public sector industrial projects (which the United States and American companies spurned). Indo-Soviet ties expanded in the late 1950s and early 1960s as the Sino-Soviet rift deepened and Sino-Indian tensions increased, culminating in the 1962 border conflict. Indian purchases of Soviet arms began in 1960 but accelerated following the Sino-Indian war. Then as now Soviet terms for arms sales—price, credit facilities, and importantly, coproduction arrangements—made the Soviet Union a very attractive source. Indian dependence on the Soviet Union for arms supplies was further strengthened by the decision of US and other Western suppliers to stop arms sales following the 1965 Indo-Pakistani conflict. Although the Soviet role after the 1965 war in bringing India and Pakistan together at the Tashkent Conference led it to seek a more equidistant approach in its dealings with the two countries during the late 1960s, Soviet economic and military assistance to India continued to expand.

The high point of Indo-Soviet relations was reached in 1971 with the signing of the Indo-Soviet treaty of peace and friendship. India, concerned about the deteriorating situation in then East Pakistan and prompted by the dramatic opening of US-China contacts, sought to enlist the Soviet Union as a counterweight to China and the US in the event India again had to go to war with Pakistan over Bangladesh, as in fact it did in late 1971. The very effective Soviet support given to India during the Bangladesh war greatly underscored Indian perceptions of the Soviet Union as a reliable friend. However, both the limitations of the 1971 treaty, which committed the parties only to consultation in the event of threats to each other's security, and India's insistence on maintaining its independence of action, meant that the basic character of the Indo-Soviet relationship did not substantially change after 1971. Moreover, with India's regional predominance confirmed by the Bangladesh conflict and US interests in the Subcontinent at a low, the 1970s were a period of relatively low superpower involvement in the region.

The Soviet invasion of Afghanistan in December 1979 dramatically changed the South Asian regional security environment. But, to the surprise of some observers, it had relatively little effect on the Indo-Soviet relationship except to reinforce India's reliance on the USSR for arms supplies. India's expressed concern has been the renewed security ties between Pakistan and the United States brought about by the Afghan crisis, rather than the implications for its own security of Soviet troops at the Khyber Pass. Although India has called periodically for the withdrawal of foreign troops from Afghanistan, it has generally supported the Soviet position in Afghanistan in international fora, repaying in kind similar Soviet support for India in 1971 and 1965.

Nor has the extraordinary continuity of Indo-Soviet relations over the past thirty years been significantly disturbed by changes in the Indian leadership. Although the Janata government (1977-1979) expressed its desire for "genuine nonalignment," there was little if any effect on the actual conduct of relations with the Soviet Union. Rajiv Gandhi, despite his well-known interest in Western technology and market-oriented economies, visited Moscow twice during his first year in office.

The continuity of Indo-Soviet relations also owes much to the strength of the military and economic ties which have developed between the two countries. Since 1965 an estimated 75 percent of India's arms imports have come from the Soviet Union (90 percent during the 1970s). Despite India's efforts to diversify its arms supplies since the late 1970s, the Soviet Union has delivered to India over $4.0 billion worth of military equipment since 1980 alone. While no major new arms purchases were announced in 1986, the first deliveries of MIG-29 fighter aircraft (India is the only foreign country so far to receive this top-of-the-line plane) and Kilo class submarines were received in 1986. India also announced that it would be the first non-Warsaw Pact country to receive Soviet MI-26 helicopters.

The economic dimension of the Indo-Soviet relationship has become surprisingly important but is troubled by disparities between these two economies. The new $1.3 billion Soviet credit announced during Gorbachev's 1986 visit is to be used largely for the modernization of projects originally sponsored by the Soviet Union and for new projects in areas such as power generation and oil exploration. But the utilization of the credit is likely to be limited by Indian preferences for technologies that the Soviets can't provide. A prominent example of this problem in 1986 was India's decision to decline a Soviet offer of a nuclear power plant because its technology was outmoded and unsafe.

Indo-Soviet trade, which is conducted on a rupee-ruble exchange basis, has been hampered by the very limited Indian market for Soviet goods. The trade has been dominated by an exchange of Indian consumer goods for Soviet crude oil and petroleum products (the latter comprised 70 percent of non-military Soviet exports to India in 1985). Because of the drop in oil prices, Indo-Soviet trade in 1985-86 fell 25 percent short of the targeted amount. However, Indo-Soviet trade has acquired considerable political support in India because a large number of Indian enterprises are producing consumer goods for the Soviet market which could not easily be sold in the Indian market or in other foreign markets.

As 1986 drew to a close the only major uncertainty in Indo-Soviet relations arose from possible future developments in Sino-Soviet relations. As mentioned above, efforts by the Indian press to pin down Gorbachev during his visit to Delhi on the subject of Soviet support for India in a Sino-Indian conflict, and his coyness in response indicated the great sensitivity to a possible shift in Soviet policy. The absence of a Soviet comment on the Chinese intrusion at Sumdorong Chu in June 1986 provided some evidence of a possible slight movement in Soviet policy. But whether this develops into a significant, not to mention dramatic shift will depend on the extent and pace of change in Sino-Soviet relations. Most observers do not think Sino-Soviet rapprochement will be rapid. This prospect, and the impediments to closer Indo-US relations, to which we now turn, suggest that the Indo-Soviet relationship is not likely to change substantially in the foreseeable future.

Relations with the United States

As in other areas of Indian life, 1986 opened with considerable optimism toward relations with the United States. The 1985-86 annual report of India's ministry of external affairs, issued in March 1986, noted that US-India relations were marked by greater understanding and cooperation. In the same month Prime Minister Rajiv Gandhi expressed the hope that relations between the two countries would continue to grow closer.

But 1986 turned out to be a year of two steps backward for each step forward in Indo-US relations. Efforts to develop stronger ties in the economic and military areas were offset by increasingly sharp disagreements over the more central question of US involvement in South Asian security affairs, particularly its security ties to Pakistan. Against a background of long and sometimes bitter distrust, these renewed irritations together with Rajiv Gandhi's domestic vulnerability produced an atmosphere which by year's end approached the sour low points that followed the Soviet invasion of Afghanistan and the Bangladesh war.

Similarly sharp swings in Indo-US relations have in the past led observers to compare the relationship to a roller coaster. The principal cause of the ups and downs has been the match or mismatch of Indian and US geopolitical interests in the region. India has always sought to minimize US involvement in South Asia, while the US has been involved or uninvolved largely as a function of its competition with the Soviet Union. As mentioned above, Indo-US relations in the 1950s were strained by the US security ties to Pakistan under the SEATO and CENTO alliances and by the US rejection of Indian nonalignment. Relations improved after the 1962 Sino-Indian border war as the US came to regard India as a countervailing power to China. Indian wariness toward the US persisted, however, because the US weapons supplied to Pakistan were used during the 1965 Indo-Pakistani War and because following that war the US halted the modest supply of arms to India that had begun after the 1962 conflict with China.

The divergence in US and Indian security interests widened in 1971 with the signing of the Indo-Soviet treaty, the US opening to China, and the US "tilt" toward Pakistan in the Bangladesh War. The mid- and late 1970s, however, saw Indo-US relations return to a more even keel as a result of India's regional predominance and the downgrading of US interest in the region.

The Soviet invasion of Afghanistan made South Asia once again an arena of intense US-Soviet competition and sent the Indo-US roller coaster diving down again. India has viewed the renewed United States-Pakistan security relationship, in particular the supply of arms to Pakistan under the five-year, $3.2 billion aid package launched in 1981, as unwarranted and destabilizing interference in the region. The US views its assistance to Pakistan, including 40 advanced F-16 aircraft, as necessary support to a "front-line state," and argues that its military transfers to Pakistan are intended for use on the Afghan border and do not in any event significantly alter the India-Pakistan military equation. India objects that more than the arms per se, the US relationship is destabilizing because it signals or may be seen by Pakistan to signal a US commitment to Pakistan in the event of a conflict with India. Since 1981 the United States has not gone out of its way to disabuse India of this notion. Finally, India links US support for Pakistan to larger US strategic objectives in the Indian Ocean. India views the Indian Ocean region as lying within its rightful (if not actual) sphere of influence and has objected vociferously to the buildup of US military facilities at Diego Garcia and of US naval forces in the Indian Ocean.

Several developments during 1986 gave an even sharper edge to Indo-US differences over regional security. First, as has been described above, the deterioration of India-Pakistan relations focused greater attention on the US role in Pakistan. Second, the Reagan Administration proposed to bring forward for Congressional approval a new, six-year, $4.2 billion aid package including additional F-16s and M-60 tanks. Third, Indian suspicions that the United States has sought bases in

Pakistan in exchange for its aid were given some substance by reports that Pakistan had provided to the US a site for intelligence-gathering facilities near Pakistan's border with the Soviet Union. It was also admitted by the US that American P-3 antisubmarine aircraft were using Pakistani facilities, although not on a permanent basis. The seriousness of India's concern over the US buildup in the Indian Ocean and of its claim to influence in the region was indicated in October 1986 when it announced plans to build its third naval base, at Karwar on the western Indian coast. By the time the base is completed in the late 1990s it is expected to be the largest in Asia.

Perhaps the most inflammatory development in Indo-US relations during 1986 was US Defense Secretary Caspar Weinberger's announcement that the US would consider providing airborne warning and control systems (AWACS) to Pakistan. Pakistan had requested the AWACS to help fend off cross-border attacks by Afghan aircraft. The announcement rankled Indians all the more because it was made during Weinberger's October visit to Pakistan, immediately following his visit to India, the first ever by a US defense secretary. Indian analysts argued that the AWACS would not be very useful along the mountainous Pakistan-Afghan border and were instead intended for use against India. At year's end it was not clear whether the US would provide AWACS to Pakistan, and if it did, what kind and whether on a lease or sale basis, but it was clear that the possibility had greatly intensified Indo-US differences.

Finally, the evidence in 1986 of an impending Pakistani nuclear capability added to the strains in Indo-US relations. Some India observers saw the US willingness to proceed with a new and larger aid package despite Pakistan's nuclear program as indicative at best of US hypocrisy on nuclear nonproliferation and at worst of a tacit US signal to Pakistan that it could proceed in its nuclear program, at least up to the point of testing, with impunity.

In the background of these security-related difficulties in Indo-US relations were more familiar differences on global and other regional political issues. During 1986 Indian officials including the prime minister and the external affairs minister frequently criticized US policies and actions on disarmament, Nicaragua, Libya, South Africa, and the Indian Ocean. As a Third World leader, India has long been critical of the US in several areas, usually without much impact on bilateral relations, but the tension in 1986 reached a point where US Secretary of State George Shultz and Indian External Affairs Minister Shiv Shankar, meeting in New York in September, felt the need to jointly affirm that mutual differences on global issues should not be taken as animosity.

Table 7.1
Foreign Collaborations Approved
by the Government of India, 1981-1985

	Total	With US Companies Number	With US Companies % of Total
1981	389	85	21.9
1982	591	110	18.6
1983	673	134	19.9
1984	752	147	19.5
1985	1024	197	19.2
Total/Avg.	3429	673	19.6

Sources: Indian Investment Center, New York; Business International, New York

Beginning in 1982 with then Prime Minister Indira Gandhi's visit to the US, both India and the US have sought to improve Indo-US bilateral relations and at least to limit the damage to the relationship being caused by differences in regional security matters. For its part the Reagan Administration has emphasized strengthening Indo-US economic and military ties—especially in the high technology areas of greatest interest to India—in the hope of offsetting the negative impact of geopolitical differences. While there has been some progress in both areas, it has been difficult and slow and may have inherent limitations.

Much of the attention devoted to enhancing Indo-US economic ties in recent years has focused on increasing joint ventures between American and Indian companies. The US Embassy in India announced in 1986 that about 850 active joint ventures, a majority of them formed in the two previous years, had made the US the number one new investor in India. Other data (Table 7.1) make it clear that Indo-US collaborations have expanded regularly over the last several years. But it is also apparent that the US share of new collaborations has not increased, which suggests that these ties are not likely to become a major influence on overall Indo-US relations.

American collaboration and sales in the high technology area will also continue to be constrained by the proprietary nature of American technology and by US restrictions on dual-use technology transfer. A very visible example of the latter difficulty was the US decision in early 1987, after more than two years of intensive debate within the US government and negotiations with India, to sell a Cray supercomputer to the Government of India. Despite the December 1986 agreement on safeguards for the supercomputer sale, the US finally approved a less than state-of-the-art machine out of concern that the technology would leak to the Soviets. At this writing, India had not indicated that it would accept the inferior machine.

Overall trade between India and the US has grown in recent years. The US and the Soviet Union have periodically swapped places as India's number one trading partner and India in 1984-85 had a small trade surplus with the US. But the relatively small US share of Indian imports and the likely slow growth of Indian exports suggest that trade will not soon carry much weight in Indo-US relations.

The newest element in Indo-US relations is the cautious interest on both sides in establishing a defense supply link. For years such a relationship has been stymied by US policies on arms supply to the Subcontinent, by US restrictions on the sale of defense technology to India, by US terms (coproduction, price, and credit) unacceptable to India, and by India's perception of the US as an unreliable supplier. But the Reagan Administration's determination to develop this opening to India, symbolized by Secretary Weinberger's October 1986 visit, and Indian interest in US military technology have led to some breakthroughs. In 1986 the US approved the sale of GE404 engines for India's indigenously developed light combat aircraft. Other significant transfers have included GE turbines for Indian Navy frigates, radars, and night vision devices. Preparations were being made for other Indian purchases. By November 1986 twenty US military teams had visited India in as many months to discuss India's defense needs. And, according to the US Defense Department, over 300 requests for approval of defense-related technology sales were received from India during the past few years, 92 percent of which were approved.

The defense supply relationship is unlikely, however, to become a panacea for Indo-US relations. India still regards the US as an unreliable supplier and thus is emphasizing the transfer of defense technology rather than weapons systems. The US will continue to be selective in its release of military or dual-use technology. The Soviet Union will continue for the foreseeable future to supply the staples of Indian defense requirements on terms that the US cannot match. Most importantly, such a necessarily limited defense relationship cannot to any great degree compensate for the deep differences on security and political matters that now divide the two countries. Indeed, it will likely remain hostage to these differences. One skeptical Indian observer, writing in the *Times of India* following Defense Secretary Weinberger's visit to Delhi, argued that in the absence of change in US policies toward South Asia, the US effort to draw India into an arms supply relationship was merely "an invitation to bleed ourselves to death."

India and the Rest of the World

Although South Asia and the superpowers have always been the first and second priorities respectively in Indian foreign policy, India has also consistently pursued an omnidirectional policy aimed at expanding its global influence. Through its relations with the Third World, Europe, and the Middle East especially, India seeks to enhance the effectiveness of its policy of nonalignment and to acquire a status commensurate with its present and future roles. India's conduct of its relations in these parts of the international community during 1986 were not marred by the same kinds of difficulties that India encountered in its own region. But the regional difficulties undercut somewhat the effectiveness of India's wider policies.

The Third World has always had a very prominent place in India's foreign relations. India has vigorously sought leadership roles in Third World organizations and has spoken out forcefully on Third World issues. India's chairmanship of the Nonaligned Movement (NAM), which Rajiv Gandhi inherited from his mother and relinquished in September 1986, exemplified this leadership. Rajiv Gandhi also spoke out frequently on issues of importance to the Third World such as disarmament and apartheid. Gandhi attended the nonaligned disarmament conference in Mexico in August 1986, visited the front-line states of southern Africa in May and advocated sanctions against South Africa in the Commonwealth mini-summit in August. India boycotted the Commonwealth games to indicate its solidarity with South Africa and was the first nation to permit the Southwest Africa People's Organization (SWAPO) to establish an embassy.

Europe has become a higher priority in India's foreign relations over the last 10-15 years. India has sought these ties as a way of diversifying its relations with the West away from the United States, and balancing its relations with the Soviet Union. The Western European countries have also become increasingly important sources of economic cooperation and arms supply. During 1986 four European leaders visited India, including Chancellor Helmut Kohl of West Germany (which has supplied India with submarines and other advanced military equipment). Actually, the most difficult of India's relations with Europe were those with its former colonial power, the United Kingdom. Indo-British relations were plagued by the issues of Sikh terrorists based in

Britain and the new British regulations governing immigration by Indians.

Also very important in India's foreign policy has been its links with the Arab nations. India has assiduously cultivated these relationships in an effort to limit automatic Arab support for Pakistan, as well as to protect its access to Persian Gulf oil. During 1986 the prime minister of the People's Democratic Republic of Yemen, the Iranian foreign minister and the king and queen of Jordan visited India, while the Indian external affairs minister visited Iran, Iraq, Kuwait, and Bahrain.

Until recently, India has not given much attention to its relations with East Asia other than China. But this has been changing as India has sought economic advantage in its relations with Japan and Korea and political advantage in its relations with Southeast Asia. Over the period 1981/82 to 1984/85 India's total trade with Japan grew more rapidly than that with any other country, and in June 1986 India and Japan signed an agreement to further expand trade and joint ventures. And in October 1986 Rajiv Gandhi travelled to Indonesia, Australia, New Zealand and Thailand where he offered India as a mediator in the Kampuchean crisis and praised New Zealand for its anti-nuclear stand.

Conclusion: Narrowing Options

India's foreign relations in 1986 were marked overall by narrowing options and increasing defensiveness. India's national security seemed at greater risk than it had just a year or two before. The establishment of a stable, positive regional order so necessary to Indian security in the longer term appeared more distant. Among the main causes of these trends were India's deteriorating relations with its South Asian neighbors, greater uncertainty regarding Chinese, Soviet and US approaches to the region, and the increasing subordination of foreign policy to domestic politics.

India's foreign policy resources remain impressive, however. Its size and geography, a diversified and robust economy, leadership in international fora, military strength, and a wealth of human talent in diplomacy and other fields could all be tapped. In the months and years ahead, India will need all these resources as well as creative national leadership and policies to ensure that the trends of 1986 do not persist.

Suggestions for Further Reading

Rajiv Gandhi: A Mid-Term Assessment

Hardgrave, Robert Jr. and Kochanek, Stanley. *India: Government and Politics in a Developing Nation.* New York: Harcourt Brace Jovanovich, 1986.

Kohli, Atul. *The State and Poverty in India: The Politics of Reform.* New York: Cambridge University Press, 1987.

Rudolph, Lloyd I. and Rudolph, Susanne H. *In Pursuit of Lakshmi: The Political Economy of the Indian State.* Chicago: University of Chicago Press, 1987.

Mehta, Ved. *A Family Affair: India Under Three Prime Ministers.* New York: Avon Books, 1982.

Weiner, Myron. *India at the Polls, 1980.* Washington DC: American Enterprise Institute, 1983.

Politics: The Failure to Rebuild Consensus

Akbar, M. J. *The Seige Within: Challenges to a Nation's Unity.* New York: Penguin Books, 1985.

Kohli, Atul, ed. *India's Democracy: An Analysis of Changing State-Society Relations.* Princeton, NJ: Princeton University Press, 1987.

Roach, James R., ed. *India: 2000: The Next Fifteen Years.* Riverdale, MD: The Riverdale Company, 1986.

Religion and Politics

Brass, Paul. *Caste, Faction and Party Politics, Volume 1: Faction and Party*. Columbia, MO: South Asia Books, 1985.

Esposito, John L., ed. *Islam in Asia*. New York: Oxford University Press, 1987.

Kapur, Rajiv. *Sikh Separatism: The Politics of Faith*. Boston: Allen & Unwin, 1986.

Singh, Kushwant. *A History of Sikhs* (Two Volumes). Princeton, NJ: Princeton University Press, 1984.

Tully, Mark and Jacob, Satish. *Amritsar: Mrs. Gandhi's Last Battle*. London: Pan Books, 1985.

The Economy

Ahluwalia, Isher J. *Industrial Growth in India*. Delhi, India: Oxford University Press, 1985.

Bardhan, Pranab. *The Political Economy of Development in India*. New York: Oxford University Press, 1984.

Society

Centre for Science and Enviornment. *The State of India's Environment, 1982: A Citizens' Report*. Delhi: 1982.

Galanter, Marc. *Competing Equalities: Law and the Backward Classes in India*. Berkeley: University of California Press, 1984.

Kakar, Sudhir. *The Inner World: A Psycho-Analytic Study of Childhood and Society in India*. New York: Oxford University Press, 1978.

Sakala, Carol. *Women of South Asia: A Guide to Resources*. Millwood, NY: Kraus International Publications, 1980.

Culture

Barnouw, Erik and Krishnaswamy, S. *Indian Film*. 2nd Ed. New York: Oxford University Press, 1980.

Dimock, Edward C., et al. *The Literature of India: An Introduction*. Chicago: University of Chicago Press, 1978.

Vatsyayan, Kapila M. *Some Aspects of Cultural Policies in India.* UNESCO, 1972.

Vatsyayan, Kapila M. *Traditional Indian Theater: Multiple Streams.* New Delhi, 1980.

Foreign Relations: Elusive Regional Security

Bhargava, G. S. *South Asian Security after Afghanistan.* Lexington, MA: Lexington Books, 1983.

George, Timothy, Litwak, Robert and Chubin, Shahram. *Security in Southern Asia 2: India and the Great Powers.* Hampshire, England: Gower Publishing Company, Ltd., 1984.

Thomas, Raju G. C. *Indian Security Policy.* Princeton, NJ: Princeton University Press, 1986.

Ziring, Lawrence, ed. *The Subcontinent in World Politics: India, Its Neighbors and the Great Powers.* New York: Praeger Publishers, 1982.

1986: A Chronology

JANUARY

10 India and Pakistan sign a bilateral economic cooperation document after talks between the finance ministers of each country in Islamabad. Pakistan agrees to allow the trade of forty-two items in the private sector.

13 The defense secretaries of India and Pakistan meet in Islamabad to begin work on an accord to end two years of clashes on the disputed Siachen glacier in Kashmir.

18 India and Pakistan exchange draft agreements pledging not to attack each other's nuclear installations. This step follows an informal, oral understanding reached between Prime Minister Rajiv Gandhi and President Zia-ul Haq of Pakistan, during their meeting on 17 December 1985.

19 Gandhi dismisses three ministers and appoints them to top posts in the Congress (I) party. Arjun Singh (commerce minister) is appointed to the position of Congress vice president.

22 Three Sikhs are convicted and sentenced to death for the October 1984 assassination of Prime Minister Indira Gandhi.

Written by Owen M. Crowley and edited by Marshall M. Bouton.

25 The scheduled transfer of Chandigarh, the joint capital of Punjab and Haryana states, to Punjab is deferred because of the failure of the two states to agree on which areas would be transferred to Haryana in exchange. Under the 1985 Punjab peace accord, Chandigarh is to be made the capital of Punjab, alone.

26 Sikh extremists seize control of the Golden Temple and begin dismantling the Akal Takht (the holy seat of temporal authority), deeming the government's 1985 reconstruction of the shrine sacrilegious. The shrine had been damaged during a 1984 military operation to rout extremists from the Golden Temple.

31 The Government of India announces price rises in petroleum products in an effort to stem rising oil imports and reduce the trade deficit. In response to protest, Prime Minister Gandhi reduces price increases on 5 February.

FEBRUARY

1 Pope John Paul II begins a ten day tour of India.

The doors of the Babri Mosque in Ayodhya, Uttar Pradesh are opened after thirty-five years by court order. The mosque, known to Hindus as Ram Janmabhoomi Temple, had been closed because of a dispute between Muslims who claim it as a mosque and Hindus who believe it to mark the birthplace of Rama. Communal violence in three states follows the reopening.

7 India and the United States agree on the sale of $500 million worth of computers and technology from Control Data Corporation. Approval of technology transfers has been a central issue in Indo-US relations.

25 The government introduces a bill into Parliament limiting Muslim men's financial responsiblity to women after divorce to three months' support. The bill is intended to placate the Muslim community after the Supreme Court ruled in the 1985 Shah Bano case that a wealthy lawyer was required to support partially his estranged wife. The bill is passed by both houses on 9 May, generating much comment and criticism.

27 Minister of External Affairs B .R. Bhagat characterizes the Sri Lankan government's actions against Tamils as "having all the elements of genocide" and demands that Sri Lanka reach a settlement with Tamil guerrillas within a month. A heated series of diplomatic exchanges follows, and on 6 March the Indian Cricket Board announces that India's team will not attend the Asia Cup matches in Colombo.

28 Finance Minister Vishwanath Pratap Singh presents a $40 billion budget to Parliament for the 1986/1987 fiscal year starting 1 April. As compared to the 1985/86 budget, the emphasis is placed more on poverty alleviation, agriculture and rural programs. Taxes on luxury items are increased.

MARCH

7 Central rule is imposed in the state of Jammu and Kashmir. Congress (I) officials say that this is in response to a breakdown of law and order against which state Chief Minister Shah failed to take action. Central rule involves the dissolution of the state legislature and the direct rule of the center-appointed governor.

15 Prime Minister Gandhi travels to Sweden for funeral of slain Swedish premier Olof Palme.

24 The Government of India rejects a $350 million settlement offer by Union Carbide Corp. for claims arising from the 1984 gas leak in Bhopal.

30 United Kingdom Foreign Secretary Sir Geoffrey Howe visits India. Discussions center on India's desire for a strong treaty to facilitate the extradition of Britain-based Sikh militants.

APRIL

3 Prime Minister Gandhi establishes a new commission to resolve the dispute between Punjab and Haryana over the transfer of their joint capital, Chandigarh, to Punjab.

8 Prime Minister Gandhi declares that if Pakistan acquires a nuclear weapon, India would have to "seriously think" of its nuclear options.

9 Newly appointed Punjab Police Commissioner Julio Ribeiro demonstrates a new hard-line policy by vowing to take four lives for every police officer killed by Sikh extremists. This follows the killing of five officers by extremists on 5 April.

Intensified violence in Punjab in March and April results in 120 deaths by 5 April. The strategy of extremists is changing from attacking Sikh moderates to attacking Hindus, apparently in order to encourage Hindu out-migration and Sikh in-migration.

15 Prime Minister Gandhi strongly criticizes the US attack on Libya.

29 An official Indian delegation begins a six-day visit to Sri Lanka to discuss possibilities for settling the ethnic strife in that country.

30 Central government commandos raid the Golden Temple and seize it from Sikh extremists, who took it over in January. In contrast to the 1984 raid, the action meets little resistance and only two are killed. The raid splits Sikh moderates. Chief Minister Surjit Singh Barnala is later ordered by Golden Temple high priests to do penance for ordering the raid.

MAY

12 Gurkhas (ethnic Nepalis who emigrated to India after 1950) riot in the West Bengal city of Darjeeling in protest against alleged discrimination.

Prime Minister Gandhi reshuffles cabinet.

14 Prime Minister Gandhi begins a five-day official tour of southern Africa, visiting Angola, Tanzania, Zambia and Zimbabwe. He expresses India's solidarity with the front-line states and calls for an end to apartheid.

15 President Giani Zail Singh orders the suppression of the Thakar Commission report on Indira Gandhi's assassination, citing security considerations.

25 Visiting British Labour Party leader Neil Kinnock discusses possible terrorism among Britain's Sikhs, Commonwealth sanctions against South Africa, and new, more restrictive British immigration statutes.

JUNE

21 The transfer of the city of Chandigarh to the sole control of Punjab is postponed for a second time because of difficulties stemming from Punjab's governing Akali Dal party's insistence that only predominantly Hindu areas of Punjab be traded for the capital. A new transfer date is set for 15 July. Sikhs and Hindus riot and violence in Punjab reaches an all time high.

25 Mizoram rebel leader Laldenga of the Mizo National Front agrees to end the group's twenty-year insurgency in return for statehood for Mizoram. Mizoram is in the northeastern part of India, bordering Burma.

28 Congress (I) wins all of the thirty Rajya Sabha (upper house of Parliament) seats it contests in elections.

JULY

5 Akali Dal dissidents who split with the party following the 30 April Golden Temple raid elect their own party president, Parkash Singh Badal.

Prime Minister Gandhi arrives in Mauritius for a two day visit. He calls for the dismantling of US bases in Diego Garcia and mandatory sanctions against South Africa.

10 The transfer of Chandigarh is deferred for the third time because of difficulties in attaining agreement between Punjab and Haryana on the areas to be exchanged. At year's end, the transfer still has not taken place.

15 The death toll in Hindu/Muslim rioting in Gujarat reaches fifty. The violence is attributed to long-standing communal tension and to caste conflicts over access to education and government employment.

17 A consortium of international donors meeting in Paris pledges $4.5 billion in aid for India for the 1986/1987 fiscal year, a sixteen percent increase over the previous year.

21 The seventh round of Sino-Indian border talks begins despite Indian accusations that China has recently intruded into Indian territory in the northeast. The two countries fought a war over the demarcation of the Sino-Indian border in 1962, and the issue has since been the chief obstacle to improved Sino-Indian relations.

25 Fourteen Hindu bus passengers in Punjab are separated from the other passengers and killed by four Sikh

gunmen. News of the attack leads to anti-Sikh riots in Delhi.

AUGUST

2 Prime Minister Gandhi arrives in London to attend a "mini-summit" of seven non-aligned nations. India and five others decide to impose fresh sanctions on South Africa. Gandhi leaves 5 August for a Mexico summit on nuclear disarmament.

10 Lt. General Arun S. Vaidya, former Indian army chief of staff who oversaw the 1984 Operation Bluestar raid on the Golden Temple, is killed in Pune, Maharashtra by four gunmen. A Sikh terrorist group claims responsibility.

13 The central government through new legislation acquires control over law enforcement in Punjab, Gujarat, Rajasthan, and Jammu and Kashmir. The government also announces its intention to create a five kilometer-wide militarized border zone to stop Pakistan from aiding Sikh terrorists.

SEPTEMBER

1 The eighth summit of the Nonaligned Movement begins in Harare, Zimbabwe. Prime Minister Gandhi steps down from his post as chairman of the Movement at the end of his term.

5 Arab terrorists storm a Pan American airlines flight in Karachi that originated in Bombay. Twenty-one people are killed, most of them Indian citizens. Prime Minister Gandhi strongly criticizes Pakistan's handling of the attack.

9 Nicaraguan President Ortega arrives in India for a three-day visit.

OCTOBER

2 Prime Minister Gandhi escapes an assassination attempt in old Delhi. On 10 October, Gandhi cites evidence that Pakistan-based Sikh terrorists were involved.

3 US Secretary of Defense Weinberger arrives in India for a visit. Talks focus on technology transfers. Weinberger asserts that the decision to sell a supercomputer to India has been made "in principle." He leaves for Pakistan on 14 October, where he announces that airborne warning and control systems (AWACS) would be provided to Pakistan. On 15 October, India awards General Electric a contract to supply ten of its F404 aircraft engines.

13 Prime Minister Gandhi begins an official tour of Indonesia, Australia, New Zealand, and Thailand. During the trip, Gandhi calls for a moratorium on nuclear testing and greater South-South cooperation.

22 In a cabinet reshuffle, Minister of Internal Security Arun Nehru, known as a hard-liner on the Punjab issue, is dropped from his post.

Prime Minister Rajiv Gandhi launches construction of India's newest and largest naval base at Karwar in Karnataka, on the western coast of India. When completed in 1995-1996, the 3,200 hectare base will reportedly be the largest in Asia.

NOVEMBER

6 Farooq Abdullah is sworn in as chief minister of Jammu and Kashmir, and the state legislature is called into session for the first time since central rule was declared in March. Abdullah and Rajiv Gandhi agree that their parties will cooperate in running the state and in the state elections to be held in early 1987.

8 Tamil Nadu police arrest hundreds of Sri Lankan Tamil militants and seize a large cache of arms. Rebel leaders are released after a few hours' detention.

15 India begins Operation Brasstacks, a series of military maneuvers of record size near the Pakistan border. Resulting tensions reach a high point in January 1987 when the armies of India and Pakistan move to forward defensive positions.

16 The second summit meeting of the one year old South Asian Association for Regional Cooperation (SAARC) opens in Bangalore. Cooperation in development, trade and fighting terrorism are discussed. Prime Minister Rajiv Gandhi also reviews bilateral isses with Pakistan's Prime Minister Mohammed Khan Junejo and Sri Lankan President Junius Jayewardene in separate meetings.

25 Soviet leader Mikhail Gorbachev arrives in Delhi for a four-day official visit. 400 thousand people are bussed in to greet him and the day of his arrival is declared a public holiday. Prime Minister Gandhi joins Gorbachev in condemning the US strategic defense initiative and the two leaders sign the "Delhi Declaration" calling for the banning of the use or threat of use of nuclear weapons. The two countries pledge greater technological cooperation and expansion of trade.

30 Sikh militants kill twenty-four bus passengers in the Punjab district of Hoshiarpur. Demonstrations follow in New Delhi and other northern cities.

DECEMBER

1 Punjab Chief Minister Barnala orders 150 militant figures arrested, including Parkash Singh Badal (leader of a breakaway Akali Dal faction) and the newly elected leader of the Sikh Temple Management Committee, Gurcharan Singh Tohra.

4 The Government of India, under the authority of the Terrorist and Disruptive Activities (Prevention) Act, draws up rules under which the movement or presence of any person or persons may be restricted in any location declared prohibited by the government.

7 A short story published by a Bangalore newspaper touches off two days of rioting because it is perceived to be insulting to Muslims.

9 Parliament draws Chinese protests by passing a bill making the union territory of Arunachal Pradesh into a state. Parts of this northeastern territory are claimed by China and were disputed in the 1962 war between India and China.

10 During a three day visit by a US State Department representative, the United States agrees to safeguards for the sale of a supercomputer to India. Details of the agreement are kept secret.

Parliament amends the ninety-eight-year-old Indian Post Office Act to allow virtually unrestricted government access to private mail. Opposition politicians protest that the government would use its powers under the act to intercept and censor mail for partisan purposes.

20 On a visit to Darjeeling, Prime Minister Gandhi rules out the division of the state of West Bengal in order to grant autonomy to hill areas as demanded by the Gurkha National Liberation Front (GNLF). He also refuses the GNLF demand that Nepalese who settled in India after 1950 be granted citizenship.

India and Pakistan begin talks on controlling cross-border smuggling, drug trafficking and terrorism. India maintains that Pakistan offers refuge and training to Sikh terrorists.

21 The army is called out in the union territory of Goa because of clashes between Konkani and Marathi language supporters.

Glossary

Abdullah, Farooq. Chief minister of Jammu and Kashmir leader of the *National Conference* party. Son of the famed Kashmiri leader, Sheikh Abdullah, Farooq led his party in coalition with *Congress (I)* in the March 1987 state assembly elections.

Akali Dal. Ruling party in the state of Punjab until May 1987 when *President's Rule* was imposed in the state. It is associated with members of the Sikh religion.

Aksai Chin. High desert plateau northeast of Kashmir that is claimed by India but has been controlled by China since the 1962 Sino-Indian war. Disagreement over China's occupation of this area, which links Tibet to China's Xinjiang province, is a major obstacle to improvement of Sino-Indian relations.

All India Anna Dravida Munnetra Kazhagam (AIADMK). Ruling party in the state of Tamil Nadu, led by *M. G. Ramachandran.* The AIADMK stands against the adoption of Hindi as the national language of India.

All India Sikh Students Federation (AISSF). Militant Sikh student group.

Anti-Defection Bill. Bill passed by Rajiv Gandhi's government in 1985 forbidding members of Parliament and state assemblies from changing their party affiliation without standing for election again.

Apna Utsav. Government of India-sponsored national cultural festival held in New Delhi in November 1986. The festival, attended by 6000

Written by Owen M. Crowley and edited by Marshall M. Bouton.

Cross references are *italicized.*

artists from all over India, was intended to demonstrate the vibrancy and diversity of Indian culture.

Arunachal Pradesh. Formerly the North East Frontier Area, this region's status was changed from union territory to state in December 1986. China's claims to sovereignty over much of this region makes it a key element in the Sino-Indian border dispute.

Asom Gana Parishad (AGP). Ruling party in the northeastern state of Assam representing the interests of native Assamese. It was formed just before the December 1985 elections from members of the pro-Assamese All Assam Gana Sangram Parishad (AAGSP) and the All Assam Students Union (AASU).

Assam Accord. Agreement signed by Rajiv Gandhi, the AASU and the AAGSP in August 1985 to end six years of violent student agitation against immigrants to the state from neighboring Bangladesh. Under the agreement, all migrants who arrived since March 1971 were to be expelled and those who arrived since 1967 were to be deleted from the electoral rolls.

Babri Mosque. Known to Hindus as the Ramjanmabhoomi temple, this mosque was built on the site in the state of Uttar Pradesh that is believed to be the birth place of Lord Rama. Dispute over this mosque has led to recurrent violence between Hindus and Moslems.

Backward Classes. Classes recognized by the Constitution as disadvantaged and allowed remedial treatment. In practice, backward classes have been defined in terms of caste membership.

Badal, Parkash Singh. Leader of a dissident faction of the *Akali Dal* which broke off after a April 1986 raid on the *Golden Temple* by government commandos. He had previously been a supporter of the *Punjab Accord.* He was arrested for sedition in December 1986.

Baluta. Autobiography written by a *dalit,* Daya Parwar. A leading example of *dalit* literature based on the experiences of "untouchables."

Bandh. Protest through general strike or closure.

Barnala, Surjit Singh. Chief minister of the state of Punjab government from October 1985 to May 1987. His increasing inability to control violence in Punjab and dissention in the ruling *Akali Dal* party led to his removal from office through the imposition of *President's Rule.*

Bharatanatyam. Classical dance form of Tamil Nadu. The revitalization of this form in this century helped spark a general revival of classical Indian culture.

Bharatiya Janata Party (BJP). Party formed from elements of the *Jan Sangh* party, with support mainly in northern India. Its attempts to broaden its social base by taking a more secular course has cost it valuable *Rashtriya Swayamsevak Sangh* support.

Bharatiya Lok Dal (BLD). Party formed in 1974 by Congress dissidents that drew its support mainly from the backward classes of Bihar, Haryana and Uttar Pradesh.

Bhindranwale, Jarnail Singh. Sikh priest and principal leader of the militant Sikh separatists in the early 1980s. He was killed in the 1984 *Operation Bluestar* raid on the *Golden Temple.*

Bahujan Samaj Party (BSP). Party formed in 1984 representing *scheduled caste* interest. It is influential mainly in Bihar, Haryana and Uttar Pradesh.

Chakravyuha. Play by Ratan Thiyam using traditional techniques on a modern stage. This production, supported by Sangeet Natak Akademi, won high critical acclaim for helping to revive traditional Indian theater.

Chandigarh. Joint capital of the states of Punjab and Haryana. The transfer of Chandigarh to Punjab under the *Punjab Accord* was scheduled for January 1986 but has been indefinitely postponed.

Chandralekha. Contemporary *Bharatanatyam* dancer from Madras. Her philosophy of dance emphasizes the centrality of the human body in dance against the idea of "divine origin" asserted in the classical treatise on dance, the Natyasastra.

Communist Party of India (CPI). The oldest communist party in India, characterized by a pro-Soviet stance. its electoral strength has been in decline for many years and its only remaining stronghold is in the state of Kerala, where it won sixteen out of 146 Kerala state assembly seats in 1987.

Communist Party of India (Marxist) (CPI(M)). 1960s offshoot of the CPI. The CPI(M) is the ruling party in West Bengal and holds thirty-nine out of 146 state assembly seats in Kerala.

Congress (I) Party. Party of Prime Minister Rajiv Gandhi and the dominant Indian national party since Independence. Congress is the principal inheritor of the mantle of the independence movement. The "I" stands for Indira Gandhi, who led this faction after a Congress Party split in 1969.

Dalit. Literally meaning "ruined, trampled," this term has come to refer to "untouchables," or members of *scheduled castes.*

Damul. Film that won the best film award of 1985 in India. As a result of the impact of TV on box office sales for small-budget films, "*Damul*" had to be premiered on television.

Desh bachao. Phrase that literally means "save the motherland" and expressed Rajiv Gandhi's theme of national unity for the December 1984 parliamentary elections.

Doordarshan. India's state television network. No privately-owned television stations are allowed in India.

Dowry death. The killing of a woman by her husband's family in retaliation for the failure of her family to pay in full the promised amount of her dowry. This usually takes the form of "accidental death" of the woman by burning in her kitchen.

Foreign Exchange Regulation Act (FERA). Law regulating foreign investment in India. Foreign ownership is normally limited to 40%, except in certain high technology industries.

Golden Temple. Holy seat of Sikh religion, located in Amritsar, Punjab. The Golden Temple has been a center of Sikh militant activity.

Goondas. Miscreants often involved in rioting and looting that is frequently politically motivated and is attributed to communal problems.

Gurdwara. Sikh temple.

Gurkha National Liberation Front (GNLF). Militant organization based in the Darjeeling area of the state of West Bengal that demands the creation of a separate state for Nepalis in India, known as Gurkhaland, as well as the adoption of Nepali as an official language of India.

Hegde, Ramakrishna. Leader of the ruling *Janata Party* in Karnataka and one of the few opposition figures considered to be a potential national leader.

Hum Log. Television soap opera begun in 1983 that won a huge and loyal following. One of the first programs on *Doordarshan* to be co-produced by a private firm, it demonstrated the potential appeal of popular televison programming.

Indo-Soviet Treaty of Peace and Friendship. Treaty signed in 1971 which commits India and the Soviet Union to consult in the event of threats to each other's security.

Jan Sangh. Hindu-chauvinist party formed in 1951 with strength mainly in North India. Much of its political cadre is drawn from the *Rashtriya Swayamsevak Sangh.*

Janata Party. One of the principal opposition parties, and ruling party in Karnataka. Janata headed a national government coalition in 1977-1979, the only non-Congress party to do so since Independence.

Jati. Caste or sub-caste unit that defines acceptable interactions in marriage, dining and other caste-related practices.

Jatra. Folk theatrical form popular in West Bengal state. Since the 1950s, themes have ranged from social issues and politics to mythology.

Kalakshetra. Art academy in Madras founded by Rukmini Devi to study and revitalize South Indian classical dance.

Lalit Kala Akademi, Sahitya Akademi, Sangeet Natak Akademi. Academies set up by the Indian government to document, encourage and popularize Indian culture in literature, the performing arts, and fine arts, respectively.

Liberation Tigers of Tamil Eelam (LTTE). Leading Sri Lankan Tamil militant group which seeks a separate state for Sri Lankan Tamils on the island of Sri Lanka. Its headquarters and training camps are located in the southern Indian state of Tamil Nadu, a major source of friction in Indo-Sri Lankan relations.

Lok Dal. Break-away faction of the Janata party formed in 1979 due to opposition to *Rashtriya Swayamsevak Sangh* involvement in the *Janata Party.*

Lok Sabha. Lower house of India's bicameral parliament.

MacMahon Line. Northeastern border of India with China charted by British cartographers but undemarcated. It is recognized by India as the legitimate border with China. China disputes this border and overran it in the 1962 Sino-Indian war.

Manushi. Bi-monthly feminist magazine published alternately in Hindi and English.

Mizoram. A former union territory, granted statehood after the 25 June 1986 signing of the Mizoram Accord between Prime Minister Gandhi and Mizo National Front (MNF) leader Laldenga. The MNF had been leading a guerrilla movement for Mizo autonomy. The Mizo accord is an example of Rajiv Gandhi's policy of reconciliation with disenchanted ethnic groups.

Monopolies and Restrictive Trade Practices Act (MRTP). Law regulating firms that command a major share of the market in their product. Reducing this act's application has been a major element in Rajiv Gandhi's program of economic liberalization.

Mukherjee, Pranab. Former protege of Indira Gandhi and leader of a dissident faction of *Congress (I)*, Mukherjee was expelled from the party in late 1985 for criticizing Rajiv Gandhi's policies.

Muslim Women's Bill. Bill passed into law in May 1986 that frees Muslim men from the responsibility to financially support their ex-wives for more than three months after divorce. This bill was introduced by the government in response to the protest from the Muslim community that followed the *Shah Bano* Supreme Court decision.

National Conference. Dominant party of Jammu and Kashmir, led by *Farooq Abdullah.*

National Film Development Corporation (NFDC). Government of India-financed institution that supports the production of art films.

Nehru, Arun. Former minister of state for internal security and cousin of Rajiv Gandhi. He was removed from office by the prime minister in October 1986 because of his opposition to Gandhi's policies of reconciliation, especially in Punjab and Mizoram.

Operation Bluestar. Military assault on the *Golden Temple* in June 1984 to flush out Sikh extremists using the temple as a refuge. Operation Bluestar led to widespread Sikh alienation and protest.

Operation Brasstacks. Indian military maneuvers of record magnitude near the Pakistan border from November 1986 to January 1987. The size of the maneuvers and Pakistan's response of deploying its troops near the border created a war scare in both countries.

President's Rule. Suspension of a state's assembly and direct rule of the state by the central government through the centrally-appointed governor. Although president's rule is intended to be put into effect when a state of emergency exists, it has sometimes been used by the center to topple opposition-controlled state governments.

Punjab Accord. July 1985 agreement primarily between the central government and the states of Punjab and Haryana intended to resolve the crisis created by Sikh grievences over treatment of their community and the state of Punjab by the central government. Under the Accord, the sharing of river waters was to be adjudicated between the two states, Sikhs discharged from the army after *Operation Bluestar* were to be rehabilitated, and Haryana and Punjab were to transfer their joint capital, *Chandigarh,* to Punjab in return for the transfer of some Hindi-speaking areas of Punjab to Haryana. The agreement remains largely unimplemented.

Rajya Sabha. Upper house of India's bicameral parliament.

Ramachandran, M. G. (MGR). Leader of *All India Anna Dravida Munnetra Kazhagam* in Tamil Nadu.

Rao, N. T. Rama. Chief minister the state of Andra Pradesh and leader of its ruling *Telugu Desam* party. His move to assist the backward classes of his state by extending reservations for education and jobs has led to clashes between upper and lower castes.

Rashtriya Swayamsevak Sangh (RSS). Militant Hindu youth organization associated with the *Jan Sangh* party. The RSS draws its membership mainly from urban and lower middle classes and seeks the consolidation of a Hindu nation.

Scheduled Castes. List of "untouchable," or "harijan," castes and tribes drawn up under the 1935 Government of India Act and subsequently revised. Legislative seats as well as government posts and places in educational institutions are reserved for members of these castes.

Self-Employed Woman's Association (SEWA). Ahmedabad-based labor organization that provides services such as day-care, legal protection, cooperative banking, and vocational training to women working in the informal sector of the economy. SEWA's work is a prominent example of the increasing role that private, grass-roots organizations play in Indian development.

Shah Bano. Divorced Muslim woman who successfully sued her ex-husband for maintenance. The Supreme Court's ruling in 1985 caused an uproar among Muslims who saw this as a state intrusion into their religious affairs.

Shariat. Islamic law based on the Koran and traditional interpretations of its teachings. Muslims in India have the option of applying Islamic law to matters of marriage, inheritance and adoption.

Shiv Sena. Militant nativist communal organization based largely in the towns of northern India. It was founded in Bombay in 1966 to agitate against South Indian immigrants to the state of Maharastra.

Siachen Glacier. Disputed area in the mountains of Kashmir and the site of many recent minor skirmishes between India and Pakistan.

Simla Agreement. Peace pact signed in 1972 by India and Pakistan, formally ending the 1971 war between India and Pakistan over Bangladesh and affirming the line of control between Indian and Pakistan in Kashmir.

Singh, Arjun. Former Congress (I) vice-president, removed in October 1986 to become minister of communications. Singh's removal from the party vice-presidency was apparently in response to criticism of Singh emanating from the party.

Singh, V. P. Former finance and defense minister under Rajiv Gandhi, Singh ran into political difficulties resulting in his April 1987 ouster from government because of his efforts to hunt down tax evaders and eliminate corruption from India's government arms deals. He was the principal architect of India's new liberal economic policy and is considered by some to be a potential prime minister.

South Asian Association for Regional Cooperation (SAARC). Organization formed in 1985 to enhance regional cooperation in social, economic and cultural development. The SAARC members are Bangladesh, Bhutan, India, the Maldives, Nepal, Pakistan and Sri Lanka. The second SAARC Summit was held in Bangalore, India in November 1986.

Telugu Desam. Ruling party in the state of Andra Pradesh, formed in 1982 and led by *N. T. Rama Rao.* This party survived a 1984 attempt by the Center to install a Congress (I) chief minister in place of Rama Rao, marking a new trend of resiliency of opposition-led state governments.

Tohra, Gurcharan Singh. Leader of the powerful, separatist-oriented Shiromani Gurdwara Prabandhak Committee (Sikh Temple Management Committee), jailed for sedition in December 1986. Tohra had previously supported the *Punjab Accord.*

Tripathi, Kamalapati. Congress working president who was forced to step down in November 1986. His ouster is part of Rajiv Gandhi's attempt to remove the old guard, which he perceives as an impediment to his program of change, from *Congress (I).*

Varna. The four broad hierarchical categories of the Hindu caste system. In descending order of status, the *varna* are Brahmin, Kshatriya, Vaishya, and Shudra. Untouchables fall below these categories.

About the Contributors

Myron Weiner is Ford Foundation Professor of Political Science and director of the Center of International Studies at the Massachusetts Institute of Technology. His publications include *India at the Polls, 1980, Sons of the Soil: Migration and Ethnic Conflict in India* and many other books and articles.

Francine R. Frankel is professor of political science at the University of Pennsylvania. She is editor and contributor for *Caste, Class, Ethnicity and Dominance: Patterns of Politico-Economic Change in Modern India* (forthcoming) and author of *India's Political Economy, 1947-1977: The Gradual Revolution.*

Ainslie T. Embree is professor of history at Columbia University and director of Columbia's Southern Asian Institute. Past president of the Association for Asian Studies, he is the editor of *The Encyclopedia of Asian History* (forthcoming) and author of *India's Search for National Identity* among many other publications.

John P. Lewis is professor of economics at Princeton University. He has served as chairman of the Task Force on Concessional Flows at the World Bank and of the Development Assistance Committee of the OECD. His recent publications include *U. S. Foreign Policy and the Third World: Agenda 1983* (with Valeriana Kallab).

Joseph W. Elder is professor of sociology at the University of Wisconsin, Madison and president of the American Institute of Indian Studies. He has produced several films on South Asian culture and society, including *The Fourth Stage: A Hindu's Quest for Release* (with David Thompson) and *Dadi and Her Family.*

Girish R. Karnad is a playwright, director, actor and author. Mr. Karnad currently serves as co-chairman of the Joint Media Committee of the Indo-US Subcommission on Education and Culture. He is the recipient of the Sangeet Natak Akademi award for playwriting (1970/72) and the Padma Shri award of the Government of India (1974).

Marshall M. Bouton is director of contemporary affairs at The Asia Society, New York. He has served as special assistant to the US ambassador to India and director of policy analysis for Near East and South Asia in the US Defense Department. Dr. Bouton is author of *Agrarian Radicalism in South India.*

Index